PHILOSOPHY AND RE
IN THE CRISIS

For Phaedra and her generation

PHILOSOPHY AND RESISTANCE IN THE CRISIS

Greece and the Future of Europe

COSTAS DOUZINAS

polity

First published in 2013 by Polity Press

Polity Press
65 Bridge Street
Cambridge CB2 1UR, UK

Polity Press
350 Main Street
Malden, MA 02148, USA

ISBN-13: 978-0-7456-6543-6 (hardback)
ISBN-13: 978-0-7456-6544-3 (paperback)

A catalogue record for this book is available from the British Library.
Typeset in 10.5 on 12 pt Sabon
by Servis Filmsetting Ltd, Stockport, Cheshire
Printed and bound in the USA by Edwards Brothers, Inc.

The publisher has used its best endeavours to ensure that the URLs for external websites referred to in this book are correct and active at the time of going to press. However, the publisher has no responsibility for the websites and can make no guarantee that a site will remain live or that the content is or will remain appropriate.

Every effort has been made to trace all copyright holders, but if any have been inadvertently overlooked the publisher will be pleased to include any necessary credits in any subsequent reprint or edition.

For further information on Polity, visit our website: www.politybooks.com

CONTENTS

PROLOGUE:
THE AGE OF RESISTANCE

The strange story of this book

I was born in Greece. I have lived most of my life in Britain. Dual identities create tensions. When I arrived in London in July 1974, after the fall of the Greek dictatorship, I was told in no uncertain terms, by an elderly gentleman walking his bulldog in a park, that Britain does not belong to Europe or indeed to any other continent. Britain stands on her own beyond geographical classifications. By contrast, the Greeks used to be supremely Europhile. Most would have gladly moved their government from Athens to Brussels. The gentleman's denunciation of Europe was part of Britain's post-imperial *tristesse*. Greece's love for the European Union was part of its post-dictatorship search for identity. I could not have predicted that some forty years later the policies of the Union would bring my two home countries close.

My early experiences as a graduate student and young lecturer in my adopted home were positive. Familiarity with the classics and the history of philhellenism, visits to the Aegean islands and the antiquities, and the hospitality and warmth of Greeks had contributed to the welcoming of the young graduate. As soon as my accent betrayed my provenance, people volunteered stories of appreciation for the culture, memorable holidays and strong relationships. I thought that we Greeks enjoyed something approaching positive discrimination: I was treated everywhere much better than my Italian, Turkish or German colleagues.

Suddenly, in 2010, a different cold and hostile Britain emerged. Newspapers and broadcasts kept talking about the cheating corrupt lazy Greeks, a nation I did not recognize. Every aspect of life had failed, every Greek was immoral. The debt and deficit had metamorphosed

1

a whole people overnight. It was a line of argument propagated by the then Greek government in its attempt to attract sympathy and loans from the European leaders. In lectures and seminars, in conferences and pubs, friends and strangers became distanced, occasionally aggressive. I was trying to explain that many criticisms and attacks were based on ignorance of facts, that the media and the government were presenting a distorted view, that austerity was liable to fail, to no avail. For the first time, I felt a 'racism-lite' affecting me. It was ideological not ethnic.

When, early in 2010, the *Guardian* asked me to write about the austerity measures that Premier Papandreou had announced I responded eagerly. On 4 February 2010, *Comment is Free* published an article entitled 'Greeks must fight the neo-liberal European Union.' It condemned the injustice and ineffectiveness of these early 'voluntary' measures, which were a gentle slap compared with those that have been imposed since by the European Union and the IMF. The article predicted their failure, their disastrous effects, the unravelling of the social bond. It concluded: 'The future of democracy and social Europe is in the balance and the Greeks are called to fight for all of us.'[1] Most responses below the line expressed versions of the emerging anti-Greek feelings. Some celebrated the fact that the pending exit from the Eurozone would make holidays in Rhodes and Zante cheaper. Intellectuals could not believe how modern Greeks, 'descendants of the founders of philosophy and democracy', could deteriorate to such a degree. Greece had become the black sheep of Europe and the bar of legitimate attacks had been lowered considerably. The hostile reactions as well as a growing number of supporters of the Greek resistance made me continue the writing. Some thirty articles appeared in the *Guardian* and other newspapers, charting the trajectory of the Greek tragedy. The early articles were translated into many languages and led to a series of public lectures and conferences in Europe, Latin America, Asia and Greece. Without wishing it, I became an unofficial representative of suffering Greece.

In the process, I reconnected with my country of birth and with friends I had not met since the days of the Colonel's dictatorship. Talking to them, I was shocked by the large number of parties, groups, tendencies and groupuscules on the Left. This acronym soup often expresses ancient enmities and small ideological oppositions. It is the result of the defeats of the Left and the hardening 'narcissism of small differences' that followed it. People from different groups have a broadly similar analysis of the crisis and of the response to it. When I pointed out this fact, they became hesitant, embarrassed, unclear:

'You may be right but you don't know how wrong these people were in 1981/1989/2001.' I tried to organize joint events with the groups that agreed on the basics. I was soon disappointed. As someone who had no link with any of the parties and groups, I was viewed by many with suspicion.

When I was asked to publish a collection of articles and speeches in Greek my response was initially negative. Two events convinced me that I should go ahead. On 25 February 2011, I gave a press conference in Athens in a building called *Hepatia* where 300 undocumented immigrants were staging a hunger strike. I was also an immigrant – a very different 'luxury' immigrant of course, since I came to London for graduate studies with a scholarship. When I was asked to come to Greece to help the struggle of the *sans papiers* I did not hesitate for a moment. The government's inhuman treatment confirmed my view that human rights are often used to legitimize power while excluding large groups of vulnerable people from protection.[2] The *Hepatia* strikers demanded a 'humanity' different from that of rights, courts and government commissions. Meeting the strikers, I recognized in their bright but exhausted faces the dual nature of *homo sacer*: they were hostages of the state of exception without legal rights or safeguards; playthings and sacrificial victims in the hands of the sovereign. But these legally non-existent people had removed the sovereign's ultimate weapon, which was to control life and let people die. They were the 'last free men' of Athens. The second invitation came from *Stasis Syntagma*, as I called the movement of *aganaktismenoi*, who occupied Syntagma and many other squares in 2011. On 17 June, speaking to thousands alongside Manolis Glezos, the man who lowered the swastika from the Acropolis in 1941 and is a world symbol of resistance, I gave the most emotionally charged talk of my life. The thirteen minutes given to each speaker were not enough to explain how the occupations had transformed the political stage, reviving the direct democracy of classical Athens; how they had changed the power balance, thus creating a possibility of victory for the resistance; how the future of Europe depended on the outcome of the Greek resistance. Yet I was able to say all that and more in the limited time dictated by the 'axiom of equality' of the squares. When equality becomes an axiom, public speaking becomes aesthetic performance and political praxis.

Stasis Syntagma changed the pessimism and 'left melancholy' that had descended on Greece. Everything was possible again. Europe and the world started looking at the Greek resistance with hope. The change can be dated. On 16 June, after a huge rally at Syntagma,

3

Prime Minister Papandreou resigned and asked the opposition to form a government. A *Guardian* leader argued for the first time that the new austerity measures were catastrophic, that the Greeks cannot accept them or bear their effects and that the only solution is to suspend loan repayments and have a substantial 'haircut' of the debt. A few days later most non-Greek media started discussing these options. The change in public opinion was the direct result of hundreds of thousands turning up every weekend in Syntagma and the other squares. The resisting Greeks alongside the Spanish *indignados* were showing a different way out of the economic crisis. An informal international solidarity movement to the suffering and resisting Greeks started taking shape. This book aims to assist this new International.

The original version was written in August 2011 in Dryos, a village on the Cycladic island of Paros. It was published in Greek in December of that year. I returned to the book and wrote this new version in August 2012, again in Dryos. The experience of writing a book over such a short period is strange. With no library and few books around, a life's preoccupations, obsessions and dreams come to the surface and claim their dues. Manic writing, absentmindedness and a solitary daily *tour d'horizon* does not make for good holidays either. Both in 2011 and 2012, I met friends rarely and kept asking them monotonously about the ideas I was writing that day. Maria Comninou and Angelos Papazissis, Nicos Douzinas and Annic Paterneau, Nicos and Anna Tsigonia were my Dryos interlocutors, informants and critics. They kept telling me that this is not a way to have a break. Daily swimming and occasional visits to the Resalto bar and DJ Apostolos, perhaps the best music bar in the Aegean, recharged the body and replenished the spirit. Akis Papataxiarchis, Chris Lyrintzis, Maro Germanou, Alexandra Bakalaki, Athena Athanassiou and Dimitris Papanikolou gave me advice and encouragement. Costas Livieratos of Alexandria Publications was a careful editor of the Greek version, improving it immensely. Joanna Bourke was the main victim of my daily mood swings, from elation to depression and back. Joanna is a soul companion, an inspiration for ideas and the most insightful critic. Her presence is felt on each page. I am personally responsible for mistakes and exaggerations. We are collectively responsible for continuing to resist the destruction of the country.

The Greek edition of the book was written in outrage and despair. The outrage is still there, a year later, but there is also hope. The bad news, first. Many things have changed since 2011 but most remain the same, a little better here, a little worse there. The burdens on the people have increased hugely. New taxes, salary and pension cuts are on the way. Unemployment stands at 25%, youth unemployment at 55%. Twenty young men and women with postgraduate degrees have contacted me in the last year to help them find jobs in the UK. This brain drain is undermining the future, whatever happens to the immediate problems. In early September 2012, a 'leaked' troika 'non-paper' suggested that a six-day week should be introduced, the minimum salary abolished altogether and labour protections removed to attract investment and drive up competitiveness. People in employment should not be 'advantaged' at the expense of the unemployed, the cynical gloss went. This was the way successive waves of measures are launched. A stalking horse is sent out to test reactions and when the actual measures are not as awful as advertised, the government is praised for its steadfastness. This time looks different. German economists and industrialists have started arguing that 'special economic zones' with tax breaks and no protection for the workers should be introduced; some believe that the whole of Greece should be turned into a 'special zone'. A special zone is a euphemism for an economic ghetto or company town. These measures test how far the rearrangement of the social fabric can go in conditions of extreme economic crisis. Greek work practices are getting close to those of China. The austerity first tried in Greece is being exported to Portugal, Ireland and Britain, with Spain and Italy following close behind. A return to Victorian capitalism kept in place by an authoritarian state is perhaps what awaits us all. Greece may be the future of Europe.

Now for the good news. In April 2010, I concluded an article in the *Guardian* that 'commentators fear that the Greek malaise is part of a wider attack on the euro. Now that the measures are proving worse than the disease, their imposition may mark the return of radical politics. The defence of the common good and democracy, a proud Hellenic tradition, shows the political way out, not just for Greece, but also for the whole of Europe. As the Icelandic volcano reminded us, the eruption of life-changing events is still a historical possibility.'[3] The back cover of the Greek edition of this book published in 2011 took my hopes further: 'Europe used Greece as a guinea pig to test the conditions for restructuring late capitalism in crisis. What the European and Greek elites did not expect was for the guinea pig to occupy the lab, kick out the blind scientists and start a new experiment: its own transformation from an object to a political subject. The meaning and limits of democracy are renegotiated in the place it was born.'[4] Friends told me at the time that I was excessively optimistic or, even worse, I had lost touch with reality. The squares had emptied, the movement was in abeyance, a new government had been sworn in, the usual left melancholy had returned.

Where did I base my optimism? Meeting people at the *Hepatia* hunger strike, in Syntagma and the other occupations up and down the country, I was reminded of the scary and thrilling days of 1973. The occupations at the Law School and the Polytechnic in Athens started the process of decay and eventual overthrow of the military dictatorship. The students walked down the streets with their heads held high, weighty academic tomes in their hands, badges of identity and pride. In 2011, in the midst of the catastrophe that has befallen Greece, people smiled at strangers in occupied squares and streets again, with that momentary twinkle in the eye so different from the empty gaze prevalent in Greece today. There is no immediate comparison of course between the ridiculous Colonels of the 1970s and the democratically elected government of 2011. But the will to resist and the determination to bring the country back from the brink are similar. My optimism was confirmed by the astounding results of Syriza, the radical Left party, in the double elections of 6 May and 17 June 2012. The seeds were sown in Syntagma Square, in popular assemblies up and down the country, in the many instancs of civil disobedience and solidarity, in the 'can't pay won't pay' movements. Without the occupations, the power system would have probably survived intact. On 6 May, the occupiers and resisters met again in polling stations and voted for the Left. The radical Left won all the big cities where the occupations took place. In places where civil disobedience campaigns had dominated, it won handsomely. Direct democracy acquired its parliamentary companion.

The book has various points of departure and arrival. The articles and lectures forming its foundation expressed despair, outrage and anger. Their reconstruction attempts to interpret these emotions creatively. The first version was a quick political intervention. The new version is more theoretical. As a result, the book's chapters and sections belong to different genres. Hegel said that the daily reading of the newspaper has replaced the morning prayer. Perhaps a more theoretical approach must complement daily journalism. Parts of the book belong therefore to what we could call 'philosophical journalism' and take the essay form. Vignettes from daily life help to illustrate the destruction of the social bond. The main part of the book uses theoretical concepts and strategies from radical philosophy in order to explore the 'age of resistance'. It also uses the opposite tactic: starting from the experience of resistance, it tests the interpretations of political philosophy. Most chapters bring practice and theory together, hopefully enriching both in the process. A light psychoanalytical approach permeates the whole as does a concern with jurisprudential themes.

The different styles and schools of thought examined, criticized and synthesized make the book somewhat heterogeneous. Its chapters and sections can be described as a 'multiplicity of singularities'. The book's organization and style 'perfoms' the plural action of the 'multitude', one of its key theoretical concepts. The multitude remained plural and singular in the occupations, united only by a common political desire, and so does the book.[5] Its narrative starts with the 'state we're in' which examines the political, moral, legal and semiotic aspects of the crisis. The second part is theoretical. It presents disobedience and resistance as motors of social health and political change and moves to theories of political subjectivity. The final part brings the first two together, examining the types and subjects of disobedience in the light of radical philosophy. The reader may plot her own trajectory moving in and out of different chapters and sections, all of which retain a certain autarchy.

A word of warning. After I started my academic career I did not get involved in Greek politics. I am not in a position therefore to advise the Greeks, an attitude of many expatriates that I find morally and aesthetically problematic. But a lifelong exploration of normative matters and my eschatological and soteriological readings (Benjamin, Schmitt, Taubes and Agamben among others) mean that I did not always avoid the temptation. These deviations are effects of a *deformation proffesionelle* instead of a belief that I have the answers others have missed. The long absence from Greece and my academic interests and readings mean that the sociological and anthropological musings of the book may not be fully informed. Errors of interpretation may have crept in; but after the avalanche of ignorant commentary on Greece a considered response is timely. Parts of Chapter 9 appeared in 'Athens rising', 20(1) *European Urban and Regional Studies* (2013).

Resistance spreads throughout Europe as fast as austerity. Greece may become the future of Europe in a second sense. The anti-austerity anger is simmering just below the surface in Italy and Spain and is about to explode. Europe is following Greece both in its catastrophic spiral and in the rise of resistance. Which side of Greece will become the future Europe? Will Europe get mired in austerity and decay or will it join the age of resistance?

The age of resistance

Identity politics and humanitarian campaigns dominated the 1990s and early 2000s. This changed after the collapse of the financial system in 2008 and the imposition of austerity policies. Mass resistance returned to public spaces and marks the politics of the twenty-first century. A series of protests, spontaneous insurrections and occupations and the desire for radical change broke out everywhere. They include the Paris *banlieues* riots in 2005, the Athens December 2008 uprising, the Arab spring, the Spanish *indignados* and the Greek *aganaktismenoi* occupations, Occupy Wall Street, Occupy London and similar occupations around the world. Some uprisings started after an unexpected catalyst, such as the police killing of Grigoris Alexopoulos in December 2008 in Athens, or Mark Duggan in August 2011 London, or the self-immolation of Mohammed Bouazizi in Tunisia in 2010. Others were triggered by what was happening elsewhere. Tunisia inspired Egypt; Puerta del Sol modelled itself on Tahrir Square and, in turn, Syntagma followed the Spanish example and was then imitated by the world Occupy movement.

Unprecedented and innovative types of resistance and revolt now appear regularly. Their timing is unpredictable but their occurrence certain. This persistence cannot be explained simply by technological innovation, such as the "Facebook revolution", nor is it mere coincidence. Standard political science, obsessed with the machinations of governments, parties and parliaments, cannot understand these spontaneous events and dismisses them as non-political. The miscalculations of politicians and commentators are striking. The Arab spring is a case in point. Hilary Clinton stated on 25 January 2011 that 'our assessment is that the Egyptian government is stable'. Mubarak was overthrown a few days later. Peter Mandelson tried to save Mubarak junior, when the Egyptian revolution was almost over, stating that he 'has been the leading voice in favour of change within the government and the ruling party [and not] the putative beneficiary of a nepotistic transfer of family power, the continuation of "tyranny" with a change of face at the top'.[6] Similarly, traditional Marxism proved unable to comprehend changes in the social composition of working people and their influence on the politics of resistance.

A number of radical commentators, on the other hand, argue that we have entered a period of upheaval. For Michael Hardt and Antonio Negri, the movements share certain characteristics: the use of encampments, internal democratic organization, the struggle for the commons and against private and state property.[7] They are right: the various resistances are linked in an emerging world movement. But what led to the explosion? What made it spread around the world? Alain Badiou argues that history has 'woken up'; we live in 'times of riots and uprisings'.[8] For Badiou, events in Paris 2005, Athens 2008 and London 2011 were 'immediate' non-political riots. Tahrir Square counts as a 'historical' insurrection, albeit with many qualifications and reservations, since it did not rise to his 'idea of communism'. We are still in an 'intervallic' age, Badiou claims, the long stretch between two revolutionary periods. He is right: France and the Western world do not live in revolutionary fervour. But revolutions start only after people have taken to the streets, stay there and challenge the established order. Whether radical change follows and what type it takes depends in most cases on the emergence of a political subject as well as on unpredictable events and contingencies.

The politics of resistance, the 'street' and the square are well ahead and an excellent corrective to both mainstream and radical political theory. We need new theoretical approaches and perhaps new political strategies. Despite differences, the new resistances form a sequence, both because they trigger each other, and also in a more profound sense. Their simultaneous emergence and similarity of form results from common socio-economic and political conditions. The historical variations and political specificities make the insurrections differ in scope and intensity. The Arab spring had different aims from the Spanish *indignados*, the Greek *aganaktismenoi* and Occupy. However, the systemic pressures and the political reactions are similar. Biopolitical neo-liberalism and the post-Fordist economy of services treat people everywhere as desiring and consuming machines. Debt for consumption is the main motor of the economy. Intermediate institutions such as parties, unions, even churches have been weakened, as has the principle of representation. People become directly integrated into the economy without mediations. The obedient worker can withdraw abruptly and even violently, however, should the supports of integration fail. The frustration of cultivated expectations and certainties can lead to violent disengagement from dominant behavioural patterns. It can take the form of a violent 'acting out' or of innovative political actions. The riots are politics at degree zero, the occupations an emerging new democratic politics.

A sequence of uprisings will dominate the world political landscape in the next period. Ours is an age of resistance. The possibility of radical change has been firmly placed on the historical agenda. This book discusses its socio-political as well as its ethical and cultural conditions. I hope that its arguments are widely applicable. Most examples, however, come from Greece, to which I now turn.

Greek tragedy: a chronicle

As the reader knows, Greece has been subjected to a long list of claims and counterclaims about debt and deficit, the state of the economy and its people's moral standing. The beginning was totally unexpected. Late in 2009, George Papandreou, the recently elected prime minister, announced to universal shock and without prior warning that the Greek debt had grown to 120% of GDP and the deficit to 15.4%. Austerity was necessary, the Greeks were told, to bring the country back from the brink of debt default. When a first tranche of voluntary measures failed, the government asked the International Monetary Fund, the European Union and the European Central Bank for a loan. In May 2010, a €110 bn three-year loan was agreed. The quid pro quo was a series of strict austerity measures. A 'troika' of representatives of the lenders was appointed to supervise the application and effectiveness of the measures. The austerity measures attached to the loans were set out in 'memoranda' of agreement between the government and the troika. The first bailout led to an increase of the debt. The country's credit rating fell to junk status and by the summer of 2011 Greece again could not meet its debt repayments. A series of further financial agreements accompanied by new austerity measures. An EU summit in July 2012 partially restructured the debt and introduced a 'haircut' of privately held bonds. In February 2012, a new government agreed a second loan of €130bn which would go towards the payment of private bondholders and the recapitalization of banks who took the 'haircut' and previous loans. The whole package was calculated to bring debt down to 120% of GDP by 2020. Memorandum No 2 was agreed, introducing new austerity and privatization measures.

If the first memorandum was a tragedy, the second looked a farce, which, like all farces and unlike tragedies, does not lead to catharsis but to the endless humiliation of its protagonists. After the 'great success' and 'breathing space' given to Greece by the second bailout, the Athens bourse hit bottom. One more great triumph unravelled before our eyes. The operation 'succeeded' but the patient died. In September 2012, the troika is demanding a further €14 bn of cuts, tax rises, privatizations and further labour law 'liberation' before it approves the payment of the next loan instalment. The story goes on; political time has been condensed. When this book is published Greece will look again very different from the time of writing. In the meantime, Spanish and Italian bonds reached the levels that had made Greece seek help. Greece was picked as the hare leading the southern race to the bottom.

Austerity aims at rearranging late capitalism in conditions of severe crisis. The contraction of the state through 'fiscal discipline' is only part of a wider project affecting every part of society. The cumulative effects of austerity are staggering. The early measures affected the public sector with a 30% reduction in state spending that was mainly made up of up to 50% salary and pension cuts and an estimated 150,000 job losses by 2015. The private sector, exploiting the civil servants' salary and pension cuts, started applying similar measures in order to improve 'competitiveness'. Economists of all persuasions explained that labour costs played a small part in the improvement of competitiveness, to no avail. Eventually, the second memorandum slashed the minimum salary by up to 32% and abolished collective bargaining and various other long-established labour protections. Sector specific measures were accompanied by increases in direct and indirect tax, a VAT increase to 23%, the doubling of some public transport fares and road tolls, and the imposition of a property tax collected through electricity bills. The economy shrank dramatically by –24% over five years, the largest in peacetime. In 2012, unemployment stood at 25% and youth unemployment at 55%. Austerity led to a developing humanitarian crisis with homelessness, mental illness and suicide at unprecedented and growing levels. Hospitals cannot work for lack of basic medicines, schools have no textbooks or fuel for heating, and tax collection has come to a virtual stop. These measures are part of a wholesale radical restructuring of life. Its effects will be more radical and long lasting than any economic measures. Greek society is collapsing before our eyes.

Let us briefly explore the politics of the crisis. Three governments ruled the country between 2009 and 2012. First was a Pasok (Socialist) government led by George Papandreou following a landslide victory in the October 2009 elections. It was replaced in November 2011 by a coalition of Pasok and right-wing New Democracy led by banker Loukas Papademos. Finally, following two elections on 6 May and 17 June 2012, another coalition of New Democracy, PASOK and the Democratic Left parties, led by Antonis Samaras, the leader of the Right, took office. On the popular side, resistance against austerity grew throughout 2010 and 2011. More than 25 one-day general strikes, sectional and professional strikes, Ministry occupations, non-

11

payment of new property taxes, of increased transport fares and road tolls and various other types of protest were used. The general strikes were accompanied by marches and rallies in Athens and other cities leading to confrontations with the police. The success of the early campaigns was limited, however, and no major change in government policy was achieved. By May 2011, the resistance seemed to be running out of steam. There were many reasons for that. Regular strikes and demonstration in central Athens had turned many against this type of protest. The leading role of the Left turned away those who had traditionally voted for mainstream parties. The most important reason, however, was the gradual and graded imposition of austerity. Different sectors and groups were picked successively by the government, preventing anti-austerity alliances. The first memorandum in 2010 targeted the wider public sector and civil servants. This was the easiest target. Excessive bureaucracy, the state's limited welfare function and the continual attacks on state corruption and inefficiency by the two parties, which had used it over the years to build their power base, had fuelled traditional anti-state feelings. The government and mainstream media started believing that the worst had passed and a major legitimation crisis averted.

The sense of complacency came tumbling down on 25 May when the Syntagma Square in central Athens, and soon afterwards squares in some sixty cities, were occupied by a motley group of people calling themselves *aganaktismenoi* (indignant) in a tribute to the Spanish *indignados*. The Syntagma occupation started spontaneously and drew strength from the mobilizations of the previous period. Unlike earlier occupations, however, it rejected the logic of representation, party belonging or political leadership and opened to large parts of the population who were not politically active or were voters of the established parties. The occupations and encampments lasted for three months. On 16 June, a major demonstration and rally in Syntagma and the heckling of ministers and MPs led Papandreou to the brink. He offered to resign and form a government under the leader of New Democracy who refused, however, the poisoned chalice. It was the first major victory of the resistance movement. On 28 and 29 June, the *aganaktismenoi* attempted to encircle Parliament and put pressure on MPs to stop them voting into law the measures agreed with the troika. Trade unions and parties had also called for a two-day general strike and a march on Parliament. A huge police operation kept Parliament open and carried out a brutal attack on the protesters, with hundreds of people injured. Despite popular disaffection and the chasm between manifesto promises and government action – Papandreou was elected a few months earlier, promising to reverse the neo-liberal measures of the right-wing: 'There is money' for redistribution he had insisted – Parliament did not stop the measures. At that point, the right-wing New Democracy was not supporting the austerity packages for petty party advantage. The Papandreou government, assisted by small parties, held onto its large majority. Parliamentary democracy had failed spectacularly to represent the people. Chapters 10 and 11 discuss *Stasis Syntagma* in great detail.

June 2011 marked a change in the government's response. The multitude standing opposite Parliament was now treated not as a peaceful protest but as fundamental threat. The riot police surrounded Syntagma and eventually removed the encampment in late July. In early September, smaller numbers started assembling but police repression showed that the government was determined not to allow the permanent occupation of the symbolic square again. Nevertheless the combination of popular anger and catastrophic economic performance kept the government on the brink. In a 'last chance saloon' gamble, in late October Papandreou announced a referendum on continued membership of the Eurozone. It was neither a late recognition of the repeated humiliations visited on Greeks by their government and European allies nor a reassertion of sovereignty. It was an irrational 'acting out' and an attempt to regain the initiative by a regime that had lost touch with the people. The proposal had two targets. First, it was a threat to the Greek people, telling them that unless they accept the new catastrophic measures, they would be condemned to leave the Eurozone and suffer a further collapse of living standards. Secondly, it was addressed to backbench Pasok MPs, who had started stirring in response to popular pressure and the catastrophic opinion polls. They were asked to give a vote of confidence to Papandreou, under the James Callaghan principle that 'turkeys do not vote for an early Christmas'. Both blackmails failed and turned against their perpetrator.

The reaction of the Greek people to the referendum proposal and another summit agreement on 27 October bringing a new tranche of austerity measures was devastating. The military parade of 28 October in Thessaloniki commemorating the Greek resistance to the Axis powers in 1940 was abandoned when protesters occupied the street and the President of the Republic had to flee. School parades in many cities and towns were similarly interrupted. The political elites, who felt unassailable for thirty years, were now sensing the popular anger physically and were unable to comprehend or contain it. At the same time, the European leaders interpreted Papandreou's gambit as a veiled threat. The Europeans have been traumatized by popular rebuffs in constitution referenda. 'Referendum' is a dirty word in the corridors of Brussels. It brought back the fear elites feel when the people momentarily enter the political stage. Chancellor Merkel and President Sarkozy called Papandreou to a meeting in Cannes and told him that he could not hold the referendum. The referendum was cancelled, a large number of government MPs rebelled and Papandreou resigned on 9 November. Like many desperate acts, the referendum call backfired and turned into a long suicide note. The European involvement in Papandreou's downfall was highly problematic, however. The picture of a prime minister dragged in like a miscreant by the headmistress to be reprimanded does not augur well for the Union. The decision to hold a referendum is a national political decision and, in theory, Greece remains independent. The 'bailout' is a loan to Greece. A loan to a sovereign state does not give the lending governments the power to treat another country like a protectorate.

Papandreou's resignation led to protracted negotiations between PASOK and New Democracy and the creation of a coalition government by the two erstwhile enemies under Lukas Papademos, a former governor of the Bank of Greece. The resignation was a major victory after the long struggle of the Greek people. Following the Arab spring, it was a reminder that Western governments too can fall when they abandon basic principles of democracy, decency and independence. The second bailout and memorandum agreements were voted into law by the new government and the agreed haircut of privately held bonds was implemented, changing private debt into government loans. Strikes, demonstrations and rallies continued. When Papandreou resigned the leadership of Pasok, Evangelos Venizelos, his greatest rival, replaced him. The second memorandum was the result of backstage negotiations by a government without an electoral mandate. It could not be implemented. Early elections were called on 6 May. Syriza, the Coalition of the Radical Left, saw its vote jump from 4% in 2009 to 17%. The New Democracy and PASOK parties, which had alternated into government with a combined 80% of the vote in the last forty years, collapsed to 32%. PASOK fell from 43% to 12.5% and New Democracy from 32% to 19%. With the mainstream parties unable to form a government, elections were held again on 17 June. New Democracy polled 29% with Syriza a close second at 27%. A second coalition government of New Democracy, PASOK and the smaller Democratic Left party was formed under Antonis Samaras, the New Democracy leader. The new coalition set out to implement the earlier agreed budget cuts, which had by now increased because of the recession. An extra €14 billion of savings must be found, with a new round of salary and pension cuts, tax increases and job losses. But the political temperature has changed. With the Left as the main opposition, the Greek people are sensing the taste of a possible end to the system that brought them to the edge of abyss.

Greece was the first victim of capitalist correction. Greek GDP amounts to only 3% of the European economy. But the symbolism of the pressure worked. Soon after Greece, Portugal and Ireland followed. As I write in August 2012, Spain, Cyprus and Italy are following the same path. If Greece is the future of Europe, perhaps in another sense resistance might become Europe's future too.

Part I

Crisis

— 1 —

THE QUEEN'S QUESTION

The debt's debt

In the summer of 1918, Constantin Cavafy and E. M. Forster met in Alexandria and became lifelong friends. Forster reports that Cavafy,

> half humorously, half seriously, once compared the Greeks and the English. The two peoples are almost exactly alike, he argued: quick-witted, resourceful, adventurous. 'But there is one unfortunate difference between us, one little difference. We Greeks have lost our capital – and the results are what you see. Pray, my dear Forster, oh pray, that you never lose your capital.' That was in 1918. British insolvency seemed impossible then. In 1951, when all things are possible, his words make one think – words of a very wise, very civilized man, words of a poet who has caught hold of something that cannot be taken away from him by bankruptcy, or even death.[1]

Giorgio Agamben, commenting on Cavafy's mysterious statement, writes in 1993: 'The only certainty is that since [1918], all the peoples of Europe and perhaps the whole world have gone bankrupt.'[2] The Greeks, the Europeans, and perhaps everyone, have been bankrupted. Greece was declared substantively bankrupt in 2010 albeit in 'orderly fashion' and only temporarily. Temporary default is a little like temporary death. It lasts forever unless the departed exits on the other side. Posthumous life is unlikely; the temporary is the mask of the permanent, resurrection the fig leaf of death. Formal default was avoided through loans by the European Union and the International Monetary Fund used to repay old loans, thus increasing the overall debt. They are accompanied by the harshest austerity measures and deepest depression in peacetime. All this is well known and there is no

19

point in adding a further (and perhaps ill-informed) layer of economic analysis.[3] This is perhaps the time to sit back and serve the debt of (non-economic) thought, something not in great evidence. For Right and Left, the urgent demand has been 'act now', 'act decisively', 'this is no time for contemplation'. Everyone agrees that the overwhelming responsibility is to save the Euro/Greece/Spain/Europe whatever the cost. The humanitarian catastrophe, the huge fall in living standards, the fire sale of the remaining public assets are necessary steps towards this rescue. If 'rescue' means that Greece stays in the euro and keeps repaying its gargantuan debt, redemption is unlikely but not impossible.

Cavafy and Agamben may have had something different in mind. What if Greece, and perhaps Europe, have been bankrupted not economically but morally, culturally, politically? The book explores another sense of debt and bankruptcy: moral and political debt and the bankruptcy of social ethos. Every newspaper and news broadcast agonizes over the 'euro or drachma' dilemma. The debt of thinking, debt's debt, poses different questions. What is the gain if Greeks keep the euro and lose their soul? We will escape temporarily and partially the endless repetitions of the economists and concentrate on what gives meaning to life: the political, ethical, semiotic and cultural aspects of crisis and resistance. The debt's debt leads to thinking.

The Queen's question

Two spectres hover over Europe and the world: bankruptcy and resistance. Bankruptcy of states, banks, companies and individuals; resistance of people, communities, nations. In this chapter, we leave resistance hovering to concentrate on debt. Its ghost has been appearing for some time. Its arrival had been predicted. If bankruptcy is the death of a political economy and a form of life, this is the chronicle of a death foretold. The world financial system collapsed in 2008 under the weight of its own contradictions. Financial speculation and virtual capital imploded when finally the real economy claimed its dues. Billions of dollars were transferred from the taxpayers to financial institutions, giving a temporary respite to the banking system. Following the collapse, people started losing homes, jobs and businesses but no philanthropy was forthcoming. No funds were available to save schools, hospitals and family homes. A new type of political economy emerged in those turbulent months: socialism for the rich, capitalism for the poor. Or, to paraphrase Bertolt Brecht, you go to jail for fiddling your benefits but you get huge bonuses for bankrupting a bank.

The Queen, during an official visit in November 2008 to the London School of Economics, an elite school consistently preaching the neo-liberal doctrine, asked a prominent professor of economics a simple question: 'If these things were so large, how come everyone missed them?' How come your brilliant models failed to predict the most dramatic event in recent economic history? How come that you can go to bed and have a good night's sleep, one could add, when you know that your theories have destroyed so many people? The professor's answer is not known. A year later, after a British Academy seminar, eminent economists blamed 'a failure of the collective imagination of many bright people, both in this country and internationally, to understand the risks to the system as a whole'. [4] The Queen's question reversed the tale of the Emperor's new clothes. Her innocent question imitated the child who, faced with the sycophantic praise of the Emperor's clothes, followed his eyes' evidence: the Emperor is naked. The Queen became for a moment the demystifying child questioning those who represent the contemporary sovereign. It is a rhetorical question that can have only one answer: economics is not an exact science and cannot deliver the 'objective' knowledge it claims to possess. Mainstream economics is not a royal road to knowledge. Not only is the Emperor naked but there are also more competitors for the Emperor's title than during the Roman tetrarch. At least three major schools of economic theory have been used in the current crisis. The dominant neo-classical school, various types of Keynesianism and, finally, Left and Marxist approaches. They base their analyses on the same data but end up with widely diverging explanations of the crisis and its solution. George Osborne and David Cameron appear to have sound arguments. Nobody can claim on the other hand that Vince Cable or Robert Stiglitz are not 'good' economists or that Paul Krugman and Yannis Varoufakis have miscalculated. They are right within the parameters of their theoretical premises and ideological axioms. Economics is not an 'objective' science, but a field contested by various approaches and schools. As Max Weber first argued, immanent critique runs out when we reach incommensurate premises. Stronger force instead of better argument carries the day.

Monetarist and neo-classical policies have dominated the last thirty years. It was during their watch that the collapse of 2008 and of 2010–11 happened. The world was made to follow their prescriptions, which proved catastrophic. The disaster cannot be blamed on some miscalculation but to flawed premises. The dominant school of economics turns out to be a false emperor. Its high priests and priestesses could not have predicted the coming of the financial meltdown, precisely because their training and socialization did not allow them to see it coming. Alan Greenspan, the Governor of the American Federal Bank and high priest of the religion, stated in late August 2008, a few days before the collapse of Lehman Brothers on 18 September, that the economic system was sound, people should have trust and go on acting normally. As his huge Titanic moved inexorably towards the iceberg, Greenspan was a visually impaired captain. If my experience and instruments tell me that there is no iceberg on the horizon, he seemed to be saying, the evidence of my eyes and the warnings of a few miscreant crew must be wrong.

In October 2008, Greenspan gave evidence to a congressional committee about the banking debacle. Henry Waxman, its chairman, reminded him of an earlier statement: 'I do have an ideology. My judgement is that free competitive markets are by far the best-organized economies.' In light of this, Waxman asked whether Greenspan felt that his 'ideology pushed him to make decisions that he wished he had not made'. Greenspan's answer was striking: 'I found a flaw in the model that I perceived as a critical functioning structure that defines how the world works.' Financial institutions should have avoided risky speculation. 'I made a mistake in presuming that the self-interests of organizations, specifically banks and others, were such as that they were best capable of protecting their own shareholders and their equity in the firms.'[5] Absolute trust in the prudence of the markets and wilful ignorance of evidence compel a simple conclusion: neo-classical economics is a strong ideology with toxic effects.

Let me give another example. Between 2010 and 2012, European leaders held a number of summit meetings and reached various agreements with the IMF, which would guarantee the repayment of the gargantuan debts of the South European states, the elimination of deficits and economic recovery. On each occasion, the mainstream media reported the meetings breathlessly and celebrated the decisions. Economists from across the ideological spectrum, on the other hand, found the measures inadequate and predicted that only a radical debt reduction (whether debtor or creditor led) or an exit of the weaker members from the Eurozone followed by devaluation of the new currency would jumpstart the economy. Without such radical solutions, bankruptcy and decades of economic depression loom large. On each occasion, the adopted measures proved wrong or inadequate so soon after the 'triumph' that the ink had not dried yet on the press communiqués. The failure of diagnosis and cure is also evident at a lower level. In April 2010, the staunchly neo-liberal IMF predicted that austerity Greece would have –1% growth in 2011 and move to steady growth in 2012. In April 2011, it changed its forecast for the year to –3% growth. It turned out to be –7%. Finally, in April 2012, the IMF predicted –4% for the year. The Greek government is predicting –7% and most economists a –9% contraction.[6] It does not take great knowledge to explain the abject failure of the 'experts'. The Greek economy has experienced a 24% contraction over five years. Public spending cuts and tax increases during such a deep depression reduce demand, increase unemployment and halt growth. The slow-down shrinks tax revenues and increases spending for unemployment and other benefits. The deficit increases, causing the fiscal targets to be missed, leading to new austerity to plug the ever-increasing fiscal gap. The European south is caught in a deadly recession spiral that can be halted only with a radical change in policy. If the IMF functionaries were first-year economics students, they would have failed their exams. Unfortunately, their diktat makes millions fail their lives.

Liberal orthodoxy is like a ship the compass of which fails every time it approaches an iceberg. The Queen's question implied that people must learn to live without the illusion of 'objective' expertise. For a brief moment, the repoliticization of the economy and its removal from the clutches of snake-oil salesmen appeared a possibility. The moment passed quickly. With some banks rescued by public funds and others closed, the toxic debt crisis moved to states and companies. The country bailouts were neo-liberalism's revenge for its 2008 humiliation. Only that on this occasion, the outcome was easily predictable and the victims are not banks and hedge funds but whole populations.

Debt's desire

It is the bad luck of the Greeks that the poor man's Greenspans have been running the state for a considerable period of time. As deficit, public and private debt grew, the political and economic elites turned a blind eye and continued drawing cheap loans. The evidence is not hard to find. Excessive borrowing and debt increased after entry to the euro, with its strict 3% deficit ceiling reminding us that the best place to smoke is next to a non-smoking sign. But unlike Greenspan and the embarrassed LSE economist, the Greek captains precipitated the pending doom. Considerable evidence exists that the Greek government 'doctored' the macroeconomic figures in 2001 to gain entry to the euro. The spiralling loans and mounting debt were used by the ruling elites to oil the wheels of state patronage and party clientelism. In an unprecedented first, the incoming government challenged the statistics of their outgoing predecessors twice and had the deficit and debt revised upwards. In 2004, the New Democracy government claimed that its Pasok predecessor had lied. The Papandreou government repeated the tactic in 2010, claiming that New Democracy too had lied. It upgraded the deficit to 15.4% triggering the European intervention. To cap it all, every set of measures adopted increased the debt. The Greek debt was 120% of GDP in 2009 when austerity was imposed. It is 165% in 2012, it will move to 190% in 2014 and, after the pain of a dozen years, will reach 129% in 2021 (the initial calculation was that it would be 'only' 120% but then who can believe any of these forecasts), still above the 2009 position. Unlike their name, the austerity measures are multipliers of debt which keeps increasing and metastasing like a malign tumour.

The repeated revisions of deficit and debt have enriched the English language with the pejorative term 'Greek statistics'. The revision of statistical data was initially interpreted as an attempt to defame party opponents and justify austerity policies. Was this type of creative accountancy petty politics, stubbornness or simple idiocy (a good Greek word meaning 'private')? Information is now emerging that an element of skulduggery may have been involved. In September 2011, the Papademos government sacked six members of the Greek Statistics Commission, because they stated that the deficit was falsely revised upwards. According to Zoë Georganta, a member of the Commission, the deficit was increased to 15.4% to make it larger than Ireland's at the top of the list and allow the IMF to impose stricter austerity.[7] In a further twist, Mr Roumeliotis, the Greek representative to the IMF at the time, stated that the Fund knew that austerity would fail before its imposition. Both he and Dominique Strauss-Kahn, the then IMF Head, had warned Papandreou not to accept the troika plan, he claimed, to no effect.[8] To clarify things, I do not (need to) claim that dark conspirators schemed Greece's downfall. Conspiracy theories do not help us understand history. But conspiracies do happen from time to time. One hopes against hope that the accusations will be properly investigated. They are not central to my argument. I do not have access to (or interest in) the minds and hearts of politicians and bankers. Without an account of the obvious and predictable consequences of actions, the revelation of motives cannot explain much. Whatever the motives, a combination of systemic pressures and conscious decisions has created the monster that is eating up Greece. This is what I call 'the desire of debt': a long series of decisions and actions, of intended or unintended consequences, which consistently and inexorably led to the Greek tragedy.

'Debt's desire', as a double genitive, raises two questions. Who desired the debt and why? Secondly, what does the debt desire? What is the debt's debt? The two meanings of debt, 'what is (financially) owed' and 'what is morally due', come together. The only consistent explanation of the debt trajectory, beyond party political calculation, is that the Greek elites desired and sought the debt, first by crazy borrowing and spending and then by deliberate increases in its calculation. 'Unserviceable' debt, 'crippling' deficit, potential bankruptcy were either desired or wilfully neglected. What does the debt desire? It is not difficult to detect. Because Greece owes, the Greeks must destroy the old and adopt radical new economic, cultural and moral values. They must abandon their 'lying, lazy, cheating' ways in order to service the debt. The debt, condemned as dismal and catastrophic in its evil effects, will allow the return to the path of virtue, morality and honour. Like the Platonic *pharmakon*, the debt is poison and cure, curse and blessing. It is the cause and effect of the Greek passion and the promised (and endlessly deferred) resurrection. How did we get here?

Mainstream European imagination has created two major sociopolitical models, classical liberalism and social-democracy. For classical liberalism, the market is an efficient and neutral mechanism for resource allocation. The belief in markets is accompanied by a commitment to a weak state and a strong rule of law. The state should intervene minimally in the economy but maintain a strong policing function to enforce agreements and repress challenges to the social order. Distribution is based on property, merit and increases in marginal productivity authenticated by law and contractual entitlements. Individual rights, modelled on the foremost right to property, and personal responsibility characterize the liberal citizen. The social democratic model, on the other hand, believes in a strong state, which regulates resource allocation according to social needs registered in democratic elections and negotiations with the social partners. It protects social and economic rights, emphasizes community belonging and social solidarity and transfers resources from richer to poorer areas and people to ensure a minimum standard of life.

This basic political division was blurred in the last thirty years by the convergence of classical liberalism and social democracy into what has become known as neo-liberalism. Neo-liberalism inherits aspects from both systems. It extends the market mechanism to the social state, privatizing public utilities and social amenities. It weakens economic and social rights and turns the law from arbiter of social conflict aspiring to neutrality into a detailed regulatory mechanism. Finally, the state remains strong. But this is no longer the protective state of social democracy (*état providence* is the apt French term) but a state of behavioural controls, extensive surveillance and emergency powers deemed necessary to uphold order and keep resistances in check. The neo-liberal age started in the 1980s when the deregulation of financial transactions, privatization of public assets and utilities at bargain prices and taxation regimes favouring transnational corporations were introduced throughout Europe. The commitment to full employment and the welfare state was dropped as the Europeans revised redistributive plans to fit strict expenditure constraints and balanced budgets. Century-old gains of the trade union and radical movements were reversed. The new orthodoxy suggested that competitiveness and productivity would improve if the power of the unions was curtailed (something pioneered by Mrs Thatcher in her attack on the Miners Union), labour law protections weakened and employment security abolished. The Maastricht single market treaty started one of the largest transfers of capital and power from labour to business, a process now reaching maturity. Neo-liberals believe that monetary stability, improved productivity and competitiveness lead to growth and translate into economic rewards for the employed part of the population. Increased consumption, rising property and equity values will make the masses adopt 'popular capitalism'. The 'seduced' two-thirds of the population will support an unfair economic system which offers them improved standards of living unless they become unemployed or ill. The unemployed and underemployed third, on the other hand, is largely abandoned, opts out of the political system and is treated as a security threat and policing matter.

What is the logic behind these strange policies? Capital accumulation no longer depends exclusively on the extraction of surplus value in the primary and secondary sectors of the economy. These have largely migrated to the developing world with its minimal wages and rudimentary labour and environmental protections. In the Northern economies, profit takes two forms: rent for services and interest for capital. Late capitalism increasingly works through consumption funded by debt and rent. People, companies and states are treated as consumers who must borrow to spend. They survive (or fail) on debt. Debt and indebtedness have become integral to life from birth to death. Student loans and loans for personal consumption, enterprise loans and mortgages make a large part of the population permanently indebted. Borrow to spend, invest in stocks and shares, act as desiring machines is the motto during periods of growth. The exchange and employment contracts create an (often illusory) sense of freedom. But an unbridgeable gap between creditor and debtor characterizes debt. Debt generates feelings of moral failure and guilt for the debtor that pursues her, ghost-like, throughout life. The term 'moral hazard', the most widely used ethical concept during the crisis, indicates how morality has been almost exclusively identified with a Northern Protestant work and cultural ethic of sin, guilt and punishment. In late capitalism, creditor and debtor are involved in a master and servant struggle. But the creditor, unlike the factory boss, is removed from the production process and has no sympathy or interest in the hardship or the debtor.

Many infamous 'financial products' of the last twenty years were mis-sold to people encouraged to cash their equity or insurance policies.[9] The gargantuan financialization of the economy looked like a giant pyramid scheme, which, like all such schemes, eventually came to a (temporary) end in 2008. The financial crisis soon infected the 'real' economy. Huge transfers of taxpayers' money to 'bailout' failed banks inflated state deficits and debt. The 'credit crunch' that followed starved the economy of investment. The accompanying recession hit tax revenues and turned the financial crisis into one of sovereign debt. It was an almost perfect storm and was not just economic. The political aims and effects of the crisis and of austerity as the preferred solution are evident both in Greece and in Europe. Recent institutional measures such as 3% deficit ceiling for Eurozone members (breached by every state before the recent crisis and covered through creative accountancy and backstage political agreements), the European stability pact as well as the markets' 'attacks' on sovereign states were preparations for the final neo-liberal push. The imposition of austerity on the European states derisorily named PIIGS (Portugal, Ireland, Italy, Greece and Spain) started with the rapid increase of the interest rates of sovereign bonds, which eventually made market borrowing prohibitively high. Their main aim was the completion of the neo-liberal project. When the society of indebted consumption came to an abrupt end, it exposed the dark side of the credit relationship. Accumulation through rent and interest must be strictly policed, since the loan, unlike the labour contract, does not automatically create the conditions for its reproduction. Drawing rent and interest in periods of economic hardship requires the cultivation of physical and moral

27

fear since, unlike wages, they do not have an acceptable or 'natural' level. The market pressure on sovereign bonds is precisely a way of pressing the debtors to accept extreme austerity. 'Debtors beware', the lenders seem to be saying, 'either you destroy the social state or you go bankrupt'. Their threats are not unlike a protection racket. If a debtor challenges the terms or the protection fee, the goons beat him.

The close link between the European Union, the International Monetary Fund and German policies is well known. It is a universally accepted truth that the strong euro, low interest rates and the German policy of reducing labour costs have helped the German balance sheet, but have been catastrophic for Southern Europe. EU states are Germany's larger trade partner. The trade imbalance, which allows Germany to become the beneficiary of the extensive privatization of state assets in Southern Europe, was the result of the cheap loans that euro membership gave to Greeks, Spaniards and Italians. When the banking collapse put an end to the period of excessive borrowing and consumption, austerity became the next phase of neo-liberal consolidation. State action should be cut deeply and remaining labour market 'rigidities' removed. The first group of European states 'bailed out' was placed in a position similar to developing countries under the IMF's 'Washington consensus'. The bailout is not a gift but a loan from governments and the IMF. The 5% interest rate on the Greek loan is much higher than that paid by the lending governments to the central banks who give them the loan money, thus producing an extra little windfall for the lenders. The bailout funds are used mainly to repay previous loans. Indeed, according to the second Greek agreement, the loan can be used only for that purpose. It is a case of borrowing on the Visa to pay the MasterCard. The overall debt increases and the vicious spiral continues its downward revolution.

We can now understand better what the debt desires. The stakes behind austerity is a top down rearrangement of capitalism towards its late predatory stage. A major aim of austerity is precisely to reduce workers' salaries, rights and social benefits, seriously downgrading the position of European working people in the global division of labour but at the same time ensuring the continuing profitability of capital. As Paul Mason recently put it, 'the race to the bottom, to be like China, is on, and we're all going to do it. So your wages will meet the Chinese somewhere, and so will your social conditions . . . abolish minimum wages, abolish social protection.'[10] Greece is leading the race.

Let me move to politics. Liberal politics takes economic and deliberative forms. In the former, politics is approached as a market-like

28

activity. Individuals, groups and classes accept the overall socio-economic balance and use politics to pursue marginal improvements of interest and profit. In the latter, politics is presented as a process of argumentation where rational consensus about public goods can be reached. Neo-liberalism is a global ideology and world-view. It adopts and distorts the logic of both liberal models, turning politics into the administration of economics. Its rationality disseminates a version of social 'normality' that subjects all aspects of life to the logic of economic optimization, and a market-based distribution of goods, values and life prospects. Government has been replaced by 'governance' and is ruled by the same logic. The *homo oeconomicus* becomes *homo tout court*. Everything is subjected to a particular economic logic: the polity and the electoral system, health education and foreign policy as well as the constitution of the subject and the citizen. At stake is not 'the market economy but the market society'.[11] The neo-liberal project touches all aspects of life. The atomization of society is accompanied by a weakening of institutions. President Reagan and Mrs Thatcher, its initiators and pioneers, attacked parties, trade unions, local government and even the church. These institutions mediate between the state and civil society. Their weakening undermines the civility necessary for easing social tension and pacifying conflict.

Approached as a neo-liberal market-place of efficiency and productivity or as a town-hall debate, the principles of which have been agreed before the debate started, politics pronounces conflict finished, passé, impossible, and, at the same time, tries to foreclose its appearance. Truth-telling economists, modernizing bureaucrats and patriotic media have largely replaced political action, turning the state into the muscleman for the market internally and a superficially tolerant enforcer of morality externally in our 'humanitarian' wars. But conflict does not disappear – the neo-liberal recipes increase inequality, fuel antagonism and turn the anger against immigrants and the 'undeserving' poor. The person who was treated as consumer in the years of affluence becomes the object of police attention in the age of austerity. As resistance grows, increased police powers and surveillance mechanisms, justified as necessary in the 'war on terror', have been diverted to new but predictable tasks. A permanent quasi-state of exception has been imposed all over the Western world. Walls are built everywhere: in Mexico and Palestine, in Northern Africa and the Greco-Turkish border.[12] Ghettoes for the poor and immigrants keep appearing in city centres, while gated communities and zones for the rich pop up in protected suburbs. Prisons proliferate and prison populations create new records every year. Those seduced by the fake financial bubble must learn to abandon consumption. It is no longer the excluded one-third that suffers. All over the world, large parts of the population move from affluent to *nouveau pauvre* and from power's beneficiaries to excluded. A new 'austerity man/woman' must be created. The project is well on the way in Greece. Spain, Italy and Britain are following suit. Their governments impose deep austerity, claiming at the same time that they do not have a major problem, they are not 'like Greece'. Denial, acknowledgement and punishment form the three-step dance of the European crisis.

Reality and the Real

The desired and feared debt acts like psychoanalytical theory's Real. According to Jacques Lacan, reality must be distinguished from the Real. Reality is what presents itself as the natural state of things, immediately available to our senses. 'Let the facts speak for themselves' is the realist's mantra but the 'facts' remain stubbornly silent. Everyday routine reality is symbolically constructed and supported by what Lacanians call the 'reality principle'. As Alenka Zupančič puts it, 'the reality principle itself is ideologically mediated; one could even claim that it constitutes the highest form of ideology, the ideology that presents itself as empirical fact or biological economic . . . necessity (and that we tend to perceive as non-ideological)'.[13] What we call 'facts' emerge in the symbolic order of language, law and institutions. Dominant ideological frameworks colour them and authorized interpreters construe them authoritatively. In this approach, reality never comes in a pure pristine form; it is always mediated. The Real, on the other hand, is the point of failure of the symbolic order and the reality principle, what stops them from becoming whole, closed and complete. The Real is a traumatic 'nothing'; it cannot enter the symbolic order of language and representation. Reality bans and disavows it in order to appear consistent; we do not have direct 'experience' of the Real. Symptoms and malfunctions beyond our understanding or control manifest its work. We hover around this void or failure of symbolization, attracted and repelled by its unrepresentable vortex-like force. As the disavowed mark of failure, the Real commands that we redouble our efforts, only to be frustrated time and again.

Mainstream economics acts as the 'reality principle' of our age. In the current crisis, economists of all kinds dominate the debate and fill the airwaves with graphs, figures and repetitive clichés. Despite the repeated failures of the dominant neo-classical model, our reality principle insists that individual choices and market calculations make the world move. We see through the lenses of a particular ideology and mistake its perspective for our natural, obvious, uncomplicated state. Its artificial character emerges only at points of crisis: its unspoken taken-for-granted premises, which animate the symbolic edifice, come to the surface, become objectified and can be seen for what they are, ideological constructions. At that point, the symptoms of the repressed Real unpick the soothing clichés of reality. This is what Greenspan unwittingly admitted and the Queen implied.

If economics constructs the symbolic (mis)representation of our world, the debt acts like the Real of the situation.[14] It is the destructive kernel of reality, both disavowed (hidden, denied, neglected) and prohibited (by the demands of fiscal discipline, the stability pacts, and so on). The Greeks had no idea about the size of the debt or its significance until they were told one fine morning that they, the people, owe huge amounts although they had not borrowed and had no idea how the loans were used. As the Real of the economy, the debt becomes known only in its symptoms, in salary cuts and unemployment, homelessness and suicides presented as acts of a vengeful God. Like the Real, the debt cannot be fully revealed. Parliamentary investigations and audit commissions are not allowed to examine it. Every request by the opposition to examine the legality and morality of the Greek debt was rebuffed. In the few cases state debt has been explored elsewhere, the search gets ensnared in astronomical sums and legal minutiae. The debt is present in its effects but absent in its essence. It generates great fear and awe but also a sense of *jouissance* for the opportunities it offers. If, for Marx, class struggle is the motor of history, for the captains of the economy, debt is its fuel.

Economic and moral, catastrophic and redemptive, collective and individual, debt is abstract in its composition, unknown in its provenance, but all too concrete in its symptoms and effects. We Greeks have gone bankrupt, says Cavafy; Agamben adds, perhaps all Europeans have followed. Debt is the South's labour and epic.

— 2 —

THE BIOPOLITICS OF PLEASURE AND SALVATION

Austerity is an apposite ground for testing theories of power. Mainstream political philosophy presents power as an object possessed by the great subjects: king, state, the people or capital are figures of sovereignty. According to Michel Foucault, on the other hand, power is not an object of possession but a multiplicity of shifting relations exercised from innumerable points, 'furrowed across individuals, cutting them up and remolding them, marking off irreducible regions in them, in their bodies and minds'.[1] Power produces reality; it creates subjects of freedom and objects of cognition; it disciplines and attempts to control all aspects of people's lives. Political and legal philosophy have remained preoccupied, however, with the premodern themes of sovereignty and right focusing on the mechanisms that make power appear rational and legitimate while neglecting its operation as the 'conduct of others' conduct'.[2]

In a further mutation, disciplinary power has been superseded over the last thirty years by 'biopower', the operation of power on life processes. Practices and institutions of normalization have proliferated to such an extent that every aspect of social relations is now subjected to operations of power.[3] Disciplinary technologies defined behaviour as normal and deviant. They marked the boundaries of acceptable thought and practice and, through the exclusion of the abnormal and alien, policed bodies and souls. But the disciplinary institutions are now on the retreat and disciplining expands throughout the smooth social surface of Western societies. Global communications, new media, extreme consumerism, total surveillance through CCTV, detailed personal information held in ID cards, passports, public and private databanks all combine in the new form of biopolitical power which extends its hold to the whole of life.

Biopower extends from the depths of consciousness to the bodies of individuals and to whole populations targeted on the basis of characteristics such as gender, race, health, age or profession. These technologies of power are supplemented by 'technologies of self'. People are asked to reform their behaviour through practices of self-improvement and discipline in the name of individual health and collective well-being. Biopolitical capitalism produces not just commodities for subjects but subjects, first and foremost, the 'free subject' of desire and rights. The self is the target and product of two strategies: the first, concerned with the strength of populations, applies policies around birth rate and life expectancy, sexuality and health, education and training, work and leisure. The individual is of little interest here. The second inscribes needs, desires and expectations in the individual, making her feel free, autonomous, creative. Only as disciplined by the symbolic of power do we acquire the imaginary of freedom. Biopower is therefore dual.

Giorgio Agamben and Roberto Esposito emphasize the negative controlling aspect of biopolitics, which prioritizes the group.[4] Paolo Virno, Antonio Negri and Michael Hardt underline the potential for resistance and revolution that the biopolitical care of self allows.[5] Biopolitics and biopower complement neo-liberalism by preparing the obedient and free subject of late modernity. The negative and the positive are the two sides of the same coin. The paradox of a subject that becomes free by being subjected to state and capitalist powers lies at the centre of the European crisis and the prospects it creates.[6]

The biopolitics of mandatory pleasure

After the collapse of communism and the announcement of the 'end of history', popular capitalism and representative democracy were promoted as the future of humanity. Working people were integrated into capitalist priorities by a number of methods. The stock exchange was presented as a casino where the punter always wins; public utilities were privatized and shares were offered initially to small investors at extremely profitable prices; council houses were sold below market value and credit cards, loans and mortgages were offered at low interest rates. British Gas was the first major privatization in Britain. A huge publicity campaign with the slogan 'Tell Sid' told low-income people (the 'Sid' of the giant posters) that if they bought shares before their flotation, they would double their money as soon as stock exchange trading started.

Private and public debt and consumption linked private interest and common good. Indebtedness and consumerism was the order of the 1990s and early 2000s; 'iPhone or BlackBerry' the existential dilemma of the age. Lifelong savings were turned into financial 'products' and working people became shareholders either directly or through the investments of insurance and pension funds. The strategy aimed to link the expectations and hopes of working people with the risks and pleasures of capital investment. The indebted worker with a small shares portfolio accepts that freedom of consumer choice and personal responsibility are the main criteria for success. Proliferating individual and consumer rights deepen socio-economic integration further. In the buoyant 1990s, the dominant ideology declared that every desire could become an entitlement, every 'I want X' become 'I have a right to X'. The interests of working people started gradually to approximate those of capitalists, despite the income differential, which grew to unprecedented levels. The sub-prime mortgages scandal showed that financialized capitalism must 'invest in the bare life of people who cannot provide any guarantee, who offer nothing apart from themselves'.[7]

South European countries, locked into the dominant model through the euro, followed suit. In Greece, the channelling of individual behaviour took two forms: casino capitalism and modernization. Casino capitalism spread the belief in fast and effortless profit based on borrowing, speculation and entrepreneurialism drawing on political favours. The turn can be timed. At the beginning of the 1990s, news bulletins began to broadcast regularly the stock exchange closing prices, although very few people had any stocks or shares. The message was clear: invest your money in stocks and borrow, spend and be happy. I recall being told by a relative who was a banker in Athens to buy a particular financial 'product' called 'repo', because it was a 'safe investment with high return'. I asked him what these 'repos' were but he could not explain. When I added that I do not own stocks or shares nor I am interested in acquiring any, he was incredulous. 'I thought that you must be a smart guy, being a London professor. I am no longer sure.' Conspicuous consumption was the other side of the neo-liberal dream. Easy and cheap loans, rewards for market speculation, rapid increase of real estate values became instruments of economic policy as well as criteria for social mobility and individual well-being. 'Mandatory pleasure' was the official commandment. The 'obscene' father of psychoanalytical theory kept telling people 'enjoy', 'buy', 'live as if this is your last day'. After the flight of industry and agriculture to the developing world, debt for consumption became the main growth strategy of the West.

The official aim of 'modernization' is to bring Greece closer to its European partners by reforming and streamlining state institutions and rationalizing private economic activity. It is based on an alleged divide between advanced Western civilization and the backward Eastern world. Its ideology is a strange combination of orientalism and *orthodoxophobia*, to coin a term. The 'modernizing' project peaked around the Pasok government of Prime Minister Costas Simitis between 1996 and 2004. Its promoters were liberal academics and technocrats, educated in the West, with strong links in Brussels and Washington. They despised the 'oriental' and 'religious' aspects of Greek culture, which they blamed on Ottoman rule and backward Orthodoxy. Feeling more at home in Paris and London than Athens, they believed they could use state power to carry out a cultural revolution. It would combine neo-liberal economic policies with institutional and educational initiatives aimed at providing a social side to economic liberalism. In reality, it was the opposite. Modernization was a response to the failure of the social democratic project and the state's near abandonment of its welfare function.

A number of initiatives have been credited to the project: the introduction of private radio and television with minimal regulation; the creation of semi-autonomous institutions such as the Ombudsman and the Commission for the Protection of Private Data; large-scale funding for NGOs and 'civil society' initiatives; extensive privatization of public assets and an attempt to introduce private universities prohibited under the 1975 constitution; finally, grandiose projects such as the 2004 Olympics. They were all part of a plan to create a more open, orderly and integrated capitalism. Some initiatives, such as the creation of an ombudsman and other semi-independent state institutions and the attempt to restrict the influence of the Church, were positive. The privatization of universities and the reform of social security met resistance and failed. The overall project smacked of nineteenth-century social engineering. It was ill-conceived, normatively flawed and practically impossible.

If we put the rhetorical statements to one side, modernization was neo-liberalism with a human face. Sociologists and 'socialist' politicians believed that the legendary 'civil society' of Western Europe was a necessary prerequisite of liberal capitalism and tried to import it top down. Reforms would make the state more capital friendly and would 'socialize' liberalism. The transfer of social services, such as education, health and social security, from the public to the private sector would rationalize and improve their effectiveness, while liberating people from state tutelage. Privatization would turn citizens into consumers, giving them 'freedom of choice' and a sense of their buying power, thus making them natural allies of the reform project. If employment is high and the stock exchange keeps rising, conflict between capital and labour would be abolished or at least become hidden. Borrowing, consumption and 'bull' markets would lead to perpetual growth, improvement in living standards and acceptance of the order of things. The plan was based on a near religious faith that the philosopher's stone, transforming Midas-like economic trash into stocks and shares gold, had been found. The proliferation of financial products in search of ever greater profits led to the 'automonization of financial capital from any collective interest' and to a profound gap between financial logic and social need.[8] When the bubble burst in the early 2000s and again in 2008 the financial priorities changed. Investments lost their inflated value, devastating savings and leading to a housing market crash. It was the end of the hope of continual growth and perpetual peace. As savings and loans ran out, working people and elites started facing each other again across a thin blue line.

Modernization was a mechanistic importation of Western models without consideration of anthropological differences. The habits, conventions and values that support the Greek economy and polity differ from those of the West. Identities and social bonds are based on family, friends and the community. This 'social ethos' creates a sense of belonging and facilitates the operation of institutions and law. It is true, however, that these foundations of identity have been consistently betrayed. The ideology of fast profit, instant gratification and narcissism forms the delinquent underside of Greek life. Bribing officials, kickbacks for politicians, illegal placement of public contracts, deals between political and economic elites, tax evasion and avoidance proliferated in the age of affluence. Modernization was supposed to cleanse the state from and punish corruption. It did not happen. The seeds of the current predicament were sown during the Simitis premiership. The respected journalist Stavros Lygeros details how the government 'offered gold-producing contracts in return for unquestioned political support . . . during his premiership cronyism became so gigantic that it seriously distorted the rules of free competition'.[9] The proliferation of practices that the rhetoric of modernization condemned, and the crash of the stock exchange, brought the edifice down.

The modernizers' Manichaean distinction between the 'backward' Greek and 'progressive' European traditions forgot that 'civil society' associations and NGOs cannot replace deep and long-standing cultural roots. Membership of an animal welfare group or the card of a consumer rights association has less attraction than a MasterCard. 'Constitutional patriotism', cosmopolitanism and individualized philanthropy hold little attraction in London and Paris and absolutely none in the northern suburbs of Athens. It was not surprising, therefore, that the attempt to introduce the European model of socialized individualism failed. As a result, Greece was living a contradiction in the early twenty-first century. The economic components of neo-liberal economy had been imported but social relations remained stubbornly communitarian. Financial services and economic mentalities did not differ much from those in England or France. But the attempt to supplement them with Western social structures had failed, undermining the positive aspects of identity and augmenting its delinquent distortions. Greece had entered the age of financialized capitalism without going through mature social modernity. Neo-liberalism and the biopolitics of individual desire and instant gratification had taken root faster than their promoters would have hoped. But social 'Europeanization' had failed. The 2004 Athens Olympics symbolized the folly and vanity of the age. Simitis' departure in 2004 alongside his group of mediocre experts marked the end of the 'modernizing' experiment of free-floating politicians, celebrity academics and media 'intellectuals' who had spearheaded the campaign to 'civilize' the Greeks. Greece will be paying for many years for the bonfire of the modernizing vanities.

There is no doubt that the Greek state is in dire need of root and branch reform in order to change from a tool of party hegemony to a force for redistribution and social justice. The old duopoly of New Democracy and Pasok has repeatedly promised to reform, 're-found' or rationalize the state. In reality, after an election victory they would only replace personnel – some 7,000 officials change when the opposition wins the elections. Successive governments used cronyism and clientelism to gain or retain power; they could not indict their personal and preferred practices. The trumpeted state reforms aimed at protecting entrenched interests. Real state reform can take place only after radical political change. The modernizers' attempt to transform individual mentalities and behaviour succeeded economically, but failed socially. Greek capitalism does not need a 'civil' society, because the society of 'communities' is more profitable and efficient for deal-making. The social ethos, however, retained its ability to defend social relations and help communities and identities. Family care and help as well as material and emotional support from friends are perhaps a better way of dealing with hardship than visits from social workers, surveillance from health visitors or the fast-diminishing offerings of state largesse. The Greek ethos, with its mild nationalism, secular religiosity and familial base, remains one of the strongest in Europe. In its corrupted version it promotes neo-liberalism; it is also the most powerful force for resisting it. It became the first target of the austerity measures.

The biopolitics of collective salvation

Greece is a textbook case of the complex entanglement of population control and the disciplining of individuals. After entry to the euro, the government promoted consumption and hedonism as the main way of linking private interests with the common good. The distorted economic growth based on borrowing and the financial bubble came to an end in 2008. The austerity measures reversed priorities, impos-ing a novel and brutal biopolitical administration of population and individuals. The 'rescue' of Greece is seen as a return to fiscal 'health'. Public spending cuts, tax hikes and privatizations are the tools. People were told for some twenty years that the main concern of power was the economic success and happiness of individuals. Now the earlier policies were reversed. The politics of personal desire and enjoyment turned into a strategy of saving the nation by abandoning its indi-vidual members. Population is everything, the individual nothing.

At the collective level, austerity divides the population according to work, age, economic, gender and race criteria and demands radical behaviour reform for the sake of fiscal probity and competitiveness. The measures cover every aspect of life, from basic food consump-tion to health, education, work and leisure. People are asked to align their behaviour with the 'needs' of the nation and to be subjected to extensive controls, which aim at recovering 'social health'. The behavioural change was initially demanded of the low paid and pen-sioners; it eventually spread to everyone. Every new wave extended the measures to ever increasing groups of population pulling into the vortex the middle class and creating an oversized 'squeezed middle'. Population strategies had to be supplemented with extensive inter-ventions at the individual level. Twenty years of individual hedonism had to be brought to a rapid end. To do that, an extreme version of the 'shock doctrine' recipe was imposed in the hope that the violent introduction of austerity would reduce resistances and rearrange behaviour fast. Its economic strategy creates scarcities in the things the previous period provided in abundance and individualizes the

38

disciplining process. Money, work, rights, security and aspirations become rationed and people are asked to administer this sudden reversal without help.

Biopolitical strategy mobilizes fear and alleged scientific truth but also cultivates a sense of guilt. Undoubtedly there was tax evasion (mainly by the rich) and corruption (mainly by the powerful). A collective sense of guilt is the prime disciplining tactic. Psychoanalytical theory is of assistance here. As Slavoj Žižek argues, the superego is dual. Its moralistic part indicts us for the pleasures the 'obscene' superego demanded during the period of fake affluence. The categorical superego has now become dominant and tells the Greeks that 'you deserve to suffer because you sinned. For twenty years you have improved your living standards by means of non-productive activities. Now you must pay.' The Northerners who treat Greeks as cheating and lazy liars are the external representatives of the superego. 'Your life full of pleasures and holidays, your good food and sex, your sun and sea steal from us this little something, this *je ne sais quoi*, that would fill our lack and make us complete and happy.' The Greek elites follow suit. 'Accept your punishment because you deserve it' they intone. Moralism is the indispensable companion of biopolitics, the Protestant ethic fellow-traveller with neo-liberalism.

A second strategy targets certain 'specially guilty' groups, which are presented as the main culprits for the country's hardship. Civil servants, university professors, doctors, pharmacists, public transport operators and drivers have been picked for special vituperation. It allows everyone else to feel both guilty (since all Greeks sinned) and innocent (since others were the main cause of the travails). The 'guilty innocent' is a major moral role during the crisis. The super-rich tax evaders and the corrupt contractors of public works are periodically chastized anonymously; no investigations or prosecutions follow. The billions siphoned into Swiss bank accounts and Mayfair luxury houses 'will be rigorously pursued'. The citizens, educated in the cynicism of power, take these denunciations with a pinch of salt. Those who ruled the country for forty years cannot indict and prosecute themselves and their supporters.

Immediately after the end of the Second World War, the German philosopher Karl Jaspers gave a series of lectures on German guilt. He listed four types of guilt: criminal (commission of identifiable violations of law), political (statesmen and citizens acquiescing to a regime committing crimes), moral (responsibility for actions felt by individual conscience in conjunction with friends and intimates) and metaphysical (universal responsibility for everyone alive who, witnessing terrible crimes, failed to act out of fear and self-preservation). In the Greek case, the rhetoric of metaphysical guilt ('we are all at it') has eclipsed all physical sense of guilt and punishment.

The strategies of 'collective guilt' and 'guilty innocence' are accompanied by continual attacks on the working population. The security of work has been replaced by short periods of work and long of unemployment. Flexible, part-time, alternate, shared and piece-work, continual geographical movement in search of work, de-skilling and permanent low level retraining in new skills are mainstays of a worker's life. The life of a typical working man from the town of Veria is a good example. 'Themis trained in mechanical engineering, once did skilled work in construction, including building work for Lidl supermarkets. Now he sits by the phone waiting for random shift work sorting peaches for a local farm co-operative for €29.45 a day . . . Since construction work dried up last year, Themis has accepted anything, from travelling a 140-mile round trip daily to work on road building, which has now stopped, to carrying carcasses in a meat market.'[10] In this bleak climate, the family is expected to replace withdrawn state support. Family and community have traditionally been the foundation of identity and sociality and offer support in times of need. But, as Richard Sennet has detailed, work uncertainty and movement place huge pressure on families.[11] Once austerity had removed the flimsy state safety net, families are asked to step in. Government policies, however, undermine family values, completing the 'achievements' of the 'modernizing' project. Every part of state provision from preschool to school and university education, to health, unemployment benefit, elderly care and psychiatric support has been brutally cut. People have to fall back to family support, if it is available, with the corresponding loss of autonomy and privacy, or to learn to live a life of poverty, humiliation and disease. This total reorganization of work, life and social relations is hitting three groups hardest, the young, women and immigrants. With unemployment at 55%, the young have little hope of finding a job. They have been reduced to 'human detritus' or 'youth debris'. This is perhaps the greatest obscenity of the crisis. In the pre-crisis days of moralistic humanitarianism such massive attack on identifiable groups could be considered a crime against humanity, a *genecide*, to coin a term. Human rights groups have been absent with a few exceptions.

Women are a main target of biopolitical control. In Britain, the gender effects of austerity have been widely discussed. Women are the greatest victims of the crisis. Employers are more likely to sack women; supports of maternity and child care in the form of crèches, benefits and the like have been removed. Anecdotal evidence indicates that a similar gender bias exists in Greece but such matters are of no concern to 'macho' politicians and 'neutral' experts.[12] The *Guardian* reports that 'homelessness is rising, food banks in Athens are struggling to meet demand, and suicide rates have risen sharply along with requests for psychiatric counselling. Young couples can't afford weddings and Greece, already struggling with its lowest birth rate in decades, now has a generation of 30-somethings postponing having children because they can't afford to feed them.'[13] A short stroll in central Athens tells you that between the 2011 *Guardian* report and late 2012, the crisis has become a humanitarian catastrophe. Young homeless people on every corner, drug addicts shooting up, skeletal immigrants begging. Austerity and class indifference are destroying Greece.

Michel Foucault argued in his College de France lectures that biopower adopts racism as state mechanism and uses it as a major technology for behaviour control.[14] This is clearly happening in Greece but also to Greeks.[15] The populist Western press describes the Greeks with epithets used in the past against groups considered ethnically inferior. Calling Greeks cheats or lazy is an ideological statement with racial undertones, turning them into the contemporary colonial subjects. In equal measure, many Greeks have racialized their predicament, absurdly accusing immigrants for the travails of the country. Their inability to see in the mirror the inferiority the Germans find in the Greeks and the Greeks in the immigrants is a bitter irony. Immigrants have become the greatest victims of poverty, destitution and hostility, as jobs disappear and extreme racism is on the rise. The first two austerity governments used migrants to display toughness and ideological purity. During the May 2012 election campaign, the Pasok Ministers of Health and Public Order launched a campaign to remove immigrants from city centres, calling them 'human trash' and accusing them of crime and of spreading infectious diseases. It was just a show; those arrested returned soon to the city centre. New Democracy responded in kind, promising to 'reconquer' central Athens from the 'invaders'. Once in power, it launched a campaign called 'Hospitable Zeus' to arrest and remove immigrants from cities. Racism is spreading like wildfire. An Olympic athlete tweeted that mosquitoes spreading the 'West Nile' meningitis virus have lots of 'home-made food' to nibble on.

Greek authorities, preoccupied with debt and austerity, are not concerned if a scapegoat, any scapegoat, can be found to carry their responsibility for the disaster. Again, before the May 2012 elections, ministers launched a particularly disgraceful campaign against 'foreign-looking' sex workers. They were rounded up, tested for HIV and detained pending trial for unspecified crimes. Their names and photos were publicized in newspapers and websites. The practice copied the infamous British Contagious Diseases Acts of the 1860s, which authorized the rounding up of prostitutes and women judged to be promiscuous for mandatory venereal diseases testing and subsequent imprisonment. The nineteenth-century operation was universally condemned and contributed to the rise of feminism. An Association for the Repeal of Contagious Diseases Act was formed and special repeal journals were published. The Association was compared to the Society for the Prevention of Cruelty to Animals, since women were treated like 'female dogs or bitches' who 'may be brought before a summary jurisdiction, and, if the court thinks it fit destroyed'.[16] As Joanna Bourke drily comments, 'the legislation treated women as a whole as nothing more than contagious animals, while at the same time they identified the real "mute creatures" in class terms'.[17] The contemporary operation has added race to class and sex and offers a shameful symbol of cynical biopower. It allegedly aimed at protecting the 'health' of the Greek nation by targeting, humiliating and punishing racially 'inferior' women. The government was saving men from foreign sex predators intent on destroying the Greek gene pool. When it became known that many detained women were Greek, the publicity subsided. In the nineteenth century, middle-class women rallied to the cause of their persecuted sisters. In the twenty-first, only the Left defended the dignity and privacy of these women. In late capitalism, the proud liberal traditions have been abandoned by the liberals and are kept alive only by the radicals.

The racial attacks by mainstream parties and media legitimized the neo-Nazi Golden Dawn party which polled 7% in the 2012 elections. Electoral success has emboldened this gang to increase attacks on immigrants, gays and ethnic minorities. Groups of party members roam Athens and provincial towns at night and attack immigrants in the street but also in their shops and homes. At least ten attacks are reported daily, with some leading to serious injury and death. Non-Greek stall-holders in flea markets are set upon; their merchandise is scattered and destroyed. Party blood banks collect 'Greek' blood and give it only to Greeks in need. The party leadership has stated that it despises Parliament and trains 'storm troops' in order to enforce the law. It is a moral and political disaster. The open expression of racist and fascist ideas and the physical attacks influence young people who admire strong-arm tactics and the explicit glorification

42

of violence. The political and cultural shortsightedness of Greek, German and European leaders who tolerate and even finance through party funding this organization is shocking. Government propaganda targets the Left because they defend immigrants and equates it with the Nazis as the 'two extremes' while turning a semi-blind eye to the Golden Dawn crimes. Capitalist cynicism places its survival above that of democracy.

Let me conclude. The biopolitics of personal desire and enjoyment has turned into a prohibition on individual pleasure. Who is rescued then when large parts of the population are destroyed? Literally Greece. The various governments are saving the genetic information of the nation by abandoning its individual members. Medical metaphors are the favourite rhetorical trope of austerity. The nation is 'sick'. If the loan instalments stop, it will be like 'removing the country from life support'.[18] The immigrants are a 'health bomb' against the nation, they bring in exotic and lethal diseases, 'foreign' sex workers are spreading AIDS; they are exposed in the media to 'save families'.[19] Greece has passed from an aggressive to a defensive neo-liberalism, from the promotion of pleasure to the management of failure. Population is everything, the individual nothing. Austerity reverses Mrs Thatcher's famous statement that 'there is no society only individuals and families'. 'There is no individuals or families, only populations' is the mantra of crisis capitalism. Greece has become a giant laboratory where a post-apocalyptic humanity is constructed and tested.

Austerity law

Biopolitical capitalism has changed law's nature and operation.[20] Two superficially opposed but complementary processes have converged over the last fifty years. On the one hand, most areas of private activity are increasingly legalized and regulated; on the other, public services and utilities are released from their redistributive aims and given over to the disciplines of private profit and the market. Juridification and de-regulation have weakened the formal sources of normativity. Whether they originate in private managers or state bureaucrats, rules are no longer the democratic expression of sovereignty or the liberal formalization of morality. Policy (often a euphemism for ideological prejudices hiding under 'scientific' expertise) becomes the inspiration and discretion the administration of law. Rule and discretion, supposed enemies according to the rule of law tradition, blend into each other as two sides of the same coin. Legislators and citizens treat laws in a purely utilitarian way. As proceduralist jurisprudence keeps reminding us, laws have now become frameworks for organizing private activities, reducing market uncertainties and lowering transaction costs. Even Jurgen Habermas despairs: 'In this *postpolitical* world the multinational corporation becomes the model for all conduct. The *impotence of a normatively guided politics* . . . is only a special case of a more general development. Its vanishing point is a completely decentreed world society that splinters into a disordered mass of self-reproducing and self-steering functional systems.'[21] The World Bank welcomes the prospect. Its 'Governance and Development' report states that the rule of law is necessary in developing states 'to create a sufficient stable setting for economic actors – entrepreneurs, farmers and workers – to assess economic opportunities and risks, to make investments of capital and labour, to transact business with each other, and to have reasonable assurance or recourse against arbitrary interference or expropriation'.[22]

Biopolitical law is a sad remnant of the rule of law tradition. This great achievement of European civilization has been 'reduced to an ensemble of rules and no other basis than the daily proof of its smooth functioning'.[23] As law is disseminated throughout society, its form becomes detailed and inconsistent, its sources multiple and diffused, its aims unclear, unknown or contradictory, its effects unpredictable, variable and uneven. All major aspects of legality have been weakened. Rule is replaced by regulation, normativity by normalization, legislation by executive action, principle by discretion, legal personality by administratively assigned roles and competencies. Regulation and normalization are ubiquitous and invisible, they come from everywhere and nowhere. They mobilize non-punitive tactics, deferrals and delays, appeals and counter appeals, media solicitations and ensnaring. They both assume and engender acceptable corruptions and forgivable transgressions as an integral component of politics, business and finance. The biopolitical order normalizes and corrupts, corruption is part of its normality.

Detailed regulation emanating from local, national, supranational and international sources penetrates all areas and aspects of life. From the most intimate and domestic relations to global economic and communication processes, no area is immune from state or market intervention. Everything, from the composition of tinned food to torture has found its way in (public or private) law. The law expands inexorably at the price of assuming the characteristics of contemporary society, becoming decentred, fragmented, nebulous. The claim

44

that the legal system forms a consistent system of norms was always unrealistic. It now looks extravagant as the law starts resembling an experimental machine 'full of parts that came from elsewhere, strange couplings, chance relations, cogs and levers that aren't connected, that don't work, and yet somehow produce judgements, prisoners, sanctions and so on'.[24] Outside the trappings of central power, law is increasingly law because it calls itself law. The legitimacy of routine legality depends on law's ability to mobilize the symbols of power and the force of the police with little reference to justice, morality or democratic legitimacy. This omnivorous – public or private – regulatory activity means that some legal statements take a normative – 'ought' – form; most are just descriptive of procedures, technics and regularities. In this sense, law is well on the way to replicating life in its annals. Modern law tries to regulate the world; late modern just mimics it. In Borges' story of the cartographers of empire, the mythical map-makers, asked to produce the most accurate possible map, ended with one the same size as the territory it mapped. The law repeats the enterprise; it has undertaken the most accurate mapping of society, a process that will end up with law and the natural life of society or, with order and desire becoming co-extensive and in perfect synchrony.

The mission of modern law (and of the metaphysics of modernity) was to open a distance, occasionally imperceptible, between itself and the order of the world. Law was a form of the ideal next to religion, nationalism or socialism. It aimed to correct reality. Now this distance is fast disappearing in the vast expanse of law-life. This is a law with force but with little value or normative weight, a law that constitutes and constrains but does not signify. In the past, law making and interpretation were domains of great political struggle. Now the gap between the law's letter and its interpretations has shrunk. The law has lost its transcendence and become the surface of social relations. The great positivist theories of the twentieth century considered validity the hallmark of law and confined efficiency to an external secondary role. Today, only efficiency matters. Validity, modern law's mark of identification, is discussed in law textbooks as a relic from the past not dissimilar to natural law. Proliferating individual rights increasingly adopt and legalize the claims of individuals and identity groups reproducing society's 'natural' order. Rights have replaced right, individual interest the collective good.[25] 'Nothing is more dismal', writes Giorgio Agamben 'than this unconditional being-in-force of juridical categories in a world in which they no longer mirror any comprehensive ethical content: their being-in-force is truly meaningless.'[26]

These changes are evident in Greece. During the period of affluence, law and rights were promoted as the great emancipator. Greek academics discovered and translated Rawls and Dworkin some thirty years after their peak and tried to reconfigure law around the idea of individual rights. Austerity changed all that. The law has been reduced to a secondary role, a trigger for assertions of legitimacy and for attacks on dissidents. All aspects of law suffer from a serious 'normative deficit'. It takes two forms. First, a number of attacks on basic principles of international law, the constitution and the rule of law; secondly, a juridical biopolitics which gives legal form and disperses austerity throughout society without the normal safeguards of legal culture. Let me mention a few legal acts that undermine the rule of law.

Under international law, sovereign debt is regulated by the domestic law of the debtor state, which can suspend payments or reduce the debt if it is deemed illegal or odious or, in cases of emergency if, for example, it cannot pay salaries and pensions. The loan agreements impose on Greece an immunity waiver and the exclusive jurisdiction of English law. The waiver means that the lenders can treat Greece as a private contractor, demanding securities and threatening seizure of all its assets under the English 1978 State Immunity Act, which prioritizes the interests of the creditor.[27] Public assets can be seized by the lenders and the government cannot protect itself under international or European law since it has accepted the exclusive application of English law. The loan and memorandum agreements imposed taxation increases and savage salary and pension cuts before they reached Parliament, which was reduced to the role of rubberstamping a *fait accompli*. The law implementing the agreement was adopted with a simple majority despite constitutional provisions requiring a three-fifths majority for such onerous international agreements. The complex memorandum imposing the austerity measures was passed under 'guillotine' procedures with minimal debate. This law gives *carte blanche* to ministers to issue executive decrees which can cover all aspects of economic and social policy, repeal pre-existing laws and sign further binding agreements giving away parts of national sovereignty without Parliamentary approval (s. 1.4 law 3845/2010).[28] Another act with a single section specified that the agreements and memoranda apply from the point of their signing. They are introduced into Parliament later just for 'debate and information' (s. 1.9 law 3847/2010). Attempts by Parliament to amend the odious measures agreed will lead to the non-payment of loan instalments turning the troika into the ultimate lawmaker. Another law set up a privatization agency to sell off infrastructure assets. Under the law, if a foreign concern approved by the lenders identifies an asset of interest, it is immediately transferred to the agency, which estimates its value and then passes the freehold or leasehold to the lenders' choice. The price of the transaction is then paid to the lenders. The agency's portfolio includes utilities listed on the Athens stock exchange, buildings, plots of land, ports, airports and uninhabited islands. The agency chief told a London meeting that Greece will become 'an El Dorado for investors'.[29]

The violations of constitutional propriety go further. Large parts of executive, legislative and judicial powers have been transferred to the EU and IMF. The reduction in the minimum wage, the abolition of collective bargaining and other labour rights as well as the pension cuts violate a number of social and economic rights protected under the Constitution, European law and European human rights law. When the austerity measures were challenged in court, the *Conseil d'Etat* peremptorily rejected the appeal. Fundamental principles of constitutional law were set aside at the altar of 'saving' the nation. Judicial power became a fig leaf for governmental decisions. The attacks on sovereignty and the moral core of the legal order are endless. Major parts of legislation are introduced through administrative decrees emerging in Brussels or Athens. The troika must approve public spending and changes in taxation. Tax revenues were used to finance the social state and had moral legitimacy. As a redistributive and social policy measure, taxation forms a part of the normative universe aiming to correct reality. Under the bailout agreements, however, taxation has hit the poorest especially hard. VAT at the top rate has been imposed on food and even *souvlaki*, the Greek fish and chips. The *souvlaki* tax has been followed by increases in direct taxation and an especially objectionable property tax collected through electricity bills and leading to power disconnection if not paid. Revenues from taxation, alongside the horizontal salary and pension cuts, are used to reduce the deficit and repay the debt. According to the second agreement, loan advances will be deposited in a special 'escrow' account and will be used to pay back earlier loans. Furthermore, the Greek government has made an undertaking to introduce legislation and eventually a constitutional amendment guaranteeing that debt repayment takes precedence over all state obligations, including the payment of salaries and pensions.[30] For the first time in a democracy, a particular ideology will be explicitly introduced in the constitution. These provisions mean that the European governments are lending money, which is immediately returned to them and their banks for earlier loans. The suffering people do not feature in the agreements; they are treated as cash cows. If, according to Carl Schmitt, the sovereign is the person who can introduce the state of exception and suspend the rule of law, the 'troika' is the bearer of (economic) sovereignty in Greece.

The austerity laws and executive decrees have formal validity; they have no moral justification or democratic legitimacy. They simply offer a normative gloss to decisions and acts that have already taken place. Austerity law aims to cover and reform every aspect of social life. For legal positivism the 'law is the law'; the underlying idea is fully radicalized. Power's *fait accompli* seeks legitimacy by attaching the 'legal' predication to itself. Law is everything that succeeds in calling itself law, without any control of formal propriety, moral correctness or political legitimacy. Law has become a justification for what exists. When a government has lost moral and political legitimacy and the symbolic capital democracy offers has drained away, legality is the only weapon left. The turn to legalism would inject, the government hopes, the prestige of the 'rule of law' into illegitimate policies. The result is often the opposite. The legitimacy deficit moves from governmental policies to individual laws and eventually to the rule of law. Instead of legality supplying legitimacy to failed politicians, law itself becomes illegitimate. At that point, *anomie* enters the scene.

— 3 —

ANOMIE I: SOCIAL ETHOS AND POLITICAL CYNICISM

On social ethos

Let me start with two stories. Many church festivals on the island of Paros and elsewhere celebrating the feast day of their protector saint, a mainstay of the Aegean summer, have been cancelled. Economic hardship is not the only reason. People no longer want to meet old friends. They feel that they have lost their dignity, they are embarrassed by their daily humiliations, they don't want to admit their problems in public and they don't want to hear the difficulties of others. Bars and tavernas have emptied; the few groups around speak in low voices or remain silent. Silence is the sound of austerity. It is as if the whole place is in mourning. People are waiting for something, anything that will put an end to the long, slow torture of new cuts, more job losses, shops and businesses closing.

The second happened in late 2011. Government politicians and mainstream media started a concerted attack against university staff. The background sheds light on the incident. The Papandreou government in full agreement with the right-wing opposition passed a law during the summer vacation which leads to the gradual privatization of universities and radical reform of their governance. It is true that the Greek university needs major reforms. It must remove party political influences, become better linked with social needs, promote critical thinking and become more open to international collaborations. But it is not the failing institution the government claims. All major world universities have Greek graduates on their staff, proving that Greek education turns out successful academics and researchers. Greek society considers education to be a major tool for social mobility and appreciates universities and academics more than the

British do. The government reforms, however, undermine academic integrity, minimize internal democracy and promote all-powerful academic bosses and business involvement. The majority of academics and the normally conservative rectors refused to implement the reforms citing Article 16 of the Constitution according to which higher education is public and free. The government punished them by withholding the hugely reduced university funding. The academics persevered and won several major concessions in 2012.

The successful resistance infuriated the government, which has responded with attacks on academics and the integrity of higher education. A small number of academics were picked and condemned for nepotism, tax evasion and mismanagement of research funds. The attack aimed at identifying the resisting academics with the wider pathologies of state and society. The government hoped to derail resistance and displace responsibility to others for the sorry state of Greece from those who ruled the country for forty years. Most of the accusations were baseless, were dropped and no prosecutions were brought. But the benefits of the choice were clear: 'Look at those supposedly super-educated intellectuals', the government was implicitly saying, 'they are the profligate state-dependent power hungry destroyers of the country. All our ills start in the university'.

The stories are examples of the spread of *anomie*. It is a term used extensively by the government in its attack on protests. *A-nomie* means the absence or lack of *nomos* law. The government chose law and legality as a favourable terrain for delegitimizing the resistance. In a characteristic statement, the Minister for Public Transport declared in 2011 that the government will not let 'Greece exposed to the risk of international disrepute and marginalization, destinations of countries characterized by *anomie*. Attacking the social acceptability of the free-rider and dismantling politically its simulation of progressiveness is of paramount importance.'[1] The harassed minister conflated the mass protests that gripped Greece in 2011 with the 'free-riders' who evade or avoid tax or otherwise violate the law for personal gain. He was confusing civil disobedience with illegality and lawlessness. Chapter 7 discusses the legality and morality of civil disobedience. This chapter concentrates on the sociological and moral aspects of anomie and the unfortunate use of the term by the government.

The term 'anomie' was introduced by Emile Durkheim in his classic studies *The Division of Labor* and *Suicide* and was developed throughout his long scholarly career.[2] For Durkheim, the division of labour leads to social integration, achieved through a number of systemic and normative operations. Work relations create social ties, which are strengthened by the normative regulation professions and activities develop. Anomie emerges when systemic integration is eroded either as a result of disrupted group life or deficient social regulation. Systemic failure occurs when people become too remote from each other and relationships are 'scattered'. In such cases, interaction patterns are weakened and behavioural expectations undermined, leading to social disintegration. Equally important is the destruction of the unspoken conventions and customs supporting integration that we call 'social ethos' in this book: the informal values, understandings and habits, which regulate communal life and everyday interactions, smoothing the operation of social relations. As Durkheim put it, 'a system of ethics is not to be improvised. It is the task of the very group to which they are to apply. When they fail, it is because the cohesion of the group is at fault, because as a group its existence is too shadowy.'[3] The social ethos is not a transient convenience that can be discarded or transformed at will. Anomie is precisely the cause and effect of the erosion of social ethos. It happens both at the macro and micro-social levels. A particularly acute type of anomie results from a substantial mismatch between the social ethos on the one hand and institutional strategies on the other. When social and economic policies and laws attack and undermine popular values, habits and understandings they create extensive disenchantment, fear and aggressiveness.

Anomie both targets social ethos and is the condition of its retreat. Latin and Latinate languages translate the Greek words *ethos* and *ethikos* with two terms: ethics and morality. Ethics retains a semantic link with the original Greek *ethos*, while morality, restricted to the realm of moral rules, codes and commandments, expresses modern preoccupations. Social ethos has elements from both ethics and morality. It helps construct the identity and sense of belonging of individuals, groups and communities. In trying to describe ethos, Augustine's negative definition of time comes to mind: 'What then is time? If no one asks me, I know: if I wish to explain it to one that asketh, I know not.' Time cannot be defined but we know when it passes. Similarly, with social ethos. We cannot draw a comprehensive list of its components but we know when it withdraws under attack. In Greece, both the modernizing policies of the previous period and current austerity have seriously undermined social ethos. The pathology of their breach allows the examination of these unwritten conventions.

The social ethos includes normative and factual elements. On the normative side, we have tacit understandings, implicit prejudgements or prejudices and prereflexive ideas about the position of self, its relation to others and its standing in the community. Gadamer's philosophical hermeneutics have analysed brilliantly these prejudge-ments.[4] They form the axiological and conceptual horizon, which enables us to reach considered judgements and make decisions. These conventions are formed over a long period of time. They are learned and reproduced in the family, the school, the neighbourhood and church through example, mimesis and repetition; they are passed informally from generation to generation. The factual component includes practices, skills and dexterities, some local and specific (habits and conventions of a locality, a particular activity or a pro-fession), others general and abstract (etiquette and good manners, behaviour in public, sumptuary and food codes). These skills are rarely described in textbooks, nor are they taught formally.

We can visualize the social ethos as a group of nested dolls, from the smallest and most intense of family life to the largest but thin-nest of the national community. The family ethos teaches us how to behave towards those close and intimate; as a family member I am treated primarily as a whole person, for who I am in the totality of my being. At school, I learn to treat others and be treated as equal, for what they and I do. The conventions of work, profession or organized activity teach specific skills and aptitudes, which help judge the success of tasks. Learning that I am equal to others either within a specific community or group or in the nation as a whole gives me the sense of dignity and (self) respect. Learning to evaluate the performance of tasks and undertakings within a profession gives me the sense of (self) esteem. We keep learning and refining these skills and normative orientations throughout life. My religious father, a natural Pascalian philosopher, used to say that it is not good deeds which make a good Christian but the practice of piety: fasting, regular church going, con-fession and communion are the external marks of devotion. Imitation and repetition will eventually inscribe the values animating these prac-tices in the soul. Louis Althusser generalized the views of Blaise Pascal (and my father) defining ideology as the 'interpellation' of the subject by ideological mechanisms and apparatuses. We are 'called' to our role and function and we assume it through behavioural adjustment and obedient performance. In this sense, our mature identity develops in a dialectical affirmation or negation of the social ethos. The ethos forms the background of both socialization and individuation.

One particularly important lesson we learn through the collective ethos is how and when to follow formal rules. 'Every general norm demands a normal, everyday frame of life to which it can be factually applied and which is subjected to its regulations. The norm requires a homogeneous medium', writes Carl Schmitt.[5] This 'everyday frame of life' mediates between the abstract rule and its application in new and unforeseen circumstances. Without such unwritten conventions, the law, formal morality and social interaction misfire. Civility, a key construct of social ethos, is necessary for the operation of rules and the amelioration of their strict and unjust application. It bridges mere legality and abstract morality and allows both to function. There is more. The stability and predictability offered by the social ethos helps innovation and invention. Its regularity 'legitimizes eccentric, surprising, and inventive applications of the given rule. On the other hand, the regularity can also cause the transformation and even the abolition of the rule in question. These two types of creativity are inextricably linked.'[6] Obeying the law but neglecting the conventions telling us how and when to obey it leads to legal correctness and social delinquency. 'Work to rule' is a good example. As a form of industrial action, 'work to rule' means absolute obedience to the law, while disregarding the conventions explaining how to apply it. If, for example, my working day finishes at 5 pm, I hang up the phone on a customer, or switch the computer off at the stroke of five, losing a contract or data. This may lead either to loss of a job or to a change of the rule. Or, consider the ritual offer of friends to pay for a meal or a round of drinks. Such verbal contests often conclude an evening's outing and preserve the ethos of friendship. In periods of hardship, however, it is expected that the most affluent person will insist until the others graciously accept his offer. Background civility, adjusting the practice to the circumstances, allows the ethos of friendship to survive without punishing the weak members of the group. Keeping to the same example, a round of drinks in a London pub creates the expectation that the others will buy their rounds. In Athens, a round is seen as a gift and does not create a duty of reciprocation. Another's offer to buy the next round turns the gift into an exchange relationship and can be taken as an insult. Unlike moral rules claiming universality, the social ethos is always situated in place, activity or nation. One reason why the European Union cannot become a political union is that no common European ethos has emerged.

If we turn to what we can call 'national ethos', the conventions and habits of *filia* (friendship), *filotimia* (respect for honour) and *filoxenia* (hospitality) are, or used to be, paramount in Greece. This trinity of *filias* represents perhaps too abstract and stereotypical a view of Greekness. It may reflect the rose-tinted view of an expatriate of forty years who nostalgically remembers life in 1960s Pireas. I certainly do not claim that some essential Greek character exists, inscribed in the ethnic DNA and protected by a patent in God's book of elect nations.

Anthropological research has shown the ambiguity and double-edged character of national attributes and attitudes.[7] Gifts and friendships may conceal claims to recognition and superiority, as Jacques Lacan suggested. *Filotimia* may be the way through which hierarchies and leadership are confirmed. Finally, hospitality may involve instrumental calculations or, worse, a turn to xenophobia and racism. Jacques Derrida reminded us of the etymological link between hospitality and hostility. The stranger who enters my space may be seen as a supplicant and asylum seeker or as threatening invader. This is the reason why most civilizations have developed rules of hospitality as an antidote to hostility. Aristotle's mysterious declamation 'O my friends, there is no friend' captures the dark side of the dialectic between *filia* and *phobia*.[8] Friends can become the worst enemies; the betrayal of friends destroys the idea of friendship. Undoubtedly, biopolitics and austerity have increased atomization and individualism and have often turned *filia* into instrumental calculation and unfair advantage. Despite attacks, however, the morality of friendship and care survives.

Anomie weakens the premoral set of values and understandings and, at the same time, it is the name of their degradation. This is precisely what is happening to the Paros festivals and to towns and neighborhoods throughout the country. People have retreated to the privacy of home, solitude and despair. Greece used to have one of the lowest rates of suicide and mental disease in the world. It has now moved up sharply on both fronts. According to Durkheim, increase in suicide offers the best evidence of modernity's anomie: 'Our social organization, then, must have changed profoundly in the course of this century to have been able to cause such a growth in the suicide-rate. So grave and rapid alteration as this must be morbid; for a society cannot change its structure so suddenly.'[9] Retreating ethos unpicks the mortar keeping personality and community together. The partial victory of the resisting academics mentioned at the beginning of the chapter, on the other hand, is the contemporary version of the conservative *jus resistentiae*. It was the revenge of social ethos against the belief that law reform can change long and deeply held values and habits without persuading people first. The greatest arrogance of power is to believe it can change society radically by legislating a few policies, while destroying the values enabling their acceptance and application. The German philosopher of law Rudolph von Jhering argued that reality has a normative force that occasionally trumps the force of law. In our terms, this is the force of social ethos. It functions like a flexible and adjustable 'natural law' that keeps the place together. Every authoritarian regime dreams a magic wand that can change society to order overnight. By forgetting basic rules of social organization, it unerringly fails. The megalomania and miscalculation of the reform project turns it into the 'folly of modernization'. The right to resistance, on the other hand, safeguards 'forms of life, which have already been affirmed as free-standing forms, thus protecting practices already rooted in society. It means, then, defending something positive: it is conservative violence in the good and noble sense of the word.'[10]

Modernization and austerity have distorted social ethos. Personal integrity, social civility and the common good have been seriously damaged. The customary care for others has turned to indifference, hospitality deteriorated into exploitation, solitary depression is replacing the meetings of friends. But despite the attacks, family and communal ties have survived and remain stronger than elsewhere. This is evident in the extensive solidarity campaigns that have sprung spontaneously over the last couple of years; in schemes of social assistance, bartering of services and farmers' markets; in neighbourhood defence committees, free health centres and cooperative initiatives; in mobilizations to protect immigrants from fascist attacks.[11] This revitalization of the spirit of community, cooperation and shared perseverance, a characteristic of periods of hardship and resistance, provides a defence against austerity's undermining of the sources of self. *Filia* (friendship, love or care), a main component of many combined activity words (philosophy, philology or philokalia), remains a key predicate of character and behaviour. It persists as a defence against radical atomization; its perverted form, on the other hand, attacks the body politic like a defective immunity system. The duel between ethos and its distorted form will determine the long-term future of the country.

We observe a similar attack on what we could call 'communal morality', those values which challenge the particularity of ethos. The 'community' refers to the groups, professions and activities individuals join when they leave family care and become independent; 'morality' to the principles and rules of the professions, jobs or collectivities we belong. 'Communal morality' consists of the general principles and concepts, which confront, negate and amend our individual ethos. Let me explain. Identity is created in a complex dialectical process. It starts with our socialization in our ecosystem or life-world. We are thrown into the waters of an ancient river, which existed before our birth and will survive our sojourn in this world. The initial identity of family and local ethos matures in a continual dialogue with general and abstract values. Adult personality emerges out of a clash and dialogue between the familiar and the alien or the particular and the

55

universal. Autonomous identity arises from the negation of what is taken as given. As Hans-Georg Gadamer put it, 'experience is always the experience of negation'.[12] The young woman who goes to university or the young man who learns a skill or profession and then starts work, enters a lifelong process of comparison and juxtaposition between the habitual, well-known and comfortable and the alien, unknown and general. Exit from our comfort zone, facing the strange and abstract helps us develop our unique identity. It emerges out of the dialectical confrontation between the implicit rules and unwritten conventions of social ethos on one side and the alien and universal on the other. Recognition of the other, both the other person and universal principles and cognitive commitments which challenge the familiarity of belonging, leads to self-recognition. 'Consciousness recognizes itself in what is alien and different.'[13]

During the rapid urbanization and industrialization of early modernity, for example, the nation as well as civil and political liberties became such universal values. They secularized religious beliefs and helped develop modern identity. Because we are English or Greek, because we are formally equal before law and state, we accept our role and condition, despite the huge class, income and opportunity inequalities. References to the nation (and nationalism), to people (and popular sovereignty) or to democracy (and political participation) emphasized assumed similarities and helped set aside huge wealth differentials and power imbalances. In this sense, the normative horizon of an age influences private morality. Our personal view of virtue and the good emerges gradually as identity develops. C. B. Macpherson memorably described the capitalist subject as an infinite appropriator and consumer. In late capitalism, these trends have reached paroxysmal levels. 'Look after number one' forms the dominant value; 'be yourself' and 'shop until you drop', the categorical commands of our age. Despite neo-Kantian rhetoric, hedonism and utilitarianism are the default moral positions of a society that promotes an acquisitive form of freedom. Radicals and resisters, on the other hand, value solidarity and community. A morality based on equality tends towards care, empathy, respect for dignity. To be sure, the normative horizon we find ourselves in creates a tendency or pressure towards a particular type of personal ethics but does not determine it. Our identity is always on the move, in conversation and struggle for recognition with intimates, friends, acquaintances and strangers. Personal ethics and our idea of the good starts in the life-world but keeps developing and changing in its openness to the other and stranger. We call 'subject', this entangled and unique combination of ethos and morality, received and universal values, self and other.

56

The cynicism of power

Let me start again with three vignettes. A Volkswagen cars advert shown on Greek television has a girl telling off her father for wasting too much water when shaving and too much electricity by leaving the lights on at night. Having established her green credentials, the daughter goes on to approve her father's purchase of the advertised car. If people respect the planet by not wasting water and energy, goes the message, they are entitled to buy what is really destroying the planet, the private car.

In June 2010, the Athens public prosecutor initiated criminal proceedings against 'persons unknown' sending messages in the social media, according to which Greece would soon go bankrupt despite the first bailout. Such speculation was neither new nor particularly shocking. Many economists, including Nobel prize winners as well as British, German and American newspapers were daily reporting what was blindingly clear: the combination of unmanageable debt and austerity-induced depression would inevitably lead to default. The prosecution, however, was against the ubiquitous 'usual but unknown suspects', trying to stop people repeating what everyone knew.

In August 2012, the government launched a campaign to 're-occupy' Athens and other cities from immigrants presented as foreign 'invaders'. Thousands of people who look foreign and darker than the Greeks, an absurd and futile exercise in physiognomy, were arrested without cause. Those found without the necessary documents, only one in seven of the arrested, were taken to camps awaiting deportation, which rarely if ever happens. Amnesty International, Human Rights Watch and the UN High Commission for Refugees condemned this major violation of human rights. The government, however, called the operation *Xenios Dias* or Hospitable Zeus. Whether this is a case of postmodern irony or ignorance of the meaning of words is unclear.

The car ad, the prefecture announcement and the misnaming of the pogrom symbolize the moral condition of crisis: cynical capitalism. The cynicism of power appears everywhere. It is most striking in the soothing statements of politicians, media and 'experts' who know (or they must be presumed to know) that the gap between their austerity policies and economic recovery is unbridgeable. They go on regardless, however, under the modern principle that a lie often repeated becomes the truth and, the postmodern edict, that anything often repeated becomes boring and turns people away. Cynicism, the dominant morality in late capitalism, is a fundamental perversion and betrayal of ethics: it accepts moral principles in theory while violating them

57

brutally in practice. The German philosopher Peter Sloterdijk describes cynicism as the paradoxical ideology of 'enlightened false consciousness'. The cynic sees himself as modern and enlightened but also as discontented and frustrated. He is 'well-off and miserable at the same time [and] no longer feels affected by any critique of ideology; its falseness is already reflexively buffered'.[14] It captures perfectly the position of Greek elites. Their maxim reads: 'I know that what I am saying or doing is false or wrong, but I concoct rationalizations and keep doing it. I know that simple logic reveals the lie but I keep repeating it.'

The Greek normative horizon had been corrupted before the recent measures and petty illegality had spread. We must distinguish, however, between legitimate but marginally legal forms of assistance to family and friends and illegal or immoral cases of corruption and criminality. Sociologists and anthropologists of the Mediterranean have explained the intricate complexities of gift exhange in kinship groups and the significance of favours among family members, friends and patrons.[15] These widespread practices have a long history going back to the Ottoman period. If unlawful action is not involved, such deals and exchanges help create friendships, sustain the social bond and are morally accepted but not publicly advertised. The second kind of delinquent behaviour involves illegal benefits, payment of bribes for services and kickbacks for the placement of contracts. The infamous '*fakelaki*' or 'brown envelope' stuffed with cash helps to get a planning permission, jump the queue for hospital admission, or have the tax demand reduced. Non-payment of taxes or social insurance contributions fall into this category and are a major cause of the spiralling budget deficit. Again, however, we should distinguish between the elites and the professional middle class who could benefit from tax evasion and avoidance and public and private employees who are taxed at source. Paying the proverbial plumber in cash is a well-known middle class practice all over the Western world. These parasitical attitudes proliferated in the period of affluence with its ideology of selfishness and instant gratification and affected ordinary people. Illegality was tolerated and even approved if it did not lead to public outcry. A friend told me that when she refused an offer by the taxman to have the value of a property she inherited reduced in order to pay less tax, he could not understand her position and became furious. He was not worried about losing the fee for his 'service', but because my friend was undermining a common practice. In this climate, both conventions and moral values were distorted. Morality became arid moralism, the ethos of friendship clientelistic nepotism, family love cold calculation. This is another instance of widespread anomie, which benefits the elites but infects the whole society. It leads to the dissolution of social ethos and generalized cynicism.

Corruption is not, however, a Greek speciality. Liberal constitutionalism is founded on a strict separation between the public and private domains. For Marxism too, capitalism does not need illegal acts to operate profitably. The rule of capital is guaranteed through the formal division between economic might and political power. In late capitalism, however, this separation has been abandoned. Economic, political and cultural elites have developed close links and intertwined interests. Cronyism combined with the ideology of enrichment leads inevitably to corruption. Corruption used to be the enemy of politics; now it is part of the political game. Mr Craxi, the former Italian PM, died in self-imposed exile in Malta; Chancellor Kohl, the great unifier of Germany, resigned his position as leader of the Christian Democrats in disgrace; President Chirac was indicted with corrupt practices; and President Sarkozy may follow. If there is something special about Berlusconi's misdeeds, it is that he publicly and openly used state power to promote his business interests. In this sense, Berlusconi was the grotesque extreme of normal activity. In Greece, kickbacks to the ruling parties and politicians by the German giant Siemens and others in return for major contracts have been known for years but go unpunished. The Pasok treasurer admitted receiving one million euros for the party in the early 2000s; a parliamentary commission of enquiry concluded that the corrupt practices led to a loss to the state of €2 billion. In August 2012, the coalition government signed an out-of-court settlement with Siemens giving the company a clean bill of health. The main compensation is a €90 million Siemens fund to finance seminars training the Greeks into anti-corruption practices. This is a striking case of the poacher turning gamekeeper and teaching the poachers how (not) to do it. It is further proof that corruption is as much part of politics as spinning and the ten o'clock news.

Moral cynicism became universal after the onslaught of austerity. The reason is simple. The elites fighting for their survival had either to lie or conceal the roots of the country's predicament. The cynicism of 'as if' ('I know that I am guilty but I act as if nothing happened') is perfectly suited for the task. If the victims also accept austerity as the only way to save the country, responsibility for past misdeeds retires and resistance to the measures becomes useless and wrong. The rhetorical denunciation of corrupt practices by the government, the repeated announcements of anti-tax evasion measures, the occasional publication of tax-evader lists, all give the impression of a concerted attack on these practices. Major corruption, bribery and cronyism involve the

59

state; the first target for investigation should have been those in charge for forty years. In Britain, during the 2010 election campaign, all three party leaders apologized for the expenses scandal, which cost less than two million pounds to the taxpayer and cannot be compared with the waste, corruption and patronage of the Greek political elite. All senior ministers have operated the system they now denounce and, considering the gravity of responsibility, a Japanese-style contrition would be appropriate. Not a single politician has been convicted for corruption. The political class demands that citizens act morally would be more credible if the paragons of public morality exhibited a modicum of humility and repentance. But as we have now learned, protestations of public virtue often conceal gigantic private vices.

Let me move to other cases of political cynicism. The official attacks on the bond markets and credit rating agencies are particularly striking. When the so-called 'spreads' (the difference between the return on German sovereign bonds and those of another state) of South European bonds started rising, governments and media personified the 'markets' into a single all-powerful malign entity, an evil monster eating up suffering people. From a loving mother figure, possessor of wisdom and source of supply and succour, the 'markets' turned into a hoarding scheming father who steals and pilfers our enjoyment. Only the financial markets were followed with fear and hostility. The Greek stock exchange was showered with love and concern. The bad foreign 'markets' have gone rogue; the benign suffering local bourse on the other hand deserves our greatest sympathy. Some parts of capitalism may become diseased but its overall moral health is not in question.

The same attitude is evident in the attacks and denunciation of the credit rating firms. They are presented as criminal profiteering gangs or as foreign parasites attacking healthy nations or banks. In late capitalism, however, credit agencies are indispensably ubiquitous. They use risk analysis to assess whether money should be lent to individuals, companies or states. Having a loan application rejected because of a bad rating is a common and hurtful experience for many; it does not lead to public opprobrium. Credit agencies are integral to the operation of financialized capitalism. The 'markets' decide only in part according to the performance of the 'real' economy.[16] The traders imitate other investors and base their calculations on 'feelings' of trust and risk. They operate on a virtual level. Rumours about the trustworthiness of a debtor, about the risk of defaulting or about political stability are added to projections, ideological constructions and 'hunches'. 'The final share price is the product of "self-fulfilling prophesies", and thus has little or nothing to do with the real economic value of the asset that the stock certificate represents.'[17] The investors' behaviour may be related marginally only to reality but it can change it radically. As George Soros put it, 'there is no reality independent of subjective bias but there is a reality that is influenced by it. In other words, there is a sequence of events which actually happens, and this sequence incorporates the effect of the participants' bias.'[18] The stock exchange and the bond markets operate on expectations, beliefs and speculation about future performance; credit agencies are indispensable. Their demonization by mainstream media and governments, whose declared aim is to return to the markets, is cynical capitalism at its worst. The cheap loans that allowed the spending spree of the 2000s were the result of the positive ratings of Eurozone countries. No government complained about the arbitrariness of their good grades, which contributed to the current crisis. Indeed the power of these agencies was created by European regulations, which oblige banks and financial institutions to seek and abide by their ratings. Credit agencies have partly replaced the 'hidden hand' of the market. Financial markets without them would be like an engine without lubrication.

The moral outrage against bond markets, hedge funds and credit agencies is an impotent 'acting out' which allows us to go on accepting the overall system after voicing our moral indignation. If the outraged governments were logical and consistent, they would condemn the entire economic system that makes populations hostage to the speculation of the securities market. The culprit is the capitalist system, not its peripheral components and tools. The rhetorical attacks resemble a boy who is daily beaten by the school bully. One afternoon, he goes back home bruised but happy because he has finally realized that the bully is stupid and illiterate. We know that a chasm separates the beautiful mask from the ugly underside of capitalism, but we keep promoting the mask. We know the reality behind the falsehood, we know the particular interests hiding behind the claims of universal principle, but we still go on accepting the falsehoods. We know that the emperor is naked but, as nobody does anything about it, we go on acting as if we had never heard about it.

Of cynics and kynics

Cynicism is the dominant ideology of the elites. The most evident symptom is the exclusion and social abandonment of large parts of the population, in particular the unemployed youth. Idle young people wander around in the capital cities, assemble in street corners gazing emptily into the distance, kicking balls. They can be seen but not heard, living a ghostly life. They exist socially but not politically, forming a void in the midst of society. The unemployed and the *sans papiers* immigrants reveal the truth of late capitalism. Unemployment has become permanent and systemic; it is an inescapable part that supports the socio-economic structure. Trade unions used to campaign against low wages; today the unemployed and the immigrants have been abandoned as economically useless, 'human trash' or 'one use humans'. Paraphrasing Giorgio Agamben, we can call those rejects of the socio-political system *Homines* or *Hellenes sacri*, the people whose insignificant lives support the inegalitarian machine.

For the dominant discourse and mainstream media, the unemployed worker is responsible for his misery. He is an extreme example of the passive, defective, lazy character of the poor and of Greeks generally, according to the mainsteam media. If however the unemployed is seen as capitalism's symptom, the picture changes dramatically. His 'valueless' roguish existence becomes the symptomatic condensation of the disasters of late capitalism. When the symptom turns from secondary side effect into basic line of confrontation, the balance of power shifts. Youth unemployment, instead of being treated as negligible collateral damage, becomes the truth of austerity. Resistance grows and the excluded victim short-circuits the victimizing order. In the society of the spectacle, the image of a single unemployed young man or woman can influence the social imaginary. If people were to see her as a symbol of the innocent and unjustly punished victims of austerity and projected the torments and tribulations of the nation on her slight physique, as Mohammad Boazzizi did in Tunisia, change would come sooner.

As Ernesto Laclau argues, the universal is always an empty, floating signifier, a site of ideological and political conflict because it carries significant 'symbolic capital'. The struggle to fill the empty universal has two sides, however. Ruling elites try to occupy the universal form and have a formidable arsenal at their disposal. The Greek elite has mobilized a double hegemonic strategy. First, it tries to move the debate from responsibility for the sorry state of the country to its 'rescue', in other words, from past to future, as if the two are unrelated. The promise of state reform, of a war on tax evasion and corruption becomes a smokescreen and fig leaf for those who extensively use these tactics, and have brought the country to the precipice. The abstract and undefined 'rescue' presents the elite as the universal class which, despite some problems in the past, can subsume partial interests and work for the common good. The destroying and 'rescuing' elite hopes to avoid responsibility for past misdeeds and present catastrophes by focussing on the future. The second strategy is to move the line of confrontation from the contents of the catastrophic and proliferating measures to the question of respect for the rule of law. The term 'anomie' combines a misunderstanding of its meaning with the ideological attempt to present resistance as disrespect for the law. Every policy dressed in legal garb deserves unreserved obedience, claims the government. The argument is untenable in a democratic state; its unreality makes the attacks on dissidents increasingly ferocious.

Peter Sloterdijk has called 'kynics' instead of 'cynics' those who abandon the detached position of moral disinterestedness for the standpoint of '*a priori* pain', proximity and concern for the other. Instead of the cold irony of the rulers, this is the warm satirical laughter of Diogenes, the dog-philosopher, and of the politics of sensuality and the body.[19] *Kynicism* is a symbol of 'existence in resistance', while cynicism 'the reply of the rulers and the ruling culture to *kynical* provocation'. The conflict between *kynicism* and cynicism intensifies when 'in crisis civilizations and civilization crises, consciousnesses clash with each other'.[20] This is another and perhaps more significant 'clash of civilizations' than that advertised by Samuel Huntington. The solidarity towards the unemployed, the persecuted immigrants and the poor has developed a *kynical* consciousness that confronts the cynicism of the powerful. One side is symbolized by the rehashed enlightenment ideas of modernizers and ruling elites; the other by rational passion and bodily closeness of the occupations as well as the social solidarity that has spread throughout the country.

Against the idea of national salvation and unquestioning obedience to law, the destruction of whole generations and the humanitarian crisis give rise to non-negotiable moral principles. The morality of resistance is found close to the most vulnerable and invisible. Its categorical form is the following: 'Always act according to a maxim which, universally applied, attacks and cancels the causes that exclude and condemn to symbolic and physical death large numbers of people.' The excluded give rise to a universal moral command. As moral, the command is addressed at individuals not groups but can be realized only through political action. The moral imperative calls to a collective attack on the symptoms of social decay. This way, politics acquires a strong moral basis. This is not a moralization of politics but a politicization of morality.

63

— 4 —

THE CRISIS AS SPECTACLE

The Big Other

The analysis so far throws light onto Theodoros Pangalos', Papandreou's Deputy Premier, infamous statement when people asked where the enormous sums of the debt went: 'Τα φάγαμε όλοι μαζί', 'we spent (literally "ate") it all together'. It was the Greek equivalent of the British 'we are all in it together', accusing the whole population of profligacy and causing debt, and shifting blame from politicians to ordinary people. The opposition was rightly outraged. The majority of the low-paid population could not and did not participate in the *grand bouffe*. But this is not enough. The Pangalos statement should be taken literally and brought to its rational conclusion: if all Greeks 'ate it' together, the minister confessed his own participation in the banquet and should be brought immediately to justice. The police should initiate proceedings against Pangalos and his co-symposiasts and interrogate the corrupt actions he has freely admitted.

The Pangalos subliminal message is more complex. It exploits an inchoate and widespread feeling that the consumerist pleasures of the previous twenty years were sinful and must be followed by a sense of guilt and the appropriate penitence. In Protestant doctrine, the original sin plays a central role in the organization of self and society. Humanity can never escape its sinful genesis and must live a life of atonement through individual endeavour, perseverance and the acceptance of suffering. The Pangalos message is not dissimilar: rich and poor, powerful and powerless, we have all sinned. The content of transgression may differ between the tax evasion of ship-owner and the cash payment of suburban electrician but the form is the same. Indeed the poorer the person who evades tax, the greater

64

the problem, because it indicates an original and all-encompassing national corruption.

There is a second deeper message. If sin is congenital, if corruption and nepotism are so widespread, they are bad but also necessary and tolerable. Sociologists and anthropologists have argued that unspoken practices, conventions and customs lie behind economic systems and legal codes, facilitating their operation and mitigating their strict and unjust results. Bribing a doctor to jump the waiting list for an operation may be corrupt, the appointment of a party member to the local council undeserved and wasteful, untaxed work may starve the public purse; they are absolutely necessary, however, for the reproduction of the system, just like the sinful pleasures that accompany procreative sex.

Mr Pangalos and his provocative statement has acted metaphorically and through his considerable physique as the Lacanian 'Big Other'. The Big Other is the all-knowing centre of the symbolic order, the point around which the ruling ideology or 'reality principle' coheres in order to appear rational and consistent. The Big Other knows the answers to all questions. We don't know whether an elite conspiracy has led to the crisis but the Big Other does. We don't know whether the austerity measures are lawful and constitutional but the Big Other has the answer. We don't know who was behind John Kennedy's assassination but the Big Other knows. The Big Other guarantees that the formal position of knowledge, closure and the possibility of a final answer exists even though nobody has it. This includes the Big Other who is a convenient fiction, an impostor our desire projects in order to give us a modicum of certainty in these unsettled times.

Now Mr Pangalos enters the scene. There is no politician, civil servant or citizen who did not know that extensive corruption, patronage and tax evasion was an integral part of life. Yet, this common knowledge was also the greatest secret. Everyone knew but nobody admitted it. The elites profited from it and accepted it as part of normal life. It was common knowledge, but since it had not been acknowledged publicly it remained private. Common but private knowledge was the routine state of petty corruption. The practice could go on like Poe's purloined letter: it was the best-kept secret because it was there for all to see. The discrepancy between the widespread practice and the official lack of acknowledgement allowed society to function normally.

The stand-in for the Big Other has now admitted what the Greeks always knew. The admission was followed by a flurry of rhetorical attacks on corruption with no immediate effect. Instead of triggering investigations and punishment, the statement added to the guilt industry. People should feel guilty, was the message, and accept the radical reduction of salaries and pensions in the same way that Eve and Adam had to endure the pains of labour and the suffering of work. But if misdeeds are so widespread and common, if they form the unspoken set of practices that allow the system to work, they may be wrong but they are not punishable. Even more insidiously, if corruption is so endemic, its denunciation can only be rhetorical. If the Big Other knows, the great initial shock becomes eventually comforting. The practices will go on as before, only in more discreet and concealed ways. Their all-encompassing nature (we are *all* at it) makes outrage momentary. Indeed, one assumes that standard practice has been resumed, since no culprit has been caught and most prosecutions of politicians for corruption have been abandoned. As Mr Pangalos said in August 2012, 'we are still at it together'. The banality of corruption will encounter no Eichmann-type trials.

The crisis as spectacle

A unique feature of late modernity is the intense spectacularization of public life. During the illness of former PM Andreas Papandreou in 1996 and the late Archbishop Christodoulos in 2007, TV news followed every turn of their disease and was deluged with physicians explaining the finer details of cardiology and hepatology. A Martian in Athens would have thought that the Greek nation was training to become doctors. It was also what I thought in restaurants and bars at the time. Medical issues dominated discussions and reduced every other topic to invisibility and indifference. The news as spectacle gives people something to talk, argue and disagree about, creating a useful distraction from more pressing concerns. It is as if politics happens in order to provide copy for the media and entertainment for the public.

In the current crisis, graphs similar to the spread of volcanic ash or the advance of a tsunami dominated the screens charting the rise of 'spreads' and interest rates. The latest fad of 'data visualization' translated the destruction of families and lives into beautiful images. The Greeks learned the meaning of credit swaps, hedge funds, bond markets, offshore companies, credit rating agencies, PSI and other inscrutable acronyms. Whether they became financial experts is a moot point. This saturation with largely irrelevant information has turned the crisis into a spectacle populated by economists and experts. Two strategies are used to make the controversial cure, worse than the disease, acceptable to its victims. The first asserts that the neo-liberal diagnosis and recipe is the only available 'truth'. Understanding the problem (its history, causes and context) and discussing alternatives is peremptorily dismissed as ignorant or naive. Political decisions in Brussels, Berlin and Frankfurt, strategic choices by bankers and traders are presented as inescapable. The crisis is an act of God, a force of nature that could not be prevented. The predominant rhetorical trope is *prosopopoiea*: an abstract entity (the markets) becomes an unpredictable, inscrutable evil being. If Greece is like the *Titanic*, as Papandreou told European leaders in 2009, the 'markets' are the unforgiving iceberg. The only response in the face of such *force majeure* is to apply civil defence procedures in order to limit casualties and contain damages.

This 'naturalization' of economics can be called the 'fetishism of catastrophes'. If the economic crisis is a natural catastrophe, politics should be kept out of it, in the same way that it must be kept out of earthquake relief. Throughout 2011 and 2012, TV news boringly repeated 'it's the economy stupid', as they charted the rise of the 'spreads' in the same way they follow rising temperatures in a heat wave. 'What is the alternative?' was the rhetorical question that stopped debate. Policy proposals outside the neo-liberal dogma were dismissed because there is only one right answer. If the naturalized economy moves in unpredictably godly ways, politics becomes a region of economics and must implement its prescriptions. This is another type of post-democratic cynicism. The idea that 'there is no alternative' does not exist in politics. Democracy is precisely the expression of disagreement and conflict, a form of life through which the most imponderable problems can be put to debate and testing and solutions found. Governments and experts had to pre-empt public opinion by announcing that the most controversial problem of our times does not belong to evaluation and judgement but to the 'truths' of objective knowledge. This is why the listing of irrelevant facts and incomprehensible figures reached such unprecedented levels.

The attempt to cow people before the mystical knowledge of economists and disqualify alternatives was followed by a strategy of normalization of the extreme. It was the poor man's version of the politics of fear developed in the Anglo-American 'war on terror'. Various types of fear have been mobilized: fear of exit from the euro and the EU, of losing savings and property, of empty supermarkets and scavenging for food. 'Greece is at war,' said Papandreou in 2010. But whom does Greece fight? The only conclusion is that the Greek government under foreign mandate is fighting the Greek people. Fear is accompanied by a paroxysmal nationalism, which rhetorically attacks the foreign 'agents' of Greek travails while adopting their commands. Greece is like the Titanic, attacked unjustly, but also a proud country resisting the Germans but begging their pity. It was crowned by the tragic kitsch of an anonymous pensioner accosting the Prime Minister to donate his savings and the millionaire singer and former MEP Nana Mouscouri offering her parliamentary pension for the salvation of the nation.

The becoming-spectacle-of-the-crisis is both anxiety-producing and soothing. As people endlessly discuss the latest information and forecast or gossip about the performance and looks of politicians and bankers on the news, the spectacle worries and comforts. The same wise 'talking heads' appear daily, creating a sense of stability and trust. People who have lost their homes, jobs or families on the other hand are not seen; they appear only as numbers in statistics. This spectacularization of the crisis creates a Heideggerian 'world picture'. The 'crisis' becomes a finite and imaginary entity, both visual and fantastical. As finite, it can be understood and mastered with guidance from the experts. As imaginary, its understanding is a matter of theatrical performance and assent to expert 'knowledge', of political entertainment and cognitive conformity. The crisis as spectacle is the final stage of commodity and catastrophe fetishism. Choreographed by the experts, the spectacle presents the social disaster as a temporary deviation in an otherwise self-reliant and transparent reality. The spectacle in its frame (the graph, the fleeting videos, the TV set) generates a sense of mastery and understanding. If people behave the way the measures and the economists demand, the unfortunate fissures and fault-lines will be cured and social harmony will return. The spectacle makes people forget their woes. The wholesome image hides the pain of austerity and comforts the alienation of social fragmentation. The crisis-spectacle is organized as a three-step dance: recognition of failure, for which a recalcitrant state and resisting citizens are blamed; virile negotiations with the Europeans and the IMF which eventually achieve major concessions as a *quid pro quo* for new austerity measures; followed by frustration of expectations and failure. The virtual rescue soon unravels to be followed by another three-step choreography and a new and more vigorous set of austerity measures. Time stands still. K's 'indefinite postponement' of the final reckoning in Kafka's *Trial* is the best approximation of the crisis' temporality. Static time creates the terrain in which cynical capitalism consolidates itself and cultivates the sense of anguish, helplessness and passivity which facilitates the adoption of further austerity measures.

The media performance of Mr Papandreou was particularly instructive in this context. Papandreou offered a theatrical condensation of causes, effects and affects. The spectacle of the crisis was projected daily on to his face, which is sufficiently blunt and can assume all kinds of inflection and interpretation. In the early stage of the three-step dance, Papandreou's face was solemn and austere as he condemned the failure of state and economy, paralleled Greece to Titanic, on the edge of the abyss with 'loaded gun' in hand. In the second phase, Papandreou appeared determined to fight for the rights of Greeks who, according to the earlier scenario, were not fully deserving. Finally, a self-congratulatory tone followed the (hollow) success, reminding Greeks how hard and at what personal cost he had fought against great odds. Statesman and censor, fighter, winner, was the profile of *Papandreou Agonistes*. Unfortunately for him there was no Milton around to record his struggle. Unfortunately for the Greeks, the denouement of Papandreou's theatrics was the failure of every 'rescue' package and further punishment.

In terms of the philosophy of history, the vicious spiral the country has entered is part of historical necessity. The *ancien régime* had reached a point of no return. Papandreou, who in name and office accurately represented that regime, was doing everything in his power to ensure its demise. In this sense, his role was historical; the 'cunning of history' chose this most symbolic name to bring the edifice down, Samson-like. Perhaps the only authentic moment of Papandreou's theatrical performance came on 15 June 2011 when, after a huge rally in Syntagma Square and with almost every Greek opposed to the new austerity measures, Papandreou, looking defeated and gaunt, offered to resign and support a government by Antonis Samaras, his bitter opponent. This was George's Gethsemane and post-Oedipal moment rolled into one. 'Father, if it be thy will, take this cup from me', he seemed to be saying. Showing hesitation and indecisiveness – the signs of humanity – Papandreou asked to be released from the father's ghost with its intimations of extreme masculinity, forcefulness and autarchy. It was Hamlet's revenge against the myriad of detractors and libellers. George became momentarily the friend I knew and liked in the mid-1970s: sensitive, humble, in a state of Oedipal hurt. Within hours, however, Papandreou withdrew the offer and returned to his usual façade of Oedipal identification with the father. Hamlet was put back to his place again. Papandreou's fate was sealed; four months later he was forced to resign the premiership and, soon afterwards, the leadership of the party his father had founded.

The protagonists' roles are literally theatrical throughout the crisis.

The 'negotiations' with the troika always end up with acceptance of their demands. Greek politicians are actors on stage, performing for the domestic audience and hoping that any applause at home might lead to collateral benefits abroad. This Greek passion is performed in the form of a tragedy for the people and a cabaret farce for their leaders.

Revolution or consolidation?

The three austerity governments have adopted a revolutionary rhetoric. The country is presented as a backward place stuck in the past, with an overblown and inefficient public sector, a worthless and corrupt university and a population lacking motivation. The task is therefore to destroy the *ancien régime*, unshackle the entrepreneurial genie and drive the Greeks kicking and screaming into the twenty-first century. It may be collective amnesia or bad faith but someone (perhaps the Emperor's child demystifier or the Queen) should remind the various prime ministers and secretaries that they ruled the country for nearly four decades. If Greece is seriously ill, they provided the poison and now promise medicine banking on the dual meaning of the work *pharmakon*.

The trumpeted 'revolution' is a consolidation and intensification of capitalism. The reforms will ensure that everything remains the same, although a little worse. Instead of revolutionizing Greece, they are trying to consolidate and strengthen the socio-economic model that has dominated the country for long but is still encountering resistance. Many reforms are necessary but the overall package moves the country towards a predatory type of capitalism. The conditions of life and work and the social ethos will change irrespective of the conclusion to the debt saga. The European and Greek elites had decided to steamroll these reforms; the debt and deficit problems offered a convenient pretext for their imposition. The debt was desired because it allowed their fast and brutal introduction. This is also the reason why the emphasis some radical economists place on the debt seriously neglects the political reasoning behind the crisis and the solution imposed. The debt was the catalyst not the cause of the crisis; austerity is the method for arranging late capitalism in a period of crisis and secondarily only the answer to fiscal imbalances.

Let us examine briefly the semiotics of 'radicalism'. The name given to the deregulation of professions and skills is 'liberalization'. It includes the licence to open new pharmacies in a country where more chemists per square kilometre exist than anywhere else; the issuing of new taxi licences in Athens which already has a huge number of cabs idling in their hundreds in ranks all over town; further 'liberalization' of the law profession in a place where the 45,000 lawyers feed an insatiable litigation addiction. Treating deregulation and liberation as synonyms is as innovative a linguistic practice as the calling of the operation rounding up and locking African- and Asian-looking people, Hospitable Zeus. Neo-liberal fundamentalism joins here the inventiveness of Orwellian terminology. An associated tactic presents anyone resisting the 'revolution' as reactionary, ignorant, immoral or plain stupid. If the government is the vanguard, resisting trade union and parties, ordinary people on strike or protest and the indignant in the squares are White Russians resisting, Canute-like, the forward movement of history. They are doomed to failure and disappointment. The brilliant tactics of the alternating governments with the same policies and overlapping personnel complemented by the historical necessity to reform Greece guarantee that the old will die while the new is born. The elite politicians are simply the midwives of history.

The trumpeted radical character of the measures is the result of capitalism's enduring power to revolutionize social relations. Classical capitalism dissolved traditional communities and customs, melting everything solid into air. Late capitalism adopts 'Asian values' and commodifies community resources, like McDonalds which has replaced Big Macs with McCurry in Delhi and McSouvlaki in Delphi. The underlying message is that Greece did not develop proper capitalism and needs strong medicine. As Naomi Klein has argued,[1] the introduction of the full market society will be made easier through the infliction of deep trauma that will turn people into an 'ideological *tabula rasa*, survivors of their own symbolic death, ready to accept the new order now that all obstacles have been swept away'.[2] The medicine will be delivered in large doses, under the orders and supervision of Northern European Doctors. Local agents are not trustworthy, so the medicine must be administered without pity by foreign inspectors and emissaries.

Political semiotics

The Hegelian tradition acknowledges the radical intersubjectivity of human identity. Self is constructed in an ongoing struggle for recognition with the non-self, the other self or the objective world.

71

Psychoanalysis adds that recognition passes through the desire of the other, the big Other and the other person.[3] The desire for integrity projects the other as non-lacking, but this gesture misfires; the other is as lacking as self. The endless proliferation of desire and rights is the late modern symptom of this failure. If subjectivity is inter-subjective, it is mediated by the object. Objects are tools for negotiating the other's desire through a reciprocal recognition of self and its possessions. Property rights by turning simple possession into legally protected ownership allow its safe placement in the world facilitating the dialectics of desire. But as Marx noted when private ownership extends to the means of production capitalist domination follows. The transformation of use into exchange value and the accompanying fetishism of commodities are key components in this process. Cynical capitalism accelerates it.

In late capitalism, the desire of objects has acquired relative autonomy and has replaced the desire of the other. Her recognition becomes a collateral benefit that follows the possession of objects. Designer or branded commodities, from a humble T-shirt to the latest Apple product or sports car, are clear instances of this phantasmagoria of objects which has collapsed exchange and use value into a new type of semiotic value. Exchange value is calculated according to the logic of equivalence; money is the best example. Semiotic value on the other hand celebrates difference, sophistication and prestige through an economy of signs: the crocodile on the t-shirt, the apple on the tablet, the jaguar on the bonnet. The market in prestige is imaginary in both senses of the term: first, it is based on images, brand icons and marks. But it is also supported by our fantasy, which projects in signs and marks the status or success it expects to receive back.

The Lacoste polo shirt is not just an item of clothing or a statement of relative affluence. It is also a public declaration about the taste and discernment of its owner placing him within a select group of people who are wealthy and 'in the know' about style. Because I desire the brand and invest my desire in it, it gives me back prestige when I acquire it. Semiotic value is reflective and self-fulfilling. It is created through the imitative accumulation of projected desires. Desire creates the desired value, in other words, semiotic value is the desire for desire itself. Value is created through a performative and self-fulfilling prophesy, based on expectation, belief and the herd instinct. Material returns, strict economic value or the utility of objects is of little concern to man as desiring machine. On the side of capital, however, whether you buy a crocodile- or a tennis-racket bearing shirt or some cheaper version is strictly irrelevant, if you keep buying second, third and fourth shirts. Belief in the status-giving ability of the object is a prop only for the basic behaviour of purchasing not strictly necessary goods. There is a second important effect of cynical capitalism and the society of semiotic value. If we act according to capitalist expectations, if we serve the insatiable desire for objects, if we buy and consume ceaselessly, then we may freely believe whatever we want. We can call it the primacy of behaviour over belief, an area of overlap between cynicism and biopolitics. We may be anarchists or communists, Maoists or Trotskyists, deep ecologists or religious fundamentalists. All belief is allowed, if behaviour is controlled. As John Gray puts it, 'we are forced to live as if we were free'.[4]

All this applies also to political parties. Spin doctors, a recent word in the political dictionary, are precisely the manipulators of branding and the masseurs of logos. The convergence of mainstream parties into the mythical centre-ground has turned the political market into semiotic value trades. In Greece, Pasok and New Democracy are the brands of elite power. Their dynastic nature turned Karamanlis and Papandreou, the names of successive party leaders and prime ministers, into brand names which differentiate the 'products'. *Karamanlis* stands for development and relative affluence and is associated with anarchic urbanization and the economic growth of the 1950s and 1960s under Karamanlis Sr. The brand *Papandreou* stands for national pride and the economic rise of the petty bourgeoisie, associated with the 1981 Papandreou Sr government. In psychoanalytical terms, Karamanlis and Papandreou are the two 'obscene fathers' of the nation, telling the Greeks how good they are and promising pleasure and narcissistic fulfilment. Interestingly, the current dynastic generation has reversed the symbolism of the 'founding fathers'. Karamanlis the Younger has been identified as master of sloth while Papandreou Jr as subservient to foreign powers. With these resignifications attaching to the brand, the two dynasties have lost their aura, specificity and market share; they have collapsed into their underlying grey identity.

Against earlier predictions, the fake and perhaps even the real revolution will be streamed live.

Part II

Philosophy

— 5 —

ADIKIA:
THE ETERNAL RETURN
OF RESISTANCE

The end of history and the dawn of a 'new world order' was announced in 1989. If it was a 'new' order, it was the shortest in history. It came to an abrupt end in 2010. Protest, riots and uprisings have erupted all over the world, both in authoritarian and in democratic places. Neither the mainstream nor the radicals had predicted the wave. This has led to a frantic search for historical precedents and to hyperbolic comparisons. Paul Mason reports that a former director of Britain's Secret Intelligence Service thought that 'it's a revolutionary wave, like 1848'.[1] Mason agrees: 'There are strong parallels – above all with 1848, and with the wave of discontent that preceded 1914.' [2] Alain Badiou diagnoses a 'rebirth of history' in a new age of 'riots and uprisings' that may bring the 'intervallic' period that follows major revolutionary upheavals to an end. In the intervallic period, the revolutionary idea is 'dormant'.[3] For Badiou, this earlier period closed after May 1968, the religious turn of the Iranian revolution and the end of the Chinese cultural revolution. The interval is coming to an end. Resistance and revolution are in the air. What causes their cyclical return? The class struggle, the desire of the poor and exploited to see their fate improved, the rise of the 'multitude' and its constituent power, or the wish of people to taste democracy, can help us understand regional specificities and differences. This chapter attempts something different. It explores the metaphysics of resistance, offering a 'narrative' that explains its eternal return and traces its incarnation in philosophy and law.

Adikia

Going to the pre-Socratics in search of the mythology of resistance is perhaps a strange choice. Yet these cryptic meditations and apophthegms have conditioned the way our civilization understands itself. The Anaximander fragment, the oldest extant Greek text and one of the most commented on, reads: 'but where things have their origin, there too their passing away occurs according to necessity; for they are judged and make reparation (*didonai diken*) to one another for their *adikia* (disjointure, dislocation, injustice) according to the ordinance of time'.[4] Heidegger uses the fragment to confirm his fundamental ontology. The proper presence of beings is a 'lingering awhile'. When they present themselves, they cannot be out of joint (*adikia*); on the contrary, they are joined with others. But, as it reveals itself in beings, Being withdraws and conceals itself. In this process of unconcealment/concealment, beings are cast adrift and 'history unfolds . . . Without errancy there would be no connection from destiny to destiny: there would be no history.'[5] *Adikia* is the disorder of Being, its concealment that accompanies its disclosure and lingering.

Jacques Derrida returns to Heidegger's reading in *Spectres for Marx*. Derrida objects to the one-dimensional interpretation of *dike* and *adikia*, which emphasize jointure and care, and reinstates the centrality of *adikia*. There is disjointure and dissension in Being, a dislocation that animates the relationship with the 'other than being', the other person and death.[6] Derrida's presentation of Being as dissension turns *dike* into a response to enduring disorder and conflict (*adikia*). In the light of this correction, the fragment can be translated as follows: 'An archaic *adikia*, dissension or conflict, animates the unconcealment of Being. It endures in human history which is the unfolding (*tisis*) of *adikia*'s overcoming *dike*.' What creates this dislocation or injustice? How is the reparation calculated and paid?[7]

Sophocles' *Ode on Man*, the superb choral song from *Antigone*, gives an early indication.

> *polla ta deina kouden anthropou deinoteron pelei* (332).
>
> Numberless wonders (*deina*), terrible wonders walk the world
> but none more wonderful and terrible (*deinoteron*) than man.

Heidegger's reading of the song places power, violence and conflict at the centre of history. *Deinon*, the key word, has two meanings: first, it is man's violent and creative power, evident in *techne*: knowledge, art and law. Secondly, *deinon* is the overpowering power of *dike*, the order of the world humanity finds itself in and has to struggle with. *Techne* confronts *dike* and violently tears asunder the order of Being. In this confrontation, man stops being at home and both home and the alien are disclosed. Humanity opens paths and sets boundaries, introduces laws and institutions, masters earth and sea.[8] *Techne* and *logos* reveal the manifold of beings and ideas and humanity's own historical becoming. But *dike,* the overpowering order, can never be fully overcome. It tosses *pantoporos*: man (all resourceful and everywhere-going) back to *aporos* (without passage and resource). Humanity cannot escape disaster, caught up as it is in the endless conflict between power and overpowering, between the violence of knowledge and deed and the order of the world. Abiding disaster is the precondition of every achievement. The fragment calls it *adikia*, dislocation, disjointure or injustice. History rises on the breach opened by humanity's exercise of force on primordial *dike*.[9] There is 'aboriginal injustice in which we share, to which we belong. Older than time, than measure and law, it owns no measure of justice of equality or inequality.'[10] This dislocation is in excess of any possible restitution and opens history 'according to the ordinance of time'. *Adikia*, the absence of *dike*, is both the unending struggle between *techne* and *dike* and the limit between them; *adikia* is the cause and effect of *dike*.[11]

The sense of injustice, which prepares militants, is history's judgement and reparation for the original and enduring *adikia*. The struggle between *techne* and *dike* lies behind it. Such was the conflict between Creon's stubborness (Hegel greatly respected his achievement and predicament) and Antigone's rebelliousness or *ate*. The key passage in *Antigone* reads:

> Nor did that *Dike*, dwelling with the gods
> beneath the earth, ordain such laws (*nomous*) for men.
> Nor did I think your edicts had such force
> that you a mere man, could override
> the great unwritten and certain laws of the gods
> *(agrapta kasphale theon nomima)*
> *Antigone*, lines 448–453

Adikia endures as the world-making struggle between *techne* and *dike*. It has political, theoretical and subjective facets. Its political form is the epochally variable confrontation of human action with the 'second' nature of established social patterns and hierarchies. Its philosophical form explores the specific forms of *adikia* of each age. Such was Plato's quest for a theory of justice against the *doxa* of his time.

Similarly, Marx's identification of class struggle and communism was a theoretical response to the *adikia* or disorder of capitalism. Finally, each type of *adikia* creates its own resisting identities by inducing subjects who rebel and radically transform it. Antigone was the champion of ancient *dike*; Prometheus of modern *techne*. They have named the two types of rebellious subjectivity, the conserving and the revolutionizing. When the time gets out of joint, an affective or/and rational sense of injustice incites subjects of resistance. Resistance has therefore two forms: theoretical exploration of the ruling dislocation and political action to resist or redress it. The dissidents and revolutionaries, from Prometheus to Michael Kohlhaas and Rachel Corrie respond to the sense of injustice each epoch's *adikia* begets. The Tahrir and Syntagma Square occupiers are the contemporary children of *adikia*'s return. History moves in a combination of politics, thinking and radical subjectivity.

This approach could perhaps explain why the theory of justice is the oldest failure of human thought. Since Homer, the Bible and Plato, the best minds and fiercest hearts have tried to define justice or imagine the conditions of a just society. They have failed; indeed the successive and endless 'theories of justice' are a serial recognition of failure. Justice and injustice are not normative predications but subjective motivations. We are surrounded by injustice but we don't know where justice lies. This is the paradox of justice: while the principal has been clouded in uncertainty and controversy, injustice has always been felt with clarity, conviction and a sense of urgency. We know injustice when we come across it; its truth is felt. However, every time a theory of justice is put into practice, it soon degenerates into another instance of injustice. Justice applied leads to (feelings of) injustice. Life starts with injustice and rebels against it. Thinking follows.

The dialectic between justice and injustice does not lead to a dialectical synthesis. Injustice is not the opposite of justice; the unjust is not the contrary of the just; suffering injustice is not the logical opposite of doing injustice.[12] *Adikia* is both the gap between justice and injustice and the endless but impossible attempt to bridge it. It is what the symbolic order tries to suppress and the prolific theories of justice to legitimize, failing each time. As Jean-Francois Lyotard put it, a residue, a 'nonlinked thing'[13] or faultline beyond control founds every community and law. It is analogous to an 'unconscious affect', encountered in the 'sharp and vague feeling that the civilians are not civilized and that something is ill-disposed towards civility' which 'betrays the recurrence of the shameful sickness within what passes for health and betrays the "presence" of the unmanageable'.[14] This unmanageable *adikia* is 'radically non-historical: history itself is nothing but a succession of failed attempts to grasp, conceive, specify this strange kernel'.[15] In modernity, the reaction to *adikia* takes the form of (the right to) resistance.

The right to resistance

The fundamental legal maxim of the premodern world was *suum cuique tribuere*; give everyone his due. It was both a moral and a legal principle. The Greek *dikaion* or the Roman *jus* was the morally correct social ordering and the legally right answer to a dispute. In the premodern hierarchical order, social status determined what was due to each, what duties masters had towards slaves, husbands to wives, Greeks to barbarians. Right and wrong revolved around the *suum*, the proper to each according to his given place. They were backed by a teleology of natural ends, roles and duties, the world's *dike*. Classical *dike* was transformed by Christianity. The first challenge was the idea of spiritual equality exemplified in Paul's statement that 'there is no longer Jew or Greek, there is no longer slave or free, there is no longer male or female; for all of you are one in Jesus Christ' (Galatians 3:28). The Franciscan nominalists Duns Scotus and William of Ockham prepared the second attack in the fourteenth century when they argued that the historical incarnation of Christ made individuality the supreme expression of creation. Its knowledge takes precedence over that of universal forms. Abstract concepts have no ontological weight; they owe their existence to linguistic practices. For William, God has given individuals control over their lives and bodies similar to that of *dominium* or property.[16] For Duns, God's will has priority over his reason; the good exists because the omnipotent ordained it and not on account of some other independent quality. They prepared the age of the sovereign and his mirror image, the individual with her rights.[17]

Medieval and early modern philosophy discussed extensively the *jus resistantiae*, which was regularly exercised. Unlike classical *stasis* (revolt), however, medieval rebellions did not promote democratic rule. They removed usurpers or tyrants and returned the legitimate or lawful rulers to the throne. The rebellion was justified by the violation of agreements between feudal nobles or of restrictions and limitations rulers had accepted. As Hannah Arendt put it, 'while the people might be admitted to have the right to decide who should *not*

81

rule them, they certainly were not supposed to determine who *should*, and even less do we ever hear of a right of people to be their own rulers or to appoint persons from their own rank for the business of government'.[18]

The great revolutions changed that. The third estate or the 'common man' entered politics by revolting against the established order and the aristocratic and royal elites. The rise of the people is exemplified by the first article of the French Declaration of the Rights and Man and Citizen, the greatest perhaps modern normative maxim: 'All men are born and remain free and equal in rights.' It transformed the premodern principle of *suum quique tribuere*. It brought together the classical maxim of due deserts and the Christian command of universal equality by disengaging the *suum* from social status and giving it, rhetorically at least, to 'all men'. The premodern (moral and legal) *jus*/right, discovered by natural reason in a fixed ontological universe, turned into a bunch of individual rights belonging to all. The confrontation between hierarchical teleology and individualist ontology could be resolved only through revolution. Resistance and revolution were raised to normative principles: the 'right to resistance to oppression' was a key principle of the French Declaration. The declaration, 'an act of war against tyrants', proclaimed resistance as modernity's *techne* and the right to revolution as freedom's due.[19] The constitutionalization of the right to revolution was as radical a normative innovation as was the proclamation of universal equality. The rights of man emerged through revolution; resistance sustains their vitality as one of modernity's weapons against *adikia*.

German idealism celebrated the revolution because it incarnated freedom into history but rejected the Declaration's revolutionary right. Once constituent power has been constituted, the right to revolution retires. Immanuel Kant typically went to great lengths to dismiss the right as a contradiction in terms. The law cannot tolerate its own overthrow: 'Revolution under an already existing constitution means the destruction of all relationships governed by civil right, and thus of right altogether. And this is not a change but a dissolution of the civil constitution; and a *palingenesis*, for it would require a new social contract on which the previous one (which is now dissolved) could have no influence.'[20] Kant's reference to the rebirth of a people accepts that revolution is the expression of constituent power, the world-making strength of the multitude. The dismissal of the right to revolution is symbolic of the conservatism that colours the turn of constituent into constituted power.

Kant's ethico-political dislike was adopted by the victorious revolutionaries. The 1793 Declaration started to weaken the revolutionary right by activating it only in relation to the listed rights. Only their violation (and no other injustice) could justify resistance, indicating that rights had started their long mutation from revolutionary maxims into supports of the established order. The first epigrammatic article of the Universal Declaration of Human Rights (1948) repeats the French statement of equal freedom. Yet no right to resistance is found in the much longer epigonal recitation. On the contrary, the preamble states that human rights are given in order to prevent revolution and Article 30 prohibits radical challenges to the political and legal system.[21] Articles 15, 16 and 17 of the European Convention of Human Rights repeat and augment this self-serving conservatism, by allowing states to declare a state of emergency and derogate rights, outlawing attacks on the established order and prohibiting political activities by foreigners. These articles and the associated criminal law provisions had dire consequences. Radical parties and groups were banned in Germany, Greece and the United States among many others, their members sent to exile, prison or concentration camps. A modest right to protest against laws and policies without challenging the social order has been included in constitutions and human rights documents. The case law of domestic and international courts shows, however, that its protection depends on the sense of security of rulers and the good conscience of lawyers and campaigners. In most cases, the right to protest is an example of the 'Speakers' corner' mentality: a place for people to 'let off steam' and for the political order to claim a variable degree of tolerance and broadmindedness.

For Kant and the legal mentality, the revolution leads to a *palingenesis*, a rebirth of nation, community or class. Constitutions and treaties morally reject and legally prohibit such a possibility. The order initiated by revolution leads to the repudiation of its founding principle. The rights of man started as normative marks of revolutionary change. Positive human rights, their descendants, have become defence mechanisms against resistance and revolution.[22] The removal of the right to revolution was an attempt to foreclose radical change by making rights an insurance policy for the established order. In this sense, the order of the world is but a species of its dislocation. But the unending confrontation between *dike* and *techne* brings back resistance through the sense of injustice that *adikia* begets. The consecrated right to resistance cannot be wished away. Every time ethical subjectivity breaks with social reality, resistance and rebellion return. Revolution and radical change may or may not follow. Revolution is the step after resistance. The right to revolution does not exist independently, therefore, nor is it free-standing. It appears historically as (the right to) resistance; people in streets and squares challenging the dominant order prepare but don't guarantee radical change.

Permanent revolution is the modern condition in science and art. Kuhnian scientific revolutions and the upheavals of the *avant-garde* have consecrated revolution as a right, if not duty. In politics and law, resistance has become a ghostly normativity, the 'right to the event' one could call it. It has been permanently exorcized but eternally returns as the most important, perhaps political, command. It has kept social systems and legal orders alive by preventing their sclerosis and reversing their ossification. The attempt to disavow or discredit resistance is doomed to fail.

The metaphysics of will

The killing of the primordial father by the band of brothers is Freud's 'just so' story explaining the emergence of morality. The confrontation between *techne* and *dike* which conditions the *adikia* of each age is the myth behind the perpetual emergence of resistance, revolt and revolution. But if revolt has been banned and the right to protest is often used to legitimize the social order how does resistance return? Let us have a look at the philosophy of right. It offers an accurate insight into Western metaphysics.

The premoderns discovered the right thing to do in the cosmos, the natural order of things. The moderns invented individual rights and gave them to select categories of people who became subjects armed with rights. Finally, late modern rights repeat, copy and legalize pre-existing desires, socially accepted demands and the claims of a proliferating collection of identity groups and lifestyle choices. Liberal philosophy presents rights as the main, if not exclusive building block of ethics.[23] Duties, responsibilities, care, love and sympathy are secondary, parasitically complementing and enforcing individual rights, the primary moral resource. The move from an ethics of the good to the legality of rights and, finally, to the legalization of desire means that ours is the morality of exit from morality. Virtue and commitment to the good survive in the will to resist domination, oppression and exclusion. It is an immutable quasi-natural will. Eric Santner recently wrote that we 'need to tell the history of political thought in the West in light of shifts in the semantic field of the concept of "will."'[24] I agree. Right and rights are manifesta-

84

tion of the language of will and the best terrain to examine will's peregrinations.

Premodern ethics and law followed the *norma agendi*, a norm of action, prescribed by divine natural, ecclesiastical or feudal law. A modern legal right on the other hand is a *facultas agendi*, individual agency, a person's ability to act. Premodern law prescribed duties and authorized a limited number of acts; modern law prescribes rights and allows limited constraints on action. A legal right is a recognized and effective capacity to enforce our will. It is individual will raised to the level of general will or of law; will given objective existence. Rights are therefore the cause and possession of the subject. They are manifestations of man occupying the centre of the world, individual will becoming sovereign. The raising of subjective will into law freed the moderns from strong ethics, the morality of duty and the pathos of tragic conflicts. The strict distinction between private good and public right allows the subject to rule over his property, body and private life. The first claim to right was that of the property owner, specifically of the creditor against the debtor. Individual rights were formed in a long process which started with the aim of protecting creditor and owner. This model of right migrated from debates about dominion and apostolic poverty into private law in the thirteenth century and from private to public law in the eighteenth.[25] Property right was the first right and the model for rights; the rights of man were modelled on the right to property.

Private or public right appears as one, individual and undivided. It claims a single source, the subject's will, a single justification, law's recognition, a single effect, the will's ability to act and shape the world. The modelling of political rights on property conditioned their operation. A yawning gap separates the will from its effects, the normative weight from empirical operation, the 'ought' from the 'is'. Formal right, the legal subject's capacity to will, is theoretically limitless. But real people are embedded in the world; class, gender or race inequalities condition them and prevent formal rights from becoming effective. We are all legally free and nominally equal, unless of course we are improper men, in other words men of no property, women, colonials, of the wrong colour, religion or belonging. This was the reason why will, the first source of right, diversified into a second adopted by the dominated and the oppressed. For the wretched of the earth, right is not about law and judges, a game they cannot play. It is a battle-cry, the subjective factor in a struggle, which asks to be raised to the level of the universal. Right is the demand not to be treated as an object or as a nobody. It is the claim of the

85

dissident against the abuses of power or the revolutionary against the existing order. Legally created rights call for obedience; the right to insubordination, as Maurice Blanchot put it, expresses the exercise of freedom.[26] 'Where there is a duty, we merely have to close the eyes and blindly accomplish it; then everything is simple. A right, on the contrary refers only to itself and to the exercise of freedom of which it is the expression; a right is a free power for which everyone is responsible, by himself, in relation to himself, and which completely and freely engages him: nothing is stronger, nothing is more serious.'[27] This second right is an exercise of free will, a justified and forceful free power. It is specific in its origin but generalizable in its operation.

Right has therefore two metaphysical sources. As a claim accepted or seeking admission to the law, right is a publicly recognized will, which finds itself at peace with a world made in its image and for its service. But secondly, right is a will that wills what does not exist or what is prohibited, a will that finds its force in itself and its effect in a world not yet determined, all the way to the end. This second right is founded *contra fatum*, in the perspective of an open cosmos, and the belief that the world cannot be fully determined by (financial, political or military) might. It eventually confronts domination and oppression, including those instituted or tolerated by legalized and dominant will. The will to change the world and create a society of equality freedom and social justice has taken various historical forms. It appeared as the republican idea in the eighteenth-century revolutions, as the socialist idea in the nineteenth century, it became linked with the communist party and state in the twentieth century and suffered as a result of their betrayal. Today, the will to change the world brings together radical equality and democracy; democracy not as a system of interest and vote aggregation but as a form of life extending into all aspects of the social fabric, from home to work to social and cultural life. This combination of equality and resistance has been called the 'idea of communism'.[28] It has nothing to do with old-style communist parties and states.

Let us conclude. The French Declaration created a dual normative legacy. First, people are born free and equal; secondly, there is a (moral and legal) right to resistance and revolution. Liberal legal philosophy has interpreted the first as a regulative principle with limited force and has retired the second. Men are not born but ought to become reasonably free and moderately equal. Yet 'even where it is recognized, the equality of "men" and of "citizens" only concerns their relation to the constituted juridico-political sphere'.[29] Liberal orthodoxy uses institutional – legal, political, military – means to spread limited freedom and formal equality. But legal equality has reproduced the gap between rich and poor. Equality of opportunities means that outcomes on the output side will closely follow the differential inputs. Inequality created in the name of equality is an extreme symptom of contemporary *adikia*; it fuels the sense of injustice, revives the dormant right to resistance and ferments the *techne* of rebellion. Resistance turns equality from a conditioned norm into an unconditional axiom: people *are* free and equal; equality is not an objective or effect but the premise of action.[30] Whatever denies this simple truth creates a right and duty of resistance. As Alain Badiou put it, 'anyone who lives and works here, belongs here'.[31] It means that healthcare is due to everyone who needs it, irrespective of means; that rights to residence and work belong to all who find themselves in a part of the world irrespective of nationality; that political activities can be freely engaged in by all, irrespective of citizenship and against the explicit prohibitions of human rights law.[32] Axiomatic or arithmetic equality (each counts as one in all relevant groups) is the impossible boundary of rights culture.[33] Late modern *adikia* pits axiomatic equality against its pale regulative version. The combination of equality and resistance projects a generic humanity opposed both to universal individualism and communitarian closure.[34]

Radical change results from the dialectical relationship between ideal and necessity, accelerated by will. Will and idea come together in a dialectical voluntarism, as Peter Halward puts it.[35] When this happens, will no longer gives passive consent to power; it becomes an active force that changes the world. History is full of such confrontations, eternally condemned and eternally returning. Disobedience is the first step. It manifests a rift between the normatively guided will and the existing political and legal reality. Dissident will does not disobey the law. Liberal jurisprudence acknowledges the legal claims of moral subjectivity, as the next chapter discusses. The obligation to obey the law is absolute only when accompanied by the judgement that the law is morally just and democratically legitimate. Disobedience is the beginning. Protests mostly challenge law's conserving violence, breaking public order regulations in order to highlight greater injustices.[36] As long as the protesters ask for this or that reform, this or that concession, the state can accommodate them. What the state fears is the fundamental challenge to its power by a force that can transform the relations of law and present itself as having a 'right to law'. Paraphrasing Badiou, we can conclude that

87

rights are about recognition and distribution among individuals and communities; except that there is a right to revolution. Politics is the 'prescription of a possibility in rupture with what exists.'[37]

— 6 —

ANOMIE II: DISOBEDIENCE, RESISTANCE, SOVEREIGNTY

Disobedience and resistance

When resistance against the catastrophic measures took off in 2011, the government's idcological counter-attack was organized around the term 'anomie'. Law and legality were chosen as a privileged ground of confrontation. We examined the sociological aspects of the government's unfortunate use of the term in chapter 3. This chapter concentrates on a second misunderstanding. The 'anomie' the minister attacked is what political and legal theory calls 'civil disobedience'. From Antigone to campaigners for the vote and workers' rights, from suffragettes and conscientious objectors to civil rights and anti-Vietnam war militants, disobedience does not equal illegality and criminality. 'There is all the difference in the world between the criminal's avoiding the public eye and the civil disobedient's taking the law into his own hands in open defiance', writes Hannah Arendt. This distinction can be missed only by 'prejudice or ill will' – both in ample supply in the Greek government.[1] Disobedience is a sign of moral conscience and of political fidelity to principles of justice that stand higher than state law and policy. The idea of a law higher than the law of the state is as old as civilization. Its source has been variously attributed to ancestors, God, the law of nature or natural right. After his death, God has been replaced by international law, which has been elevated to a higher source of legality, typically in international human rights. These different versions have one thing in common: they become effective by motivating individuals and groups to resist the commands of established power because they violate the individual or collective sense of justice. In Christian modernity, it is the voice of conscience that confirms the gap between rulers

89

and justice. As Arendt drily remarked, 'the voice of conscience was the voice of God, and announced the Divine Law, before it became known as *lumen naturale* that informed men of a higher law ... To modern ears this must sound as "self-certification", which borders on "blasphemy".'[2] Other physical or metaphysical voices have been called in to play this demanding role.

We argued in the previous chapter that no society or age has created a commonly acceptable theory of justice even though regional conceptions abound. We should therefore rephrase our definition. Disobedience is an individual moral act and resistance a collective political event. They enter the scene when a compelling sense of injustice is felt by individual and collective conscience. This sense of injustice, which differs in each society and age, and the determination to do something about it, has changed regimes, constitutions and laws and helped introduce the reforms and rights we now take for granted. Without the appeal to a law above the law and the popular will to apply it we would not have had the vote, the vote for women, basic labour rights and social protections. To be sure, a law higher than state law has all the cognitive and theoretical difficulties of the belief in God's law. But its critique and deconstruction does not defeat its motivational force. Divine and other permutations of higher law have inspired people throughout human history. A guiding idea or norm operates within historical and social conditions. We make our own history but not in conditions of our own choosing. We create the social relations which condition us. The 'higher' call, by glossing the more modest sense of injustice, becomes a guiding idea and changes the ossified relations that condition us. Disobedience and resistance are the engines of historical progress. Humanity transcends itself through its own action.

The civil rights movement started with a simple act of disobedience, in 1955. Rosa Parks, an African American, did not surrender her bus seat to a white man as the law required. As the movement against racial discrimination grew and was joined by that against the Vietnam War, it triggered a major debate among political philosophers and judges.[3] Hannah Arendt,[4] John Rawls,[5] Ronald Dworkin[6] and the American Supreme Court accepted that disobedience is not only allowed but required in certain circumstance. If the strict conditions for justified disobedience are met the courts must protect those who undertake it. Richard Nixon, on the other hand, campaigning for the Presidency in 1966, denounced the dissidents as 'anarchists' and 'extremists'. The problem was not Vietnam or racism, he argued, but the 'deterioration for respect for the rule of law', which can be 'traced directly to the corrosive doctrine that every citizen possesses the inherent right to decide for himself which laws to obey and when to disobey them'.[7] In the last few years, liberal commentators have conveniently forgotten this honourable page of liberalism and are retreating to the Nixon line. The one lesson history does not manage to teach rulers is what great folly the dismissal of resistance is. Let me present briefly the argument for disobedience, synthesizing liberalism and democratic theory.

The attack on the right to revolution by Kant and Hegel and its rejection by legal positivism led to its deletion from the legal archive. Civil disobedience made a modest entry in the writings of Henry David Thoreau but its content and scope had changed. The terminological slide from *jus resistentiae* to civil disobedience is indicative. A right presumes the existence of a law or conception of the good, which stands higher and confronts established law and power. Disobedience, on the other hand, with its emphasis on civility, seeks its justification in the constitution, the law or other institutional sources. The resister and the revolutionary demand that another legality be introduced to replace an unjust law or practice. The disobedient asks that legality be observed. The distinction echoes the early division between liberalism and democracy. Until the twentieth century, the two were enemies. As Domenico Losurdo puts it, 'the classics of the liberal tradition refer to democracy with coldness, hostility and sometimes frank contempt, [and] regarded its advent as an unlawful, intolerable rupture of the social contract and hence as a legitimate cause of the "appeal to Heaven" (in Locke's terms) or to arms'.[8] Liberalism was concerned in the main with the protection of property and individual rights; democracy with social justice and popular participation in decision-making. After the merger of the two, the liberal belief in the rule of law was supplemented with claims to democratic legitimacy. Liberals believe that power has been tamed by constitutional legality and democratic accountability. Parliament and government represent popular interests in properly legislated laws. It follows that laws enacted by a democratically elected body and respecting individual rights must be obeyed. If democracy and the rule of law are inseparable companions, resistance is inconceivable. Whoever disobeys is a criminal breaking the law as well as an enemy of democracy. The idea of the 'enemy within' could only emerge in a political system that takes itself as fundamental faith while claiming to be ideologically neutral. Liberal fundamentalism turns disobedience from a weapon of the ruled into a defence of the rulers. Dissenting citizens have no legitimate redress; violence and revolution are the only solution. Nixon was not altogether wrong after all.

91

The philosophical debate qualified this view. As Ronald Dworkin put it in 1985: 'we can say something now we could not have said three decades ago: that Americans accept that civil disobedience has a legitimate if informal place in the political culture of their community'.[9] Liberal assumptions, however, make civil disobedience highly problematic. John Locke and the social contract tradition accepted a limited right to revolution, if the state violates individual property. This remains the liberal position, suitably adjusted to contemporary conditions. Historically, disobedience was not a tool for radical change but a mechanism ensuring that the political and social order remains true to the values of the free market. It expressed, alongside the judicial review of legislation, an enduring fear of democracy. Disobedience is seen as a limitation of democratic decision-making and a constraint on the 'tyranny of the majority'. As a necessary evil, it aims to keep the rulers, including democratic bodies, within the parameters of liberal legitimacy.

The state's most important duty is to protect individual rights; disobedience is therefore justified only if policies and laws violate the principles of equal liberty (Rawls) or basic rights (Dworkin). For Rawls, 'there is a presumption in favour of restricting civil disobedience to serious infringements of . . . the principle of equal liberty, and to blatant violations of . . . the principle of fair equality of opportunity'.[10] Rawls constructs an elaborate set of conditions disobedience must meet. The breaking of laws must be motivated by respect in the rule of law, it must be undertaken as a last resort and it must appeal to society's sense of justice as incorporated in the legal system. Disobedience to the letter of the law is a way of obeying its spirit.[11] Dworkin's conditions for valid disobedience derive from his wider jurisprudence. The dissidents accept the morality and integrity of constitution and law and protest against specific governmental acts. Their motives and aims classify disobedience into three categories: conscientious objection, proper disobedience that defends the spirit of the constitution, and finally, acts which challenge policies adopted by the government.[12] Civil disobedience undertaken in order to defend fundamental rights is justified; the legitimacy of attacks on laws and policies protesters object to is less clear-cut.[13] If we accept this distinction, the civil rights movement was justified; the anti-Vietnam War campaign was problematic. The decision to go to war had been made by the legitimate government and did not violate directly the rights of Americans, the core case that 'trumps' policy decisions. The few 'genuine' conscientious objectors could be accommodated by liberal theory since conscription can be interpreted as a violation of individual moral integrity.

Dissidents did not accept the niceties of political philosophy. The rebelling students of 1968, the feminists, the Campaign for Nuclear Disarmament, and the mass protests against the communist states attacked state policies and the fundaments of the social order. As a result, liberal theories of disobedience have been supplemented by a new type of democratic disobedience that addresses the decay of our political systems. This approach draws on the principles of democratic and republican theory. According to Jean-Jacques Rousseau, the people are legislators and subjects, masters and servants of the law.[14] If democracy is reduced to a mechanism for the aggregation of votes, and citizen participation is discouraged, legitimacy withdraws. The combination of liberal and democratic approaches gives the most advanced mainstream argument for disobedience. Citizens have given their implicit consent to the constitution in a real or virtual social contract and have pledged their obedience to laws enacted by their representatives after public deliberation and a democratic 'will formation'. In return, laws must respect fundamental freedoms (the Kantian component) and promote the public interest and social justice (the social-democratic component). For neo-Kantians like Jürgen Habermas, democracy and morality, legitimacy and legality form an inseparable couple. When one is lost, the other atrophies. When both retreat, the duty of obedience weakens. But the preconditions Habermas sets for justified disobedience are more onerous than those of Rawls: 'A democratic constitution can tolerate resistance from dissidents who, after exhausting all legal avenues, nonetheless oppose legitimately reached decisions. It only imposes the condition that this rule-breaking resistance be plausibly justified in the spirit and the wording of the constitutions and conducted by symbolic means that lend the fight the character of a nonviolent appeal to the majority.'[15] The intolerance at the core of liberalism cannot be easily hidden.

The idea of the social contract was an ideological construct hard to believe in the eighteenth century and of heuristic only value today. Ideology is not false consciousness, however. It is the imaginary way through which we experience our real conditions of existence, a set of fictions that create our reality. The democratic duty to obey the government includes the right to dissent. An anti-liberal, anti-democratic or morally odious policy does not become automatically legitimate because it has been enacted in Parliament, even though its legal status gives it additional weight. In a democracy, laws don't deserve automatic or unhesitating loyalty. If state laws and policies conflict with basic constitutional values, the supposed highest expression of popular sovereignty, legality and legitimacy diverge. Opposition parties try to repeal the law; ordinary citizens take their campaign to the streets because the obligation to obey disappears and dissent replaces consent as the support of the constitution. A similar argument applies when a government enacts policies and laws that violate or reverse basic promises and manifesto commitments. In this case the mandate to rule has been obtained under false pretences. For the liberal tradition, disobedience is tolerated when basic rights are undermined, for the democratic when political legitimacy disappears. Democratic regimes are like a couple. When love stops being renewed daily and becomes routine and unexciting, the relationship comes to an end. After the end of love or trust, the relationship and democracy atrophy. The question is how long and in what condition they can survive.

Democratic disobedience combats the atrophy of democracy and the decay of 'post-democracy'.[16] It is a major improvement on the liberal version. Unlike subjective moral decisions, democratic disobedience is a collective act. Following republican theory, it prioritizes the democratic will of the people ahead of fundamental rights. Justified disobedience erupts when a large number of citizens realize that the democratic process malfunctions and major policy decisions seriously affecting their lives have no democratic or moral legitimacy. Etienne Balibar has pursued this motif throughout his long writing career. Balibar argues that democracy survives because it has an integral 'insurrectionary' moment. 'Any effective democratic constitution remains dependent on the idea of insurrection', Balibar insists.[17] Citizenship becomes active only when opposition and dissent create a 'counter power'. Power's legitimacy depends on the ability of citizens occasionally to reject laws and policies. Established powers condemn such acts as illegal and criminal; but their effective exercise is the necessary prerequisite of the political system's survival. Citizenship is paradoxical: it is 'conflictual or nothing'. The post-democratic decline of politics into governance and expert rule has made disobedience even more important. Supposed remedies to democratic sclerosis such as referenda, minority rights and judicial remedies are palliatives only. Conflict, division and active citizenship are the only hope of democracy. The right to insubordination, turning the city against itself, is the 'true *right to rights*, a kind of right to law'.[18] Balibar's argument reminds us the beginning of Athenian democracy. Solon laid down a law according to which 'whoever when civic strife prevailed did not join forces with either party was to be disenfranchised and not to be a member of the city'.[19] Conflict, resistance, insurrection is an enduring reality; it responds to the sense of injustice and keeps democratic rule alive.

The academic Daniel Markovits has tried to operationalize democratic disobedience in a more technical direction. He starts by identifying the weaknesses of civil disobedience. Disobedience challenges the lack of participation in decision-making but cannot attack the policies agreed. Its justification 'expires if the disobedience successfully triggers a political reengagement with the policy it protests against, including one in which the sovereign [people] reaffirms this policy'.[20] In periods of great crisis, however, the democratic deficit cannot be easily redressed. Citizen passivity and indifference, control of the media by economic power, endemic corruption and lack of party democracy hinder 'political reengagement'. The republican belief that people are 'sovereign' is routinely refuted. Markovits rightly argues that the liberal justification for civil disobedience does not apply to the anti-globalization protests, the most massive movement at the time he was writing, 'because the policies of international co-ordination and exchange that the anti-globalization movement protests cannot plausibly be cast as violating basic liberal principles of equality or individual freedom'.[21] Similarly, however, his type of democratic disobedience does not extend to the contemporary acts of resistance, insurrection and revolt. Tunis, Cairo and Athens did not ask the reopening of debate. The dramatic democratic deficit makes the reopening of wrong decisions useless. Democratic disobedience challenges social hierarchy and the flawed democracy that reproduces it. 'Action does not mean a failure of politics. Action is the very nature of politics.'[22] Politics happens when the people who have no claim or stake in the political game suddenly demand to be seen and heard. Democratic disobedience does not prioritize the defence of fundamental rights nor does it exclusively attack problematic policies – even though both these malfunctions are present when protesters take to the streets. The essence of democratic disobedience is to change the operation and scope of politics.

Recent decades witnessed an 'astounding silence of revolution', wrote the Italian activist Mario Tronti.[23] For Alain Badiou, 'riots' are the 'guardian of history' in the interval between revolutionary periods.[24] After a long period of low-key activity, syncopated by acts of civil disobedience, the right to resistance, Balibar's 'right to rights', has returned. Resistance challenges current policies but goes beyond them to the social conditions and institutional arrangements that allowed their dominance. Resistance is both a fact and a right. This right does not derive from positive law, domestic state or international. The 'higher' law justifying resistance is both immanent and transcendent. Resistance emerges in the historical conditions of crisis and the response of people all over the world. Its normative force and form as 'right' draws from a conception of the good that lies on the horizon of our current state. Two conflicting conceptions of the universal characterize our age, as the last chapter argued. The first accepts the order of things and identifies ought and is or, according to Hegel, the rational and the real, dressing the dominant particular with the mantle of the universal. The dissident will rests on a diagonal scission that divides the rulers from the ruled and the excluded. As a negation of the existing order, it forms an agonistic universality. It does not emerge from neo-Kantian philosophy but from the struggle of people excluded from social distribution and invisible to political representation. The right to resistance, like all proper rights, is both real and ideal.[25] It 'sublates' civil and democratic disobedience, both taking up and transcending them. Its appearance in authoritarian as well as democratic regimes turns ours into the age of resistance.

The morality of disobedience

Let us go back to the phenomenology of disobedience and resistance. For the ordinary person, disobedience is the deeply moral decision to break the law. It is the strongest mark that the morality of citizens has not atrophied. It happens when someone reaches breaking point: 'enough is enough – I can't take it any more' is the cry of the dissident who is prepared to risk punishment. It may follow an extreme injustice, like the killing of Alexis Grigoropoulos in December 2008. Alternatively, it may result after a series of humiliations that eventually exhaust moral tolerance as was the case with the civil rights movement. In normal circumstances, morality and legality represent two different types of overlapping but not identical duty: the external duty to obey the law (in formal terms a heteronomous duty) and the internal moral responsibility that binds the self to a conception of the good (autonomy). Conflicts are usually solved in favour of law. In disobedience, the duties collide and morality takes over. If both morality and legality become simple obedience to external codes autonomy dies. The duty to obey the law is absolute only when accompanied by a free judgement that the law is morally right and democratically legitimate. If that were not the case, Hannah Arendt sarcastically comments, Kant's categorical imperative would read: 'Act as if the principle of your actions were the same as that of the legislator or of the law of the land.' It would be the perfect maxim 'for the household use of the little man'.[26] This is of course the credo of positivists and failed governments. The autonomous citizen does not just obey the law; she also judges the 'legality' of the law and its relationship with justice. In acts of disobedience, autonomy and existential freedom temporarily coincide.

The decision to break the law is hard, unavoidable and traumatic at the same time. Resistance on the other hand is collective; it is addressed at everyone and aims to reconstruct the hurt community, writes Etienne Balibar. But 'at the moment of decision, of the *risk of making a mistake*' that will be paid by all, 'the subject is facing just himself.'[27] At such moments, the self is wrestling in solitude. What makes an ordinary person take such a decision? Radical philosophy must give an account of the motivational force to follow morality and break the law. Without such an account and without a conception of the ethical and political self, moral reflection becomes cynical theorizing. Simon Critchley, following Badiou, has argued that the disobedient subject 'commits itself ethically in terms of a demand that is received from a situation, for example a situation of political injustice'.[28] The 'demand' arises in specific circumstances (the killing of a young man, a deeply unjust policy) but is addressed in principle to everyone and anyone. The moral force of positive law derives from its universal form, which allows its application to a myriad future cases. The moral demand, on the contrary, draws its force from the content of the situation, which acquires universal form. Law operates deductively, situational morality inductively. The moral demand's universality makes it formally equivalent to the law but, unlike law, this is a 'situated universality'. It emanates from a unique instance or event that requires a response engaging potentially everyone (the rejection of police brutality or the claim to equality). To put it differently, the moral act responds to a wrong that takes the form of a concrete universal. 'Wrong institutes the singular universal, a polemical universal, by tying the presentation of equality, as the part of those who have no part, to the conflict between parts of society.'[29] Those who remain true to the demand become moral subjects. The wrong, its demand and the moral subject emerge together, Critchley claims. It is not previous edification or ideology that creates the radical subject but his answer to a unique event and its moral 'call'. The insubordinate subject is created by the 'normative pull of the void' or Žižek's 'normativity of the real'.

Critchley's argument emphasizes the moral significance of the situation. Philosophy knows, since the Platonic dialogues, that the rational acceptance of morality's demands does not lead necessarily to moral action. 'I may know the good', says Racine's *Phaedre*, 'but I keep following evil.' The same applies to radical action. The link between radical ideology and militant action is fragile. The decision to disobey the law rises rarely on some radical road to Damascus. The militant does not emerge by *parthenogenesis*. Antigone's defiance, Paul's conversion and Lenin's resoluteness did not emerge *ex nihilo*. Disobedient subjects cultivate, according to late Foucault, *l'art de n'être pas tellement gouverné*. Unlike Badiou's 'subjects of truth', they are prepared by values, beliefs and actions preceding the dramatic event. As Ernesto Laclau puts it, 'the subject is only partially the subject inspired by the event . . . social agents share, at the level of a situation, values, ideas, beliefs, etc. that the truth . . . does not put entirely into question'.[30] Reasons and unreason, emotions and intuition, memories and testament, conscious motives and unconscious drives give rise to acts of insubordination. Disobedience negates, resistance creates. The importance of disobedience lies precisely in starting the process of production of new subjectivities. It raises people from takers of orders and commands into self-legislating citizens. At that point, the biopolitical project to fails. If power operates as control of conduct, counter-power attacks the channelling of conduct. *Stasis Syntagma* or *Puerta del Sol* become places where people state that 'we don't want to be ruled like that'.

There is a caveat. Let me explain it through two recent cases of resistance, *Keratea* and the 'can't pay won't pay' movement. In the spring of 2011, work started in Keratea, a village outside Athens, for the construction of a major landfill servicing a large part of the Athens conurbation. The plan, which had been decided without proper consultation or an examination of alternatives, would degrade the environment and adversely affect property values. The largely conservative Keratea villagers blockaded the main road in the area for weeks and obstructed the contractors building the landfill. Large riot police units were stationed in the area and regularly fought the locals. Eventually the villagers won and the plan was abandoned in June 2011. The 'can't pay won't pay' movement was a reaction to the large increase in road tolls and public transport fares in 2010. Members of the group raised the bars in toll stations and let drivers pass without payment or blocked the ticket validation machines in Metro stations and buses allowing the public free travel. In late 2011, the movement expanded to the non-payment of new special income taxes and a property tax collected through electricity bills, as a result of which many families had their power cut off. Members of the electricians' union refused to disconnect the non-payers or reconnected them after private contractors had cut them off. These regressive taxes impose further burdens on poor and lower middle-class families who have already lost a large part of their income through salary cuts and indirect tax increases.

Keratea and 'can't pay won't pay' are well-known forms of disobedience against policies which attack a group's or locality's interests. They can be seen as instances of the 'not in my backyard' syndrome. When disobedience promotes private interests wrapped as common good it becomes hypocritical. Cynicism and nihilism is the common pathology of rulers for whom punishment is unknown and the common good is often a euphemism for personal interests. The moral quality control of disobedience, on the other hand, is strict. The first test is the willing acceptance of the risk and possibility (nowadays probability) of punishment. The second brings the specific grievance or demand under the control of a moral principle. The moral litmus test of disobedience is simple: can the good or principle, the disobedient obeys, be addressed to everyone and anyone? Can it be universalized? The answer takes account of normative and empirical considerations, the legitimacy of democracy and the moral validity of the rule of law. It is a tough, anxiety-producing moral test; if absent, it is replaced by empty moralizing, which turns private interest into public virtue.

There is nothing wrong in principle in a campaign of disobedience that starts from particular interests. Finite demands can become 'infinite' and transcend their immediate concerns. '"Infinite" here does not consist in the demands that I make, but in finding something in the situation that exceeds its limits . . . the finite demand around which a struggle organizes itself extends itself beyond the limits of the identity of the concerned group and becomes something more radical and far-reaching.'[31] The *Keratea* villagers and the 'can't pay won't pay' members participated massively in the occupations of the squares. Disobedience was not just a response to the perceived injustice of a law affecting their interests but a first step in the radicalization of subjectivity and linking the campaign with wider struggles. In this sense, the specific campaign opens to demands that leave behind local interests and specific identities. Disobedience is transformed from a personal moral act to collective political resistance. It disarticulates actions, behaviours and comportment from the political economy of consumption and debt, and the moral economy of personal responsibility and freedom of choice. This is what power fears most.

In classical Greek, *nemein* means to assign; the *nomos* assigns to places and positions. *Anomie,* on the other hand, is law's absence and lack of deontic force. When power and law are inseparably intertwined the 'ought' becomes the handmaiden of a continually degraded 'is'. This identification weakens the demand for obedience. Law's mission, until 2008, was to promote individual consumption, desire and choice. Its recent violent change has no support in social morals. For the rich and powerful nothing has changed. Those used to corruption, tax evasion and patronage continue their ways. But there is a reverse side: disrespect for austerity laws makes ordinary people join the resistance. The weakening of law's normative force and moral legitimacy explains why violations of legality proliferate. While the illegality of corruption hides behind a pretense of lawfulness ('this is how we have always done things'), the 'illegality' of resistance retains its commitment to the power of the ideal to correct reality. The *sans papiers* hunger strikers and the *Stasis Syntagma* dissidents and rebels preserve the liberal traditions after their abandonment by the liberals. Disobedience is not unlawful or anomic but a moral and civic response to government-induced anomie. Dissent keeps the promise of *nomos* and *dike* alive.

Sovereignty loosened

Sovereignty has become an endangered concept over the last thirty years, chased by cosmopolitans and human rights lawyers on the Left and American and British bombers on the Right. The end of the Cold War, the rather premature announcement of the end of history and the 'moral turn' in international and domestic politics have contributed to the waning of sovereignty.[32] Internally too disobedience and resistance have undermined popular consent to the sovereign. Let us examine the two fronts in turn.

Carl Schmitt[33] and Giorgio Agamben define the sovereign through the power to institute a state of exception and suspend normal legality in order to save the social and legal system from radical threats.[34] The decision to suspend the law, which marks out the sovereign, is both outside law's procedures and inside the law as a precondition of its operation. In Greece, the troika holds this position. Its representatives regularly inspect the books, order government ministers to adopt new austerity measures and authorize the payment of the loan instalments. They have imposed the most severe set of economic emergency legislation outside wartime. A 'task force' oversees the implementation of austerity and the sale of public assets. The most famous task force, which popularized the term, was the armada sent by Mrs Thatcher to reoccupy the Falklands in 1982. The neo-colonial status of Greece justifies the use of the term. Formally, the troika is not an organ of the Greek state. It lies outside the legal order but has near absolute power to change it. The troika's extra legal status makes it the ultimate source of law. Its diktat has suspended key provisions of the constitution, most safeguards of the social state and the basic principles of economic policy. In this sense, the Greek crisis has an element of poetic justice. The neo-colonial strategies imposed on Africa and Latin America are reimported for the first time to the continent which invented and spread them. African neo-colonialism has been operating under the name of 'structural adjustment'; Latin American as the 'Washington consensus'. According to John Williamson, the inventor of the term, the 'consensus' includes ten elements (those relating to the currency have been excluded as they do not apply to a eurozone member): 'Fiscal policy discipline; redirection of public spending; tax reform, broadening the tax base; trade liberalization – liberalization of imports, with particular emphasis on elimination of quantitative restrictions (licensing, etc.); liberalization of inward foreign direct investment; privatization of state enterprises; deregulation – abolition of regulations that impede market entry or restrict competition; legal security for property rights.'[35] As Harvard Professor Dani Rodric put it, 'stabilize, privatize, and liberalize' is the mantra of the IMF and the World Bank.[36] Every aspect of this standard recipe is now applied to Greece.

David Harvey has compellingly shown that this is the recipe book for contemporary accumulation crises.[37] They are solved through the dispossession of the weak and poor in a repetition of the great enclosures of early capitalism. It is done in a number of ways. The state rolls back regulation protecting labour and the environment, pushing down wages and production costs – this violent internal devaluation is renamed 'competitiveness'. Next, it reduces or removes social rights such as state pensions, education, welfare and health, won after long and hard struggles. Finally, it sells public enterprises at bargain basement prices. Capital takes hold of these assets and turns them to profitable use, releasing the over-accumulation crisis. All this is happening to Greece. German trade balances are seeking a profitable outlet in the sun. Perhaps a new dispensation is emerging among the elites of old Europe. We can call it the 'Athens consensus'. Greece is nominally sovereign under international law but under foreign supervision internally. The British used to send Oxbridge educated administrators to the colonies. The new colonialists are technocrats educated in mediocre business schools. If colonialism carried out 'the white man's burden' in Africa, later renamed the 'civilizing mission', the troika is carrying it out in Greece. The Greeks are well on the way to becoming the European colonials.

The external waning of sovereignty is accompanied by its internal unravelling. The sovereign represents the principle of unity of state and people. In a parliamentary democracy, the sovereign is a *Deus Absconditus*. His power to create *ex nihilo* has been passed to the institutions of state, mainly the executive and, secondarily, parliament. Its nature as *Absonditus* has been transferred to the people. They are *de jure* – ideologically – supreme, but *de facto* – empirically – they are subjected to the rule of the real sovereign. We can distinguish therefore two aspects of sovereignty. Its routine expression is evident in everyday acts of the state, in a police arrest, a tax demand or a refusal of political asylum. These acts are supported by the metaphysical manifestation of sovereignty which projects the people as united, singular, indivisible, the mirror image of the sovereign. The 'people' can wear the garments of majesty as easily as gods and kings; their power is imaginary, however, except in those rare occasions constituent power enters the stage. As Jacques Derrida has noted, the democratic majorities expressing popular sovereignty are always concerned with their size. But if the majority is calculable, it falls short of the 'general will of the sovereign or the monarch [which] cannot be divided. The One (of God, of the monarch, of the sovereign) . . . is absolutely great and thus above measurable greatness.'[38] The 'sovereign people' of liberal democracy are one further link in the chain of substitutions of the metaphysical principle of the One. It is a weak link.

Both aspects of sovereignty come under pressure by prolonged and massive resistance. In Greece, every manifestation of state power was confronted, frustrated and ridiculed. Slogans and banners reminded politicians that Argentine President De la Rúa fled Buenos Aires in a helicopter on 21 December 2001. The Greek resistance aimed at realizing the Argentine moment in Athens. It succeeded in part. Prime Minister Papandreou, his ministers and MPs could not step into a public space without being heckled. Parliament, the place symbolizing popular sovereignty and the independence of legislature from the executive, was surrounded for three months; its legislation was rejected and defied. On 16 June, following a general strike and one of the largest demonstrations and rallies in Syntagma, Papandreou resigned and asked the opposition to form a government. When this failed, Papandreou's government survived for a few months. Its perseverance was eating away at the symbolic uses of sovereignty. The people knew that overthrowing the government was within their grasp. Hurt sovereignty everywhere responds with violence. When on 28 June, Parliament was encircled, the government imposed a virtual state of emergency. The riot police attacked the protesters brutally and started a prolonged period in which repression and demonization of assorted 'others' has become the main weapon of the ailing sovereign. The disobedient attack on the icons of sovereignty was not limited to the government. When the superior courts upheld the constitutionality of the austerity measures, confirming their minor position in the ruling elite against the opinion of the majority of legal academics, the judiciary too lost respect and was ridiculed. Doctors, taxi drivers and civil servants occupied Ministries and other public buildings. The three great pillars of state authority, government, legislature and bureaucracy, lost their symbolic authority; eventually their power became seriously challenged. The people had abandoned the government and the government declared war on the people. On 26 October 2011, the President of the Republic, the formal personification of sovereignty, had to abandon the annual parade celebrating the liberation of Thessaloniki and flee after people occupied the street. A few days later the government resigned for a second time and for good. The 'street' had finished the job.

The significance of these events goes much further than the final exit of a moribund government. If history teaches anything, says Arendt, 'it is that a disintegration of political systems precedes revolutions, that the telling symptom of disintegration is a progressive erosion of governmental authority, that this erosion is caused by the government's inability to function properly, from which springs the citizens' doubts about its legitimacy.'[39] Arendt was writing about the great upheaval in the United States of the 1960s. The 1960s and our time are periods in which people learn 'to live together without loyalty, without the everyday presuppositions that the state is naturally and inexorably there.'[40] Living together without the 'everyday presuppositions' is precisely what psychoanalysis calls the traversal of the fantasy of the 'Big Other'.

Sovereignty and the psyche

According to psychoanalytical theory, a fundamental and constitutive lack marks the core of self. In our indispensable and impossible quest for wholeness, we fantasize the other person and the Big Other, as non-lacking, complete. We desire the other to be whole in order to achieve fulfilment in the recognition of her desire. As the desire for the other is mediated by the symbolic order of language and law, the law too must be seen as a coherent, rational whole, which has all the answers. The subject needs the law to be gapless, to be Ronald Dworkin's 'seamless web'. But like self, the other lacks. The symbolic order and law cannot be complete, Dworkin's hope is an illusion. No substantive principle, no procedural propriety can make the disparate rules and regulations, the unconnected commands and decisions cohere. For the law to be a coherent whole, a single author must have written it or a sole master authorized it. In psychoanalytical terms, such a master would be the other of the Other, someone or something not included in the symbolic order and therefore able to give it closure and coherence. The desire for an authoritative author standing behind social institutions animates our relationship with the law. Its signs are everywhere: in the obsession of the law with its sources; in the interminable and scarcely illuminating debates about the correct interpretation of the Constitution; in the unthinking trust in the judiciary. But, as Jacques Lacan insisted, there is no other of the Other, the masks of ultimate power are fraudulent. There is nothing beyond the structure and interdictions of language, except for the Real which cannot be symbolized. There is no real Father behind his name, no God behind the word, no single sovereign behind the law. Nothing behind signs can secure their meaning, nothing behind the law can guarantee its justice.

God, king, sovereign, the various personifications which have unerringly underpinned Western legality, are functions for the subject, guarantees that her subjection is not arbitrary or unnecessary. To paraphrase Foucault, in constitutional law the head of the king has not been severed yet. To paraphrase Pierre Legendre, even if severed, the head must be kept on the king's body. We must pretend that he is still alive, like the Soviets, those experts in the power of symbols, did, who kept President Brezhnev's death secret for long, to ensure a smooth transition or to ensure, in psychoanalytical terms, that the master signifier never dies. We desire the legislator; our desire breathes life into the 'as if' impostor. But this creation of our desire soon acquires a life of its own. The object of desire becomes the beast who kills, imprisons and tortures. Our love creates the ghostly apparition, the dreamlike whisperer of the law who is then transubstantiated into the monster we call out of fear and desire our 'mortal god' or sovereign. The progeny (sovereign) helps beget the creator (subject-citizen). God and King are not the cause but the effect of law. It is not so much that religion is the opium of the people, as Marx had it, but that religion is the desire of the people. But, as the fatherly figures retreat in late modernity, laughed out of court by children, women, gays and all kinds of people unwilling to accept the father's deceit, the possibility of leaving behind the monarch's declaration and calling the sovereign's lie opens up.

This approach helps us to understand the psychological effects of austerity and resistance. Insubordination unravels sovereignty's hold on ordinary people. Disobedience dismantles the sovereign projection of (national) unity and its symbolic support for political and legal institutions. The ideological presuppositions that keep the sovereign and the subjects in a position of superiority/inferiority become denaturalized and are seen for what they are, pure ideology. The rift in what is perceived as the natural order of things loosens the ideological unity of the body politic and undermines the 'reality principle' that helps us understand the world. Participants in the occupations reported unprecedented and draining emotions. Losing the master, even temporarily, is traumatic. Once that happens, however, everything is possible.

The elites are traumatized too. Psychoanalysis distinguishes between the 'ideal ego' and the 'ego ideal'. The ideal ego supports the subject through the imaginary projections of an ideal identity: I see myself as successful, intelligent, beautiful. The ego ideal, however, plays a more important role for the psychological equilibrium: I imagine myself from the perspective and gaze of the other, whom I desire, and try to become or do what I believe the other expects from me. This is precisely the Greek elite model. We will modernize, we will become what, we think, the Europeans would like us to be. The Greek politicians desperately search what the Europeans want in order to please them. 'What does Mrs Merkel want?' The various Prime Ministers paraphrase Freud's question. But Mrs Merkel asks contradictory things: one day she wants Greece to stay in the euro, the next wants her expelled, the third has no view either way and waits for the views of others. The jilted Greek elites, eager to attract the German lady's love, drown in anxiety, disappointment and frustration and multiply their efforts to divine and realize her desire. Psychoanalysis teaches that desire is moved by the question and its anxiety, not its (non-existent) answer. Mrs Merkel keeps hiding or changing her demands, holding the Greeks in the position of an eternally begging and jilted lover. She acts like the pastor in Michael Haneke's film *White Ribbon* who out of inexplicable love keeps punishing his children. It is the action of the Freudian superego: it imposes unreasonable demands on the self and keeps making them harder the more its victim tries to obey its cruel orders. In this sense, the Greek elites live a devastating contradiction between their love for Europe and the repeated humiliations and impossible demands the Europeans visit on them. This contradiction can become productive if it opens the possibility of exiting the immobilizing dilemma 'West versus East' or 'modern versus backward'. It can only happen after the ruling elites of the last forty years exit the political stage.

— 7 —

POLITICAL ONTOLOGIES

Resistance always returns. Its form and success depends on the historical conjuncture and the composition and strategy of its subject. The existence, nature and organization of the political agent have always exercised political philosophy. The new types of resistance place the question at the centre of theory. This chapter examines Marxist and post-Marxist attempts to capture the radical subject and revive the left agenda for a new age. The next explores the theory of the multitude, a heterodox tradition in political philosophy, which has acquired a certain prominence. Is there a subject of radical change in late capitalism?

For traditional Marxism, social classes are constituted outside politics – in productive economic activities, which distribute people into clearly demarcated positions as capitalists, workers, peasants or petty bourgeois. The material conditions of capitalism and the laws of historical motion have assigned the revolutionary role to the working class. This strong ontology determines the nature of politics, the functions of the state and the mission of the party. The working class acquires political subjectivity through the party, which recognizes and represents its interests. The party turns the disorganized and politically invisible workers into the proletariat, transforming the weak social existence of class into strong political presence. For the traditional Left, political representation is not a side effect of the size of modern states or the scale of politics but an indispensable mechanism dictated by the directive role and historical mission of the party. Its ultimate task is to unify social multiplicity and simplify the class structure and political struggle along the line capitalists/workers, as predicted by Marx in the *Communist Manifesto*.

As far as the individual is concerned, being a communist means being a member of the Communist party. Despite hardship and persecution, the militant has a clear and coherent vision and affirms a life of work and struggle. The strong link between party and militants was undermined, however, by the substitutions and reductions in communist politics. The working class replaced the people, the class was then reduced to the party, the party membership was replaced by the apparatchiks and, finally, by the leader and his cult. Both communist theory and practice failed. The communist rendezvous with history was not consummated in the communist states. In the West, history forgot to turn up at the appointed time.

The socio-economic changes of late capitalism have undermined the solidity of the working class, turning the bulk of the population into salaried workers, multiplying class positions and bringing into politics non-class identities and collectivities. The privileged political subjects of last century disappeared or contracted and survive in a spectral state. If they are still around they have decidedly abandoned their historical mission. No single party or ideology can claim to represent the class or to offer undisputed leadership. As a result, a 'Left melancholy' descended and became the permanent ailment of militants; reality had refuted their deeply held truths. As Wendy Brown aptly put it, the most troubling development is 'a Left that has become more attached to its impossibility that to its potential fruitfulness, a Left that is most at home in its own marginality and failure, a Left that is thus caught in a structure of melancholic attachment to a certain strain of its own dead past, whose spirit is ghostly, whose structure of desire is backward looking and punishing.'[1] The task of radical philosophy is to cure this ailment.

The decline of classical Marxism is related to wider cultural changes and the undermining of earlier certainties. After the post-metaphysical and anti-foundational turns, the belief that thought and being move on parallel lines was abandoned. The claim that science mirrors nature or that truth is the fruit of knowledge, strong premises of modern epistemology, have been weakened. In politics, we no longer accept that classes, fractions or people have 'objective' interests, that direct etiologies link economic processes and political superstructures or that ideology is a false consciousness awaiting demystification. The solid theoretical, political or moral grounds have been replaced by plural logics, contingent happenings, unplanned and unintended consequences, the centrality of corporeality and emotions. Radical philosophy accepts openly or implicitly that truth is no longer a reflection of reality but a commitment to its radical reform.

The collapse of the communist states and the end of the Cold War helped turn mainstream politics to morality, humanitarianism and human rights in the 1990s. The radicals too adopted a more nuanced version of ethics and turned it into a criterion of political action.[2] At the beginning of the twenty-first century, the subject was moral and the radical subject followed suit. Party membership and union activity, worker strikes, mass demonstrations and rallies declined.[3] Membership of Amnesty International seemed more radical and certainly more attractive for the young than membership of a Left party. Non-governmental organizations, small and informal groups and gatherings, carnivalesque performances and imaginative activities were the order of the day. Economic growth and a strong and confident state made radical politics a matter of protest and of controlled acts of disobedience. Protest campaigns kept a distance from the state, concentrating on local, ecological and moral issues. The emerging 'Leftist ontology' privileged difference over sameness, plurality over unity, recognition over distribution, becoming over being. With the communist parties marginalized and the socialist parties and governments adopting the rhetoric of the 'third way', modernization and, eventually, neo-liberalism, the politics of resistance moved from the smoked-filled rooms of parties and unions to the streets. The new dissidents confirmed Alain Badiou's argument that politics should be 'subtracted' from the state even though the moral substance of the campaigns was antithetical to his views.[4] The return of the examination of political ontology is a sign of rediscovered confidence.[5] It needs to be tested against the experience of the emerging new politics.

The return of radical philosophy

The collapse of the communist states heralded as the 'end of history' was in reality the end of the traditional Left. A new world order would finally achieve perpetual peace and confine political radicalism to the dustbin of history. Faced with political marginalization and theoretical irrelevance, radical philosophy started developing new tools to explain the political failure and inject a sense of purpose. A first step clarified the relationship between politics and philosophy: they are separate discourses and practices and one should not dominate the other. When philosophy uses reason in order to impose its values and theories on politics, both fail. For Jacques Rancière, 'archipolitics is the project of a community based on the complete realization of the *arkhe* of community, total awareness replacing the democratic configuration of politics with nothing left over.'[6] Plato's

Politeia, for example, created a blueprint for the ideal republic based on the hierarchy of classes and parts of the soul. When everything has its place and cannot change it, there is no politics. Theoretical thinking prevents political action. For the ardent Platonist Alain Badiou, on the other hand, politics, philosophy, art and love are the four forms of thinking. When political philosophy denies that politics creates its own truths and tries to develop an independent political logic, it becomes bad philosophy and an enemy of politics. Badiou calls his approach 'metapolitics' and contrasts it with political philosophy. 'Metapolitics' examines 'the consequences a philosophy is capable of drawing, both in and for itself, from real instances of politics as thought. Metapolitics is opposed to political philosophy, which claims that since no such politics exists, it falls to philosophers to think "the" political.'[7] Despite their differences, both Rancière and Badiou 'seek to extricate the thinking of politics from the operations with which "political philosophy" attempts to obscure, displace, or deny politics as such.'[8] The truth of politics emerges in political action. The job of the theorist is to comprehend and universalize it.

An important innovation of radical philosophy was the distinction between politics (*la politique*) and the political (*le politique*). Philippe Lacoue-Labarthe and Jean-Luc Nancy initially drew it along the lines of the Heideggerians' division between the 'ontic' realm of beings and the 'ontological' where Being unfolds.[9] Post-Marxist theorists including Claude Lefort, Alain Badiou, Ernesto Laclau, Slavoj Žižek, Antonio Negri, Jacques Rancière, Etienne Balibar and Antonio Negri have used the distinction in various forms. According to Chantal Mouffe, 'politics' refers to the practices of conventional politics. It is the terrain of routine political life, of government and opposition, parties and debating, lobbying and horse-trading that takes place around Westminster and Whitehall. The 'political', on the other hand, refers to the way in which the social bond is instituted and concerns the deep rifts in society. As Oliver Marchart puts it, this difference 'presents nothing other than a paradigmatic split in the traditional idea of politics, where a new term (the political) had to be introduced in order to point at society's "ontological" dimension, the dimension of the institution of society, while politics was kept as the term for the "ontic" practices of conventional politics (the plural, particular and, eventually, unsuccessful attempts at grounding society).'[10] Politics organizes the practices and institutions through which order is created, normalizing social co-existence in the context of persisting conflict.[11]

The definition of the political as the dimension of antagonism constitutive of society follows Carl Schmitt's understanding of politics as the relationship between friend and enemy. As William Rasch puts it, the political, is 'the ineliminable antagonism serv[ing] as the condition of possibility for the limited and channelled struggles of both domestic and international politics.'[12] Alain Badiou agrees. Every political situation includes two possibilities of action. Ordinary politics, with established interests, accepted differences and approved knowledge, gives formal recognition to consolidated identities and sanctions existing distributions and hierarchies. But every situation includes the possibility of radical break or 'event'.[13] An event persists in history and changes its route through the militant proclamation and fidelity to its 'truth' by rare individuals who, through their commitment, become its subjects. St Paul created the 'event of Jesus' by confirming his truth through his action, Lenin the 'event' of Marx.[14] The sites where these truths might emerge are close to the most anonymous and vulnerable, places considered empty or void by the dominant forces. Such is the working class in Marxism or the *sans papiers* immigrants in late capitalism. The workers have minimal social existence and no political representation, but they keep capitalism together.

The event is radical philosophy's secularization of the theology of the miracle. In the New Testament and early Christianity, miracles are called *semeia kai terata* or *signa* and *monstra* (signs and wonders). In theological semiotics, miracles do not prove God's existence; on the contrary, it is religious belief that allows their witnessing. A miracle can be recognized only by those who believe. Its wonder is that it has been predicted and offers signs of revealed truth to the believer. Something similar applies to the contemporary followers of the 'event'. For Badiou (and occasionally Žižek), the event is 'purely haphazard, and cannot be inferred from the situation'.[15] It is an unforeseeable happening arising out of the militant's fidelity, which retrospectively creates the event and confirms the philosophical prophesy. The idea of the unpredictable 'event' that changes the route of history was particularly welcome to radicals in the post-1989 gloom. It displaced the mourning of defeat and loss towards the melancholy of messianic hope. For those who had suffered the effects of failure, it was something.

Following the distinction between politics and the political, we can distinguish two axes and forms of power: *Auctoritas* (legitimate authority) expresses the 'common interest' or the will of a people to live together as community or nation I have called elsewhere 'bare sovereignty'.[16] *Potestas*, on the other hand, is the force that keeps society together through the domination of the few over the many. The function of politics is to express, condense and provisionally mediate social and economic conflict, to build legitimate authority against the permanent background of unavoidable antagonism. In the same way that 'ontic' beings exist in the space of forgetting and recollecting Being, the quest for legitimate power takes place in the field of relations of force opened by *potestas*. The new world order and neo-liberalism announced the end of conflict and at the same time tried to prevent and ban its appearance. Conflict did not disappear – the neo-liberal recipes increase inequality, fuel antagonism and turn the popular anger against immigrants, 'benefit scroungers', the 'undeserving poor' and those who resist their impoverishment. This is the reason why economic liberalism is accompanied by repressive measures and a virtual worldwide state of exception. The new police and surveillance powers introduced after 9/11 as a response to Islamic terrorism have found their métier in the 'war on dissent'. Despite fire-watching and fire-fighting, however, the conflict returned, like the repressed.

The theoretical and political failure of Marxism has led to a series of attempts to develop a non-essentialist ontology. Jacques Rancière retains the Marxist idea of social division but displaces it from class to the excluded poor. Ernesto Laclau and Chantal Mouffe update Gramsci's theory of hegemony. Finally, Antonio Negri and Michael Hardt argue that the socio-economic system of post-Fordist capitalism has created a global 'multitude' that has replaced state-bound class. We turn briefly to each, discussing their relevance for recent resistances.

Democracy and disagreement

For Jacques Rancière, normal politics (or 'police') must be distinguished from proper politics or 'disagreement'.[17] Routine politics aims at (re)-distributing benefits, rewards and positions without challenging the overall balance. Real politics on the other hand erupts when a group or class excluded from political representation demands to be included and must change the rules of the game to achieve that. Normal politics is preoccupied with questions of distribution and rational agreement, its dominant approaches, the economic and deliberative discussed in chapter 1. In both approaches, groups accept their position in the social hierarchy. *Auctoritas* or legitimate authority is presented as power's predominant if not exclusive form. Conflict and antagonism, the central reality of the politics, is neglected and *potestas* or domination discounted. In the current post-democratic condition, the attempt to replace conflict by a collaboration of enlightened bureaucrats and liberal multiculturalists has dire effects. As Slavoj Žižek has argued, when the political is foreclosed from the symbolic realm and departs politics, it returns in the real as radical evil, racism, extreme and destructive fundamentalism. The state becomes reduced to the muscleman for the market internally and a superficially tolerant enforcer of humanitarianism externally.[18]

Rancière's ontology separates the social from the political and places the excluded at the heart of politics. The social order is 'naturally' inegalitarian. Politics is precisely the attempt to challenge social hierarchies and abolish inequalities; it 'turns on equality as its principle'.[19] Equality, however, does not refer to the distribution of income and benefits. Social democratic or liberal distribution criteria are justifications for social hierarchy. Even egalitarian schemes make citizens passive. Social democracy, for example, retains the inequality between welfare managers and the recipients of state's largesse. Distribution schemes create a further problem: after they are consolidated and 'naturalized', their inherent exclusion of certain groups is concealed and forgotten. Those who challenge this state of affairs are treated as 'abnormal' or rebellious. For Rancière, therefore, equality is not the outcome of distribution but a 'presupposition' that politics puts into effect. A new political subject is constituted in excess of the hierarchical and visible groups when politics or democracy (the two are synonymous) work. In consensus politics, the dominated classes and groups accept their subordinate position; real politics exists only when the excluded challenge this hierarchy.

The economic crisis brought to the surface the deeply unequal and unjust premises of late capitalism. The consolations of *auctoritas* and routine politics receded and the devastations of *potestas*, the unavoidable rift of the political, have resurfaced. Conflict is back even though its class basis is disputed. This has turned many post-Marxists to Carl Schmitt's ontological conception of enmity. For Rancière, antagonism is the result of the tension between the structured social body, where every group has its role, function and place, and what Rancière calls 'the part of no part'. The excluded may claim political recognition by turning their demands into regional expressions of the established order. Occasionally, however, excluded groups abandon the legitimacy of *auctoritas* and challenge social hierarchy. This kind of antagonism or 'disagreement' 'is not a conflict of interests, opinions

113

or, values; it is a division put in the "common sense": a dispute about what is given, about the frame within which we see something as given'.[20]

Rancière's approach has special relevance for recent resistances. Alongside Cornelius Castoriadis and Jean-Luc Nancy, Rancière argues that democracy and politics were born together in Athens. Democracy is the institutionalization of disagreement and conflict, not a procedure for aggregating interests. The creation of the Athenian *demos* is an early example of this process. Democracy means the *kratos* (power) of the *demos*: the power of those who have no title, knowledge, wealth, experience, people who have no qualification for exercising power. The demos is not the people, the population or the body politic. It has no fixed place in the social edifice.[21] When the demos objected its exclusion and demanded to be heard as an equal partner with the rulers, it confronted the partial interests of priests and aristocrats and embodied the whole community in its unversality. Democracy is the 'power of those who have no specific qualification for ruling, except the fact of having no qualification'.[22] The demos therefore was both those excluded from the *ecclesia*, the surplus or supernumenary part, and the totality of citizens. The classical principle of equality was strictly limited, however, as the demos did not include women, metiks, slaves or strangers. Only the spread of Christianity universalized equality. Still two unprecedented ideas took root in Athens. First, power should be shared equally, an impossible ideal or horizon that is retreating as we attempt to reach it. Secondly, every time the horizon is not reached, in other words always, the principle of universality or equality (the two are synonymous in this instance) is embodied in the excluded: undocumented immigrants, the unemployed, the poor, those who fight to abolish exclusion.

Rancière finds a similar logic in the protests of Olympe de Gouges after the French revolution. De Gouges drafted in 1791 the *Declaration of the Rights of Woman and the Female Citizen*, mirroring and extending the rights of the revolutionary declaration. Its first article states that 'woman is born free and lives equal to man in her rights' while the second outdoing the main declaration proclaims the right '*especially* of resistance to oppression.'[23] De Gouges was executed for her feminism and her Girondin politics. As Rancière puts it, her argument was that if women were political enough to be sent to the scaffold, they should also be given political rights. They were both included in the political process as targets of repression and excluded from the rights of man. It was only by mobilizing this contradiction that the potential of revolutionary rights could be realized.[24] Another example is the proletariat in Marxist theory. The working class sustains capitalism through its work but does not exist politically.[25] As Rancière puts it, 'proletarian is a specific occurrence of the demos, a democratic subject, performing a demonstration of its power in the construction of worlds of litigious community, universalizing the issue of the count of the uncounted beyond any regulation, short of infinite wrong'.[26] In organizing and pursuing its own sectional interests, in becoming a class-conscious proletariat, it acts as the universal class: its emancipation will free the whole of humanity including its capitalist enemies. Normal politics is exercised when a community is limited to its recognized parts. When politics breaks out, a supplement is added and the uncounted are counted for the first time by changing the rules of counting. 'There is politics', writes Rancière, 'when the supposedly natural logic of domination is crossed by the effect of equality.' It takes place when 'those who have no right to be counted as speaking beings make themselves of some account, setting up a community by the fact of placing in common a wrong . . . that is the contradiction of two worlds in a single world: the world where they are and the world where they are not . . .'[27]

In Rancière's ontology, the political subject is not given. No class or group is the elect revolutionary agent. All societies exclude; all excluded groups can potentially rebel and rearrange the social order. The specificities of the exclusion will determine the potential subject of a society and epoch and will influence the form of resistance against inequality and injustice. Philosophers tend to discard the poor and uneducated. Only the acts and words of the excluded, however, can help us understand the meaning of exploitation and domination. The political subject of late capitalism is plebeian and conflict is the essence of democracy.

Hegemonic variations

Ernesto Laclau and Chantal Mouffe pushed the deconstruction of Marxist ontology to its logical end. Politics is not a 'level' of the social or a superstructure of the economic base. Political subjects are not constituted outside of politics in society or the economy and do not have 'objective' social positions or interests. On the contrary, social relations are contingent and are structured by the political. In this sense, 'society' is a name for the limit politics encounters as it operates on the 'social'.[28] There is 'a growing understanding of the eminently political character of any social identity'.[29] Identities and 'subject positions' are constituted through hegemonic political interventions, the outcome of which is never predetermined. The social terrain is open and takes shape when the various antagonisms traversing it coalesce in a common direction. Thought, discourse and practice (the hegemonic intervention) changes being (constitutes political subjectivity). As Laclau puts it, 'the two central features of a hegemonic intervention are the "contingent" character of hegemonic articulations and their "constitutive" character, in the sense that they institute social relations in a primary sense, not depending on any *a priori* social rationality'.[30] Pre-existing socio-economic positions offer little resistance and no assistance to the hegemonic plan; there is no ontological security or ideological solidity in class belonging. The individuals of late capitalism are malleable and fragile, aggressively egotistical and despondently melancholic. They are easily seduced and scared, imaginarily free and obediently subjugated. The militant optimism of the glorious (or catastrophic according to your view) twentieth century has subsided. Laclau and Mouffe's theory is a perfect companion for the defeated Left and the melancholy that accompanied it.

How does hegemony work? The different functions, roles and skills give people and collectivities their unique characteristics as teachers or butchers, bankers or unemployed. At the same time, these positive attributes divide the working people and create potential tensions. Identity is built out of difference, a collective subject or 'we' can be created through its juxtaposition to a constitutive outside or 'they'. This is what a hegemonic intervention does: it builds equivalences out of differences and tensions, bringing competing groups and interests together. The convergence succeeds in antagonism with an external enemy. The 'elites', 'fat cat' bankers, imperialism and the like can play that role. Negation of the enemy and opposition with an outside allows the linking of the groups inside. The hegemonic intervention must choose therefore a deep social rift that can potentially unite the groups and turn it into the central line of alliance and confrontation. Such a line transforms differences into equivalences, both splitting the social and sustaining its equilibrium. The chosen antagonism must be seen as more important than the regional conflicts and sectional tensions among groups on the same side. The historical and political conjuncture determines whether the hegemonic conflict takes the form of a class, patriotic or democratic struggle. 'There is nothing in the inherent positive qualities of some particular struggle that predestines it for such a hegemonic role as the "general equivalent" of all struggles.'[31] The way the 'they' is constructed determines the type of political subject 'we' become.

A hegemonic political agent emerges when a particular group or class adopts a universal position and manages to mobilize around it classes, groups and people. For Laclau, the universal sign, value or symbol is an 'empty signifier'; it is a word or image (solidarity, freedom, justice) without a set signified or necessary referent. Political forces and interests fight to occupy and 'fill' the signifier, turning their interpretation into its acceptable meaning. Indeed as the universal cannot be directly represented, it must be invested in a particular entity. The name *Solidarnosc*, for example, became such a universal sign in communist Poland, symbolizing resistance and uniting the opposition. In this transfer, it lost its original meaning as a workers' union. The word could have acquired another meaning and become the 'solidarity' offered to the Polish state by the invading Soviet Union, turning it into a symbol for the regime. The outcome of the struggle to hegemonize an empty signifier is never predetermined. The political force that succeeds claims *auctoritas*, the power of the common good, strengthening its position. When the rifts and crevices of the social become rearranged into two sides with one dominating the universal references, hegemony has succeeded and a hegemonic bloc is established.

In his latest book, Laclau generalizes his approach by rehabilitating populism.[32] The 'people' emerges as the universal political subject when various democratic demands (for better social security, education, health, non-discrimination etc.) are linked in a series of equivalences. This enchainment produces the 'people' as the universal political subject. In populism, struggles become integrated in a global antagonism between 'us' (people) and 'them' (the elites). The content of 'us' and 'them' is not given in advance but forms the stakes of the struggle. At this point problems start. Laclau's generalization covers every type of politics, making it difficult to distinguish between, say, the progressive Latin American populism of national independence and social justice and right-wingers using similar methods. The rise of the extreme Right and neo-fascist parties in Europe during the current crisis was partly the result of populist strategies that mobilized fears and prejudices around the 'threat' of immigrants. The different figures of the 'other', the Jew, the Moslem, the migrant, the refugee can be utilized to create series of equivalences in exactly the same way to 'solidarity' which led to a benign chain. As different particulars fight to colonize the universal, we need axiological criteria to distinguish between progressive and reactionary 'universals' or between radical and fascist rejection of austerity. Laclau distrusts all 'ethicization' of ontology, however. For him, moral ideas are empty signifiers. No solid moral imperatives exist beyond specific rhetorical tactics. As a result, Laclau abandons 'ontic' dirty politics for the abstractions of the political. 'Populism is, quite simply, a way of constructing the political' and does not require any particular ethical position.[33] But this is inadequate. Ethics is not a matter of logic or reason but of a situated response to moral demands. Care for others and *amour propre* are not the same. Chantal Mouffe may be right to claim that 'every order may be the temporary and precarious articulation of contingent practices'.[34] But the ravishes of neo-liberalism and austerity are not neutral. The crisis reminded us something we had forgotten perhaps in the period of fake economic growth. The continual self-revolutionizing of capitalism leads to extreme deprivation and destitution while offering at the same time a screen through which to explain and justify its destructive tendencies. As Slavoj Žižek puts it,

> the fate of whole strata of population and sometimes of whole countries can be decided by the solipsistic speculative dance of capital, which pursues its goal of profitability in a blessed indifference with regard to how its movement will affect social reality. Therein resides the fundamental systemic violence of capitalism . . . [which is] no longer attributable to concrete individuals and their 'evil' intentions but is purely objective, systemic, anonymous.[35]

The people whose lives were destroyed by the banking collapse in 2008 and the economic crisis of the 2010s form the core of the 'popular' pole. The socio-economically excluded (Rancière's 'part of no part') are the vanguard of opposition and resistance. Hegemonic interventions help them become politically effective. But ideological beliefs and political identities are not just discursive constructions. Class disposition and economic interest create the substratum on which hegemony works. Laclau's hegemonic approach offers a number of useful insights. But its claim to explain the totality of political action is not convincing. Resistance, uprisings and rebellions indicate the theoretical and political limitations of hegemony.

— 8 —

PEOPLE, MULTITUDE, CROWD

People and multitude

A recent narrative in the history of ideas dinstingushes two camps in political philosophy.[1] The first follows the philosophy of One and tends to unify the 'people'; the second promotes the 'multiple' and the philosophy of the Many. Thomas Hobbes is the father of the dominant tradition which places the unity of sovereignty and state – *Leviathan* as 'mortal God' – at the centre. The heretical tradition of the 'multitude', on the other hand, hails from Machiavelli, Spinoza and Marx. In this approach, the many are not united into One and do not mimic God. Let us examine briefly the two schools for ideas relevant to our concerns.

The tradition organized around the idea of the One (God, king, sovereign, people, nation etc) contrasts the multitude with the people. For Hobbes – the first and most interesting liberal philosopher – the multitude represents humanity in the state of nature before the civilizing intervention of the social contract. The contract transforms the many into a single body politic, so brilliantly captured in *Leviathan*'s frontispiece of a giant crowned figure, the torso and arms of which are composed of some three hundred figurines of men. Hobbes writes in *De Cive*: 'the *People* is somewhat that is *one*, having *one* will, and on whom one action may be attributed.'[2] The multitude, on the other hand, cannot act autonomously if it does not become unified. How do the many turn into a people? According to the social contract tradition, the sovereign emerges out of two processes. First, the premodern communities of virtue are gradually dissolved into a collection of individuals in permanent conflict (the state of nature). These free-floating atoms enter into a contract, which institutes the sovereign/

119

state. At the end of this process only individuals and the sovereign, the putative outcome of the agreement, exist. As Jacques Rancière puts it, modern politics 'begins by initially breaking down the people into individuals, which, in one go, exorcizes the class war of which politics consists, in the war of all against all'. The second operation turns the collection of individuals into a common being or *persona* that mirrors the unity of the sovereign. 'Sovereignty rests solely on itself, for beyond there are only individuals.'[3] The contract engenders the sovereign and at the same time transforms the many into one; the multitude becomes the people.

The social contract solves the famous 'Hobbesian problem of order': why do the moderns, recently emancipated from heteronomy and social stasis, obey the commands of the state? The answer is one of the greatest tricks in Hobbes' bag of marvels: 'Our obligation to civil obedience, by virtue whereof the civil laws are valid, is before all civil law.'[4] The duty to obey is an existential and legal presupposition of state and law. A rule stating 'thou shalt not rebel' would be superfluous; unless we are obliged to obedience, 'all law is of no force'.[5] Hobbes displaces politics from disagreement and struggle (*potestas*) to an originary assertion about the legitimacy of power (*auctoritas*). The presumed conflict of the state of nature legitimizes the sovereign. The duty to obey derives rationally from the contractual acceptance of the state as guarantor of social peace. Similarly, the absence of a right to resistance is the consideration citizens pay to the state for its guarantee of public order and protection from criminal mobs. While 'all human law is civil', dissidents and rebels 'are punished not by civil, but natural right; that is to say, not as civil subjects, but as enemies of government'.[6] Conflict belongs to the natural state; obedience is the cause and effect of the sovereign. It creates the state but is also created by the state since obedience is owed to positive law. It follows that the subject is obliged to obey even if it does not know the law. Such knowledge is not of 'the essence of the law'. It suffices that 'it be once known' that people must obey.[7] Immanuel Kant, Sigmund Freud, Emmanuel Levinas, Franz Kafka and Jacques Derrida remind us in different contexts that we must give our obedience to the law before we know its commands.

If we leave metaphysical abstraction, a population becomes a people discursively. The constituent power of the revolution is expressed in the 'we' of the American Declaration of Independence or the 'sovereign nation' in the French. This 'we' defines both 'who' we are and what we wish to become. Transcribed in the constituted annals of the constitution, the 'people' come into life by means of a performative announcement and its repetition. If the nation is an 'imaginary' community created through memory, tradition and narration, the people is a constitutional construction. Without the state and its organization, the united people would not have come into existence. The multitude, on the other hand, 'shuns political unity, resists authority, does not enter into lasting agreements, never attains the status of juridical person because it never transfers its own natural rights to the sovereign.'[8] As Hobbes put it, 'only the common sort of men, and others who little consider these truths' consider a 'great number of men' as the people. When a rebellion takes place it is not the people but 'under pretense of the *people*, stirring up the *citizens* against the *city*, that is to say, the *Multitude* against the *People*.'[9] Jean-Jacques Rousseau too unites the multitude through the 'general will'. However, a modicum of the multitude's constituent power is retained in the direct non-representative character of Rousseau's will formation.

After the emergence of the people and the invention of popular sovereignty, 'people' and 'nation' entered most constitutions. The figure of the sovereign, a secularized God, has been metonymically transferred from King to the nation, finally, to the united people. The democratic and republican traditions gave institutional status and ideological gravitas to the people, projecting them as the seat of power. But the 'people' as much as the nation are an imaginary community always in construction as the controversies over immigration and ethnicity indicate. The intimate relationship between state, territory and nation, established in the eighteenth century, set the scene for developments still unravelling today: every people/nation should have its own state and every state should have a single or dominant nation. As Antonis Manitakis puts it, the parliamentary system and elections allowed the 'representation of the totality of the population residing in a territory as a person with common will, as a political subject, possessor and title-holder of sovereignty'. But this people, Manitakis adds sarcastically, is a 'squeezed entity, desubstantialized, a purely formal figure without social characteristics, a legal fiction . . .'[10] People and nation promise the transformation of differences, antagonisms and conflicts into a united representable entity, the turning of the many into one. They are the mirror image of the sovereign, the invention of legal discourse and the creation of state ideology. Every time conflict breaks out and the constitutive role of *potestas* surfaces, the presumed unity of the people shatters. This is where we are today.

Let us turn now to the defeated tradition. Antonio Negri argues that behind modernity and its politics lies the constituent power of

121

the multitude. Nicolo Machiavelli, Baruch Spinoza and Karl Marx are the progenitors of the idea.[11] For Machiavelli, the historical process develops through the strength and passion of the multitude augmented by struggle. Spinoza moves from history to metaphysics and posits the infinitely expanding *cupiditas* (desire) of the multitude as the determination of politics and sovereignty. This is the sovereignty of the many, a 'democratic living god.'[12] Spinoza's multitude is a productive and constituent power. Its force creates the material world; its constitution projects its power into the future. The multitude makes the world but it does so as a counter-power to every stable and dominant power. Its force is the 'self-formation of being. . . . Political constitution is always set in motion by the resistance to Power. It is a physics of resistance . . . Political constitution is a productive machine of second nature, of the transformative appropriation of nature, and therefore a machine for the attack and the destruction of Power.'[13] The intersection of production and constitution creates the material, political, and cognitive progress of modernity. For Marx, finally, the multitude becomes living labour; its constituent power is the productive force that creates every social form.

Interestingly for our purposes, Machiavelli insisted that the reappropriation of land by the plebs renewed the democracy of the Roman Republic.[14] Spinoza described how in the jubilee years all debt was written off in Israel and citizen equality restored.[15] Similarly, Solon's *seisachtheia* in the sixth century BC, literally the shaking of burdens or debt relief, prepared democracy and the glory of Athens. Democracy, debt relief and the multitude or plebs are linked in Western political mythology. 'The city began with the clear-cut distribution of useful workers, politics begins with the motley crowd of the unuseful who, coming together into a mass of "workers" cater to a new range of needs – from painters and musicians to tutors and chambermaids; from actors and rhapsodists to hairdressers and cooks; from the makers of luxury articles to swineherds and butchers.'[16] This 'unuseful' multitude endures. It is a *'plurality* which persists as such in the public scene, in collecting action, in the handling of communal affairs, without converging into a One . . . multitude is the form of social and political existence of the many seen as being many . . . The *multitudo* is the architrave of civil liberties.'[17] The 'motley crowd' comes together and acts without unification. The many remain unique in their plurality. They are a material entity, a multiplicity of singularities acting in common, a *zoon politikon* with many limbs. The multitude acts without representatives, political parties or common ideology. Unlike the people or the nation, the multitude cannot be unified except in action. When different people bring together and co-ordinate their desires, Spinoza's *cupiditates*, a political subject emerges. It is created and dissolved in the temporariness and tension of the togetherness of singularities. If according to Carl Schmitt, law is imposed on an existing order and not chaos, the multitude is the original material which state power tries to tame and, failing that, suppress.

The great eighteenth-century revolutions, which changed the course of history, were creations of the multitude's constituent power. The constituted power that followed them, on the other hand, expressed the contradiction between the productive strength of the multitude and the principles of state and capitalism. For the contemporary proponents of the multitude, constitutionalism is the continual attempt to restrict, tame and eventually eliminate constituent power.

The victory of the tradition of the 'people' over that of the multitude has subjected the latter to the unifying action of state and capitalism. As a result, its proponents admit that no proper understanding of the actions of constituent power has developed. The multitude is a 'concept without history, without a lexicon, whereas the concept of the "people" is a completely unified concept for which we have appropriate words and nuances of every sort.'[18] It remains a spectre, haunting and threatening the unifying mission, an excess or remainder of the unity of people, nation or class. Modern politics tries unceasingly to eliminate, exorcize or tame the (excesses of the) crowd. The fear of the crowd is one of the oldest political emotions. It is the fear of the material co-presence of bodies, of their common action, of their power to change the world. But the attempt to declare the crowd finished, passé, and to ban its appearance always fails. For the theorists of the multitude, it is the many as many who create the world and humanity.

The multitude in late capitalism

Contemporary critical theory approaches the multitude as a social category similar to that of the people or the class but without their unifying action. The theory was developed in the 1960s and 1970s by the activists and philosophers Mario Tronti, Toni Negri, Paolo Virno and Christian Marazzi among others. It is an eclectic combination of Marxism, vitalism and the ontology of immanence of Gilles Deleuze and Felix Guattari. The recent interest has been triggered by the insurrections, revolts and revolutions of our age. Michael Hardt and Toni Negri's trilogy *Empire*, *Multitude* and *Commonwealth* was strategically placed to explain these events and justly acquired fame and commercial success. Negri and Hardt's work is widely known and there is no need to summarize it. This chapter will critically present post-Fordism and the multitude, two central categories of post-Marxism, adopted and popularized by Negri and Hardt. In *Multitude* the authors suggest that we need a new 'science of democracy'.[19] The recent resistances have made a major contribution to this task and this book aims to unravel it.

In late capitalism, labour and production have taken a predominantly 'immaterial' form. This does not mean that material commodities are no longer produced, or that factory production has either disappeared or moved to China – although it is true that a large part of industry has actually left the Western world, a phenomenon preoccupying 'globalization' theory. Workers and their value in East and West are not determined by the finite collection of bodily aptitudes and mental skills that are put to work, as was the case with the industrial working class and white-collar workers. The value of working people is determined by their potential for life, knowledge and work. The earlier security of employment has been lost and people are asked to develop continually new aptitudes and skills. They must be able to master evolving technologies, the Internet, new and social media. They should argue persuasively, communicate successfully, speak foreign languages, and develop analytical and critical abilities. Sympathy and emotional skills are also important; care and affect have been commodified and are key labour aptitudes. Skills and knowledge, which used to be the exclusive preserve of white-collar workers, are now required from all working people.

These developments follow a structural transformation in the 'general intellect'. Marx introduced the concept in the *Grundrisse*. For Marx, the general intellect is the work of science and technology, incorporated in machinery as dead labour and fixed capital. In late capitalism, however, symbolic or immaterial work have become major productive forces. Immaterial labour produces ideas, data, images and codes. The separate circuits of production, circulation and consumption have become integrated; horizontal, networked, global social relations are no longer the secret but the surface of economic activity. Products are created, communicated, bought and consumed on the Internet. This type of activity is the model for the rest of the post-Fordist economy. Industry and agriculture have not been abolished. On the contrary, the traditional sectors increasingly adopt the characteristics of immaterial labour. As Slavoj Žižek puts it, 'in "cultural capitalism", one no longer sells (and buys) objects which "bring" cultural or emotional experiences, one directly sells (and buys) such experiences'.[20] Working in horizontal and fluid chains is central throughout the production process. Biological and social life becomes the target of power and, turned into commodity, helps create the common substance of the multitude. Industrial capitalism turned the concrete (use value) into abstract (exchange value). In late capitalism the opposite happens: thoughts, ideas and words turn immediately into material objects. The general intellect is no longer embodied in machines but in the living worker.

Three immediate consequences follow. Permanent work has been abolished. Part-time, flexible, temporary work, long periods of unemployment following short periods of work are the rule. We must be flexible, willing to learn, opportunistic. Life has no longer routine, security, long-term planning. We must continually improve our knowledge, skills, abilities and aptitudes. Life-long learning, permanent de- and reskilling, accreditation and appraisal have become ever-present parts of life. Workers used to have a little time to themselves for rest and leisure. Now our entire life has become an indivisible commodity. People must not become attached to a particular employment or employer but treat them cynically: sufficiently close to prove dedication to their tasks but also sufficiently detached to be ready to leave for a better or better-paid job. Collaboration and networking are indispensable but with moderation. Working people must keep something back, they must not waste what gives them a relative advantage in the future. Norman Tebbit, Mrs Thatcher's beloved minister, put it simply: 'Get on your bike'. The Italian PM Mario Monti was more sophisticated. A permanent job is monotonous, he said, we need new challenges. Capitalism has socialized production and has become an immanent component of social relations. Work is disseminated throughout life, minimizing the difference between labour time that adds value and the time adding surplus value. As a result, the wage can no longer translate the value of labour power. Free time, leisure activities and hobbies, the permanently increasing time in unemployment, part-time and alternate work is used consciously or otherwise for the improvement of skills and aptitudes. 'You must have an up-to-date curriculum vitae and you should keep improving it' is the mantra of career advisers, a profession created precisely in order to meet the new organization of production. Our life has become the object of our work, a productive unpaid commodity that must be permanently improved. In this sense, we are all like working mothers: we don't get paid for a large part of our labour.

When networking becomes the main characteristic of production, hierarchy, discipline and authoritarian control by capitalists looks irrational and counter-productive. A deep contradiction develops between the co-operative nature of immaterial labour, the bosses' command and the workers' life of insecurity. One response is for the ruled to imitate the cynicism ('who cares?') and pragmatism ('look after Mr One') of the rulers. If nobody believes in values while we all pay lip service to them, social morality confirms the lies of power. But cynicism is also one way of responding to the abundance of superfluous rules and unnecessary hierarchies. As Paolo Virno puts it, working people continually encounter rules and commandments, rarely facts. 'But to experience rules directly means also to recognize their conventionality and groundlessness.'[21] Disobeying irrational rules becomes part of a strategy of disobedience or of a wider project of resistance.

The second change has to do with profit and wages. The premodern rentier economy, industrial capitalism destroyed, is coming back. The products of the immaterial labour are increasingly rented back to the people who created them. The commons of culture, nature and even our genetic information are privatized and commodified. This is why intellectual property has become such a contested field. As Carlo Vercellone argues, late capitalism is the 'becoming-rent of profit'.[22] If we move to wages, we are all salaried workers now. The content and remuneration of work differs radically but its form is similar. Even the capitalists have become salaried managers and professionals running companies owned by banks or investment and venture funds. Their putative expertise justifies their surplus wages and bonuses. The class difference has been transformed into a huge wage differential. Despite the moral outrage about 'fat cat' bonuses, bankers became prime ministers in Italy and Greece and fill the cabinets of many countries. The worker on the other hand loses on two fronts. First, people do not get paid for the continual work they have to do on themselves to become potentially employable. Secondly, wages get pushed down brutally in order to improve 'competitiveness'. In the past, the reserve army of unemployed was used in order to push wages down. Today, however, the use of technology and the privatization of the general intellect has made a large number of people structurally superfluous. Getting a wage – any wage – has become the hardest quest. As wage earning becomes generalized but also hard to get, the question of replacing wages with a guaranteed income has entered the historical agenda. For Toni Negri, this is the contemporary demand of the 'social revolutionary transition'.[23]

Professional collaboration and networking of production does not create strong political relationships. The successful use of the company intranet, being always online and in touch with colleagues – often exchanging gossip, personal and even erotic messages – is very different from belonging to the same union or party. This is one reason for the popularity of single-issue campaigns. Their members offer minimum agreement on a specific topic but no ideological or long-term commitment. Post-Fordism promotes networking but not ideological identification; collaboration is based on individualism. The main product of biopolitics is the subject; a subject that meets the functional needs of late capitalism.

The politics of multitude

This socio-economic analysis has revived the significance of the multitude as a political category. The multitude as the totality of people who reproduce themselves and capitalism through immaterial labour has replaced class and encompasses the whole working population. For Hardt and Negri, Empire, a new constitutional principle, has unified globalized capitalism and world politics in a global 'state of exception' imposed after the attacks on New York and Washington and now generalized. The model of war has been transferred from anti-terrorism and military campaigns to the containment of internal dissent and uprisings. The multitude is the cause and effect of Empire; Empire unites the multitude in a global network of economic dependence and integration while 'sucking' its life force. It is parasitically attached to the multitude's flesh which is also its greatest enemy and threat. As creator and foe of Empire, the multitude acts like an immune system, in Robert Esposito's terms, which turns against the organism that brought it to life.[24]

This analysis radicalizes one of the most challenging innovations of the Italian workerist tradition, the belief that capital can no longer control the power of working people and use it for its purposes.[25] On the contrary, capitalism reacts to the initiatives and struggles of workers and adopts social and productive forms invented by them. The imagination and networking of working people is used to develop new ways for exploiting and integrating them. This dependence on the productivity and ingenuity of workers, which can be sustained only through their relative docility and repression, makes capitalism 'constantly dream of (often brutally destructive) ways of escaping this dependency'.[26] The novelties and inventions in communications and information technology demand networking, open access to information, the sharing of resources. But the central control and disciplining imposed by owners and managers undermines collaborative invention and creation. In agriculture, science, technology, medicine and culture, the novel is created in open collaboration but is immediately transformed into a closed source of profit protected by patents and copyright. We have therefore reached the point when capitalism destroys people and the planet without reason for existence. A rupture with capital is possible and timely. What we need is to 'eliminate bosses because an industrial control over cognitive work is completely dépassé'.[27]

Negri and Hardt's philosophy of history promises the end of empire. The commodification of the general intellect, of inventiveness and imagination deters further development. As the production process has been fully socialized, capitalism has become parasitical and offers little. Policing, surveillance and repression must therefore be intensified. The multitude, the fully embedded creation of empire, is the only force that can overthrow it by following alternative strategies, such as exit, sabotage, disobedience and resistance. Preserving the Marxian philosophy of history, but not its dialectics or class analysis, Negri and Hardt argue that at an opportune moment, a sudden rupture or world-historical event will lead to 'real democracy'. The timeliness of the Aristotelian *kairos* will interrupt the linear progression of imperial temporality. The networked workers have learned horizontal collaboration and communication and will eventually transfer the principles of collaboration from work to politics. A minimal change in behaviour will transform multitude from a passive victim of empire's vampiric sucking into the active antagonist of its parasitical nature. Negri and Hardt simplify Gilles Deleuze's ideas and turn lyrical: 'the flesh of the multitude is pure potential, an unformed life force, and in this sense an element of social being, aimed constantly at the fullness of life. From this ontological perspective, the flesh of the mutlitude is an elemental power that continuously expands social being, producing in excess of every traditional political-economic measure of value. You can try to harness the wind, the sea, the earth, but each will always exceed your grasp.'[28] When the multitude finally rises Spinoza will have taken his revenge from Hobbes. The multitude, an immanent creation of empire, will bury it.

But how will the monster become the killer of Frankenstein? The hope that capitalism gives birth to its own gravediggers has not been confirmed. The argument that the multitude has been fully integrated in the circuits of empire is presented in such strong terms that its reversal seems unlikely. This difficulty becomes apparent in the rather mild concrete proposals of the authors. The universal rights of migration, settlement and minimum wage, Hardt and Negri advocate in *Empire*, are not realistic in a period of economic crisis and increased xenophobia. In the second decade of the twenty-first century, the opening of borders in Europe is more likely to lead to anti-immigrant and fascist violence rather than radical renewal. In *Commonwealth*, they call for 'a global initiative to provide the basic means of life for all, throughout the world, a global guaranteed income and truly universal health care, whether furnished through global institutions such as UN agencies, citizen organizations, or other bodies'.[29] The idea of the UN offering health care (something even the USA does not have) and guaranteed income (something that does not exist anywhere in the world) is a little fanciful. More importantly, these 'legal rights' implicate reforms in domestic and international law. No such changes can happen, however, without the conquest of power and creation of radical governments – something excluded by their insistence on direct democracy and horizontal collaboration. The hope that the multitude will move from its current imperial immanence to its assigned role as the agent of radical change is hard to believe.

The fear of the crowd

Revolutions start with a crowd in the streets. That was the case in Bastille, the Winter Palace, the overthrow of the Shah of Iran or Ceausescu, Ben Ali and Mubarak. Something 'miracular' happens when people gather and grasp the opportunity the timely moment offers. This is perhaps the reason why political philosophy fears and detests crowds and mobs. English history, in particular, is full of insurrections and riots, conveniently forgotten in the recent moralistic condemnation of the August 2011 disturbances. Thomas Hobbes, the greatest and most frank enemy of the multitude, suffered from mobs and made an honest attempt to understand their motives and effects. Indeed his invention of *Leviathan* is in part a reluctant acknowledgement and antidote to the fact that the *hoi polloi* will soon demand and gain active participation in public affairs, with the attendant dangers. Hobbes feared the London mob; *Leviathan*'s invention could not prevent the reappearance of the crowd. Riots erupted regularly and upredictably. No English elections until the twentieth century passed without extensive violence and rioting. The Luddites, the Diggers and the Levellers often resorted to fights, property destruction and looting. Their *jus resistentiae* was a defence of local communities, traditional practices and ways of life against the privatization of the commons and the violent introduction of new technologies and capitalist ways. Popular resistance failed to stem the tide of modernity. It forms alongside the radical Protestant tradition, the foundation of the anti-statist and libertarian bend of English mentality, today mobilized by the right-wing for exactly the opposite purpose. The Chartists and trade unionists, the suffragettes and the unemployed, on the other hand, fought for equality and freedom. They are the two sides of militant subjectivity, the conserving and the reforming, called to resistance by different types of *adikia*.

The rioting mob lurks behind the philosophical attacks on the multitude, that 'many-headed hydra' that destroys the achievement of the hard work and conscience of merchants. This fear survived into the twentieth century. Contemporary theorists know that the multitude has repeatedly changed regimes, constitutions and laws. The fear of revolution lies behind the rejection of the right to resistance and the obsession with public order. But revolutions have happened and will happen again. European languages record the fear of the multitude in their vocabulary. The relatively neutral term 'crowd' is accompanied by a number of negatively charged words which express fear and contempt towards a social category that acts outside accepted and tolerable norms: 'mob', 'mass', 'horde', 'throng', 'plebs', 'lumpen', 'rabble', 'chavs', the 'great unwashed' are some of the negative terms describing the multitude. Some emphasize the physical presence of the crowd, others its dispersed social identity, again others stress its position at the bottom of social hierarchy. The term 'multitude' with its positive predication had fallen into disuse; only recently it was revived and acquired general resonance.

Mainstream political science considers the crowd archaic, outdated and cruel and, at the same time, attempts to prevent its appearance. Social psychology affirms the fear.[30] Crowd theory is conditioned by the experience of violent industrialization and urbanization of early modernity. The appearance of the faceless mass of workers who left the farming hinterlands of Europe for the great cities and the repeated riots inspired great terrors in the bourgeoisie. 'In every important insurrection there are similar evil-doers and vagabonds, enemies of the law, savage, prowling desperados who, like wolves, roam about whenever they scent a prey.'[31] The protection of public order and the repression of riots was a major concern of early modern legal systems and lies behind the creation of elaborate property regulations. Protecting the 'king's peace' was one of the earliest building blocs of the common law. This almost atavistic fear of the crowd has been theorized by a number of twentieth-century psychologists. Gustave Le Bon, an early examiner, argued that the crowd is idiotic and its members uncivilized. The crowd fears its dissolution and, as a result, easily accepts to be led by demagogues for its protection. The crowd is a wild unthinking 'beast' or a 'savage', easily manipulated and waylaid.[32] It has feminine characteristics, follows violently its desires and carries up extreme actions. The crowd 'thinks' through the body not reason; it prefers images to ideas and words. Body and flesh are its characteristics, according to Elias Canetti. The man in the crowd does not care about his privacy, does not fear the touch of strangers, does not care whose body presses his; he is a man without individuality.[33]

Freud adopts Le Bon's ideas and develops them in a psycho-analytical direction. The characteristics of the crowd result from the discontent of civilization. The compression of members destroys their autonomy and at the same time relieves them of the obligation to obey the laws of civilization and to repress unhindered desire. 'Just as primitive man survives potentially in every individual, so the primal horde may arise once more out of any random collection.'[34] The relationship between crowd and leader is Oedipal. Its members invest in the leader libidinally, transforming aggressive instincts into emotional bonds and harmonious relations with others. The love for the leader or common commitment to an abstract idea unite the crowd. Often these infantile and dreamlike emotions lead to atavistic explosions and uncontrolled violence. William McDougall's *The Group Mind* popularized these ideas in the United States and Britain. The crowd loses its self-restraint, conscience and morality and does not respect non-members. Emotions such as fear, hatred and panic dominate and spread like an epidemic. The crowd's members are led by instinct and act like a horde of animals. The crowd is therefore a remnant from an older and overtaken state of humanity, perhaps from a period before civilization. The brutality and barbarism of the crowd came to an end with the rise of liberal democracies in the twentieth century, for which autonomy and dignity, values opposed to the crowd mentality, are central. We have moved from the age of the crowd to that of the individual and of difference, signs of civilizational progress.[35] But the crowd returns.

Antonio Negri in *Insurrections,* his epic hymn to the multitude, equates social theory's attacks on the crowd with those of philosophy's on the multitude: 'The *multitudo* has to become each time either

131

a nature that is mechanical and deprived of spirit, a nature closer to that of brutes than men, or a thing in itself . . . or a savage world of irrational passions . . .'[36] The hostility Negri mentions is addressed to the crowd; the multitude is not a concept that has troubled political philosophy much. Multitude and crowd are closely connected for Negri, if not identical. But when it comes to the joint work with Michael Hardt, the crowd, the mob and the mass are strictly distinguished from the multitude. The 'crowd or the mob or the rabble can have social effects – often horribly destructive effects – but cannot act of their own accord'. Its members are not singularities but indifferent wholes, they are fundamentally passive and must be led.[37] The mass, on the other hand, destroys individuality: 'the essence of the masses is indifference: all differences are submerged and drowned . . . all the colours of the population fade to grey'.[38] As William Mazzarella puts it, for Hardt and Negri, 'multitudes, in all their vital autonomy, represent the immediate recuperation of life. Crowds, in their passive heteronomy, represent the thoroughly mediated, and thus lifeless, collective.'[39] In *Multitude*, Hardt and Negri prioritize the Russian, Chinese and Cuban revolutions, the urban guerrila and the Zapatistas as well as identity politics such as feminism, the gay and lesbian movements etc. Only in *Commonwealth*, the last book of the trilogy, they find praise for the crowd and its 'jacqueries' as they call the spontaneous uprisings that 'burn out in a flash and [are] gone'.[40] These jacqueries cover a multiplicity of rebellions from peasant and worker revolts in early modernity through to anti-colonial insurgencies and contemporary food and race riots. The authors feel that they have to explain their earlier dismissal and do so in a ham-fisted way. 'It is interesting that whereas in our other works we have often taken great pains to distinguish the multitude from the crowd, the mob, and the masses, [in *Commonwealth*] we see the possibility of recuperating these social formations when their indignation and revolt are directed and organized . . . we might say, along with Flaubert . . . that we hate the crowd except in its days of rebellion, when it achieves a kind of human poetry. This poetry of the future is what has to be composed to make the multitude.'[41] The distinction between multitude and crowd or between 'jacqueries' and constituent power remains. The clause 'it is interesting' is not a sufficient answer for what is an important theoretical absence. Understanding the reasons for change of mind would be 'interesting'. Their Marxist provenance, they claim, placed emphasis on the revolutionary potential of the production process ahead of politics. Without a doubt this correction is connected with the multiform insurrections and revolts that erupted all over the world from Paris and Tehran to Athens and Cairo at the time of the writing of *Commonwealth*. The politics of the street helped correct the theoretical omission. But the revised connection between crowd and multitude remains unclear.

We can conclude that both admirers and opponents recognize that the crowd often abandons the Hobbesian duty of obedience, resists and revolts. For social psychology, the crowd's delinquency inspires fear and calls for repression. The crowd is heteronomous, mimetic and easily led, the enemy of modernization, law and reason. When it resurfaces, it brings back our uncivilized past and commits crimes: hooligans and thugs, 'hoodies' and anarchists, rioters and looters are the modern descendants of the early modern rioters. As William Mazzarella puts it, crowd theory has pathologized 'the vital energies of human groups so thoroughly that they can only appear as symptoms of modern savagery and, as such, wholly at odds with any prospect of human progress'.[42] For its radical promoters, on the other hand, the fears of power and mainstream social science confirm the revolutionary potential of the crowd. The recent widespread use of the Spinozean term *multitudo* indicates a radical re-evaluation of the crowd. Constituent power is back on the world stage and has proved that it can undermine and even overturn the principle of sovereignty. This is what motivates theoretical and political attacks against the multitude. As national sovereignty retreats, pursued by globalized capitalism, international institutions and humanitarian bombers, the multitude could deliver the final push. Can a new (and the oldest) type of direct democracy replace its failed representative form? Can the self-determining multitude create new forms of governance? *Stasis Syntagma* confirms some and corrects other assumptions of multitude theory.

Part III

Resistance

STASIS SYNTAGMA: THE SUBJECTS AND TYPES OF RESISTANCE

The stranger in me

At the Syntagma debate I was invited to speak, I was impressed by the lucky few whose numbers were drawn and were called to the microphone. Queuing before their address, they were anxious and nervous. For most of them it was the first time they had spoken in public in front of thousands. One man in particular was shaking and trembling with evident symptoms of stage fright before his address. He then proceeded to give a beautiful speech in perfectly formed sentences and paragraphs, presenting a complete and persuasive plan for the future of the movement. 'How did you do it?' I asked him later, 'I thought you were going to collapse.' 'When I started speaking', he replied nonchalantly, 'I was mouthing the words but someone else was speaking. A stranger inside me was dictating what to say.' Many participants in the recent insurrections and revolts make similar statements. Sarah, an Egyptian, tells her mother after spending time in Tahrir Square: 'I am not myself. I am somebody new that was born today.'[1] A youth in the Athens December 2008 events says: 'I had been in demos before but never participated in a riot. It was something like an initiation for me and I have to admit I felt liberated. It made me feel like I regained control of myself.'[2] A member of the 'cool' group in Syntagma adds: 'I have changed certainly . . . a different person new and old friends tell me. I have changed, I can see it myself: when I don't fear to confront people and practices in public, when I express my view and support it, when I protect myself better than before . . .'[3] The anthropologist David Graeber, describing the anti-globalization movement, writes that 'it is difficult to find anyone who has fully participated in such an action whose sense of human possibilities has not been profoundly transformed as a result. It's one thing to say "another world is possible". It's another to experience it.'[4]

Using psychoanalytical language, we can call the transubstantiation of 'the stranger in me' the work of the 'radical act'. When someone comes to the end of analysis, she traverses the fantasy that sustains her life and recognizes that the symbolic order, the 'Big Other', is not the seamless web that gives meaning to life. As Slavoj Žižek puts it 'what a moment ago evokes in us a mixture of fear and respect is now experienced as a rather different mixture of ridiculous imposture and brutal, illegitimate display of force'.[5] In more traditional language, we can call this epiphany the work of existential freedom. The subject temporarily or permanently abandons the behavioural controls of biopolitical capitalism. From obedient and subjugated, she becomes – temporarily perhaps – free. An ethical or political act that brings out the 'stranger in me' – an apt name for the unconscious – radically transforms the subject and also changes the co-ordinates of the reality in which the act emerged. This was, for example, the case with the *Hepatia* hunger strikers. By persisting in their action, despite the threat of death, they changed the parameters of a reality that presented them as inferior weaklings, condemning them and their co-immigrants to invisibility and civil death. The energy of the Real – another name for the 'death drive' – confronted physical death and defeated its power.

Many forms of resistance have emerged all over the world. Some were recognizable from previous periods of upheaval. Others are relatively new or are used in novel and imaginative ways. This chapter explores the types of resistance and disobedient subjectivity emerging all over the world, using examples from Greece. At first view they may seem radically different and unrelated. Yet they have appeared in sequences and in conversation with each other. Their surface similarities and underground links have made ours the age of resistance.

December 2008

The urban space has always expressed the inequality of social relations and offered a site of conflict. Urban legality comprises planning, architectural and traffic regulations, public entertainment, protest and expression rules, licit and illicit ways of being in public. It imposes a grid of regularity and legibility, ascribing places to legitimate activities while banning others, structuring the movement of people and vehicles across space and ordering encounters between strangers. Yet from the regular urban riots of early modernity to the Bastille, the Paris Commune, the British reform movement and the suffragettes, the American civil rights movement, May 1968, the Athens Polytechnic 1973, Prague, Bucharest, Tehran and Cairo uprisings, to name a few iconic cases, the 'street' has confronted and unsettled urban legality. Urban space offers ample opportunity for political action, which has changed social systems, laws and institutions across epochs and places. The abstract denunciation of protests for violence combines the defence of the status quo with historical ignorance.

It was therefore strange that the widespread uprising that took place in Greece in December 2008 surprised and shocked politicians and mainstream commentators. The catalyst was the unprovoked police killing of the 15-year-old Alexis Grigoropoulos late on Saturday 6 December in the Exarcheia district of Athens next to the Polytechnic and the Law School, two universities associated with student militancy for many decades.[6] Within hours of Alexis' killing, a massive wave of protest erupted. Some 800 schools and most universities were occupied throughout Greece with daily marches to local police stations and government buildings. Street happenings were combined with imaginative forms of protest. Theatrical performances were interrupted by young actors. The main evening news bulletin on state TV was stopped while broadcasting a statement by the Prime Minister, which was replaced by banners declaring 'stop watching television and get out to the streets'. A large banner with the word 'resistance' written in several languages was hung on the Acropolis hill. The huge Christmas tree in Syntagma Square was set alight, with the protesters declaring 'We are revolting. Christmas is postponed.' It was 'massive, extraordinary, beyond imagination, and, at the same time, the only thing that made sense', writes a participant.[7] For two weeks central Athens was under the control of young people, with the police keeping a distance. Banks and luxury shops were attacked, some looting took place, several cars and some buildings were set alight; no attacks on persons or casualties were reported. State institutions were paralysed and the government threatened to bring out the troops. This was averted by the Christmas break and a huge police mobilization in the New Year.

The violence against property was highly spectacular. Rioting has its own aesthetic. An implicit understanding with photographers and mainstream media offers publicity to the insurgents and dazzling photos and stirring stories to the press. As Etienne Balibar put it, the mass media have become 'passive organizers' of riots because of their news value. But there is a price to pay. The 'virtual violence' they display '*transforms* real, endemic social violence, to which it responds, *into spectacle*, thereby at once making it *visible* in its intensity and invisible in its everydayness'.[8] December enriched impressively the archive of 'insurrectional art'.

The 'sudden' awakening of a generation routinely condemned as apolitical, ill-informed and apathetic took politicians and journalists by surprise. No party planned or led the insurrection, no specific demands were put forward, no single ideology dominated. The repeated question 'What do the kids want?' paraphrased Freud's 'What does the woman want?' expressing the deep anxiety of the political class. Eventually politicians and journalists dismissed the insurrection as non-political, condemning its 'blind violence'. But it was very different for the insurgents: 'We formed neighbourhood assemblies, primary unions, groups of solidarity with people we would have never imagined standing next to us . . . by living an egalitarian moment, we changed in one night the terms of inclusion and exclusion. We were transformed from invisible solitary figures rambling around in our urban misery into political subjects who managed to challenge, not the solutions that had to be applied to the situation, but the situation itself.'[9]

According to Michel de Certeau, urban resistance takes strategic and tactical forms: 'A strategy assumes a place that can be circumscribed as proper (*propre*) . . . The "proper" is a victory of space over time. On the contrary, because it does not have a place, a tactic depends on time – it is always on the watch for opportunities that must be seized "on the wing".'[10] Strategy establishes a new place against already existing static places of authority or against structures of power. This spatial base facilitates resistance against temporal synchronicity and cyclical legality. Tactics on the other hand utilize temporality, the *kairos* or the timely; through an acceleration or disjointure of time, the propriety of place or structure is unsettled. In de Certeau's terms, the December uprising was a recognizable but transient form of 'street' resistance. It established its proper places, the Polytechnic, Exarcheia, the Law and the Economics Schools against the authoritative stability of Parliament, Ministries or the Police HQ. It used the opportunities of school, university or pre-Christmas time (the burning of the Christmas tree, the disruption of shopping districts, the occupation of schools and universities) to unsettle the propriety of cyclical temporality. But it was clearly much more than street protest. Imagine Westminster and Whitehall or the White House and Congress under siege every day for two weeks.

The December insurrection brought to the surface the simmering conflict between the rulers and those who give their active and passive consent and, on the other side, people, groups and causes who have no stake in the political order. Large numbers of people cannot formulate their most essential demands in the language of a political problem. In this sense, the insurrection was an expression of political agency at degree zero. When the director of state television dismissed protesters who raised protest banners during a live news broadcast, calling them 'disorganized rabble' and people without 'social identity', he came close to the truth, *malgré lui*. When those discarded by politics become visible (and TV news is symbolically significant) politics proper erupts. When an excluded part demands to be heard and must change the rules of inclusion to succeed, a new political subject is potentially constituted, in excess of the hierarchy of visible groups. As Jacques Rancière argues, a division is put in the 'common sense' and the 'regime of visibility' of the social space changes radically.

According to Alain Badiou, every social or political situation consists of an infinite number of elements such as classes, groups and people with varying interests, ideologies and tastes. In the midst of the differences, an empty and invisible place supports the stability of the whole. This void lies close to the most anonymous and vulnerable, people who exist socially but not politically. The December insurrection disrupted the settled state of differences by bringing the invisible to the fore and introducing them to the tribulations and joys of disobedience. It turned a usual urban protest by students or workers into something that both retained the characteristics of urban resistance but also overtook it in a radical new direction, changing the parameters of the situation. Yet this interpretation goes against Alain Badiou's explicit remarks. In his *Rebirth of History*, Badiou classifies the recent 'riots' into 'immediate', 'latent' (factory occupations in France) and 'historical' (Tahrir Square).[11] The choice of the word 'riot' to translate the French *émeute*, translated also as 'uprising' in the book, is indicative of Badiou's distancing. Calling the Tunisian and Egyptian *émeutes* 'riots' is perhaps an error in translation. But the word 'riot' is an accurate translation of Badiou's attitude towards the 'immediate' riots. Without referring to Athens, something that might have weakened his theory, Badiou calls the uprisings in Paris 2005 and London 2011 'violent, anarchic and ultimately without enduring truth ... [they] destroy and plunder without a concept',[12] downgrading their significance to irrational reactions to police repression. 'Riots' create subjects dominated by 'negation and destruction' confined to a 'rage with no purpose other than the satisfaction of being able to crystallize and find objects to destroy and consume'.[13] David Cameron, whom Badiou quotes critically, denounced the 2011 riots in clearer terms: 'It is criminality pure and simple and it has to be confronted and defeated.' Purity is Badiou's preferred term too. A riot cannot 'purify' itself. The rioting subject is nihilistic, 'always impure' neither political nor prepolitical.[14] Immediate riots lack the idea or truth of the proper event. Only the idea of 'dialectical communism' will move the riots to a higher plane and prepare radical change.

Very little in Badiou's analysis applies to December. The repeated calls to resistance, the debates in the streets and theatres, the occupations and assemblies politicized a whole generation and its parents, in other words, the majority of productive Greeks. Opinion polls at the height of the insurrection suggested that a majority of Greeks supported it. British journalists who followed the events and participated in assemblies reported that the intense and fully informed debates of the insurgents were the closest they had come across to the classical Platonic dialogue.[15] The insurgents learned the relative importance of solidarity and defensive tactics, motion and stasis, flash mobs and occupations. They understood the opportunities cyclical and ritual time offers and the importance of having a stable base. Last but not least, limited defensive violence was de-demonized despite media attempts to present the youth as violent criminals intent on destruction and looting. Badiou sees himself as the guardian of the French philosophy of the 1960s.[16] His theory must be global, explain all possible phenomena as well as the movement of history. The 'rioters' of Paris, Athens and London did not follow the 'communist idea', Badiou's indispensable prerequisite for the emergence of truth; they remained therefore apolitical and perhaps nihilistic. Badiou repeats the mainstream's dismissal of the 'mob', if not its fear. In response to suggestions by this author that December was, in his own terms, a micro-event, Badiou disagreed. Yet the Greek insurgents were political in everything they said and most of the things they did.

Etienne Balibar's discussion of the uprisings in the Paris *banlieues* is more sensitive and nuanced and anticipates the political character of the December insurrection.[17] For Balibar, the uprisings were triggered by systematic class and race discrimination against young French citizens who are treated like colonial subjects. The physical and symbolic 'secession' of a large part of society that becomes the object of repressive policing symbolizes a wider void at the heart of democracy. The poor, the 'underclass' and ethnic minorities have no stake in politics and opt out of public life. The occasional explosions of spectacular violence are their only relationship with the principle of publicity. As an Egyptian demonstrator put it, 'before I was watching television, now television is watching me'.[18] But these eruptions are not automatically anti-political: revolts can become 'insurrectional' or 'political' through a process of 'collectivization': linking with campaigns against injustice and struggles for social rights creates a 'virtual democratic citizenry' and reverses the decline of politics.[19] Similarly, the London 2012 riots had political elements. A major research project carried out by the London School of Economics and the *Guardian* newspaper found that police repression and social deprivation were the two most important grievances that led people to the streets and violence.[20] In both cases, young people who had been atomized by the behavioural controls of biopolitical capitalism and oppressive police tactics became visible and took to the streets. The Athens insurrection was different from Paris and London. In Balibar's terms, it was 'becoming political' from the beginning. The 'articulation' of the protesters with social and political movements and struggles started in December 2008 and was completed in 2011.

December was a peripatetic school, the propaideutic for the resistances of 2010 and 2011. People learned how to communicate, collaborate and stand up to police repression. The youth politicized in December crowded the squares and stood firm against the attacks of the riot police. It is not an exaggeration to say that without the 2008 insurrection, the 2011 occupations would not have happened. The sequence December–Syntagma disarticulated identities from the circuit of desire-consumption-frustration and helped the gradual emergence of subjectivities committed to resistance, justice and equality. Alain Badiou argues that the idea of communism has political, historical and subjective elements. 'Subjectivation' is the process through which an individual determines the truth of his existence and of the world he lives in. It follows and confirms the truth of an event that changes the parameters of a situation (this is the political element), placing the subject in the service of historical becoming. For Badiou the subject emerges in the process that commits him to the truth of an event.[21] Yet, the subject can emerge only after the sediments of the previous obedient subjectivity have been undermined or destroyed. This is precisely what acts of negation of the dominant existent and the refusal to obey illegal or immoral policies achieves. The sacramental baptism releases the infant from original sin. The rejection of routine politics and the discovery of new types of street action similarly turned the insurrection into what we can call a 'political baptism' preparatory of resisting subjectivities. The baptism of disobedience releases the nascent subject from the consolations of normality and the fear of normalization. The participants saw December precisely as a 'rupture in traditional Greek politics, both because it affected radically all later socio-political relations . . . and because for a moment it disengaged the subject from his/her past experiences.'[22]

Before the event, political change was a matter of consensus; dissent a matter for policing. After the rift, politics returned to normality but its terrain had changed, through the appearance of new politicized subjects. For Hara Kouki, December revealed that 'in an unjust universe the repressed learn to communicate without speaking, to step forward without mobbing, to resist without resisting . . . December, far from being an exception, contained the only normality that makes our lives possible.'[23] The year after the December insurrection, the meaning of politics was redefined. New types of activity and organization emerged and kept the December dynamic alive. 'Interrupting the normal flow and spatial arrangement of things, people start[ed] to become self-organized alongside those around them by occupying public spaces, mounting community events and forming neighborhood assemblies. Local communities, which have been erased of any political content, since the very foundation of the Greek state, appear[ed] now as an alternative political agent.'[24] The right-wing government could not survive. It was defeated in early elections in 2009. The Socialist party was elected on a false prospectus with a 42% share of the vote. A short time later, the Papandreou government recalculated upwards the Greek deficit at over 15% and solicited the intervention of the International Monetary Fund and the European Union. As the austerity measures began to descend on the country like an unstoppable landslide, new types of resistance took off. The Greek and European political elites hoped to pass the measures with minimal resistance from the usual Leftist suspects. They missed the message of December for a second time.

Hepatia

Athens, January 2011. While the Egyptian revolution was in full flow, 300 *sans papiers* immigrants from the Maghreb took refuge in *Hepatia*, a neo-classical building in central Athens and staged a hunger strike. They had lived and worked in Greece for up to ten years, doing the jobs the Greeks didn't want to do for a fraction of the minimum wage without social security. When the crisis struck, they were unceremoniously kicked out. They had no Greek documents, work or residence permits and were liable to immediate deportation. The strikers were the double victims of boom and bust. During the period of fake growth, their underpaid, uninsured work did the necessary 'dirty' jobs the locals would not do. Now that the EU and IMF austerity measures welcomed by the government led to prolonged depression, they were surplus to requirements, to be disposed of like refuse. After forty days, with several strikers in hospital with irreversible organ failure that would lead to death, the government accepted the bulk of their demands. Crucial in that victory was the campaign of solidarity and support organized by radical and social movements, who kept the topic at the centre of attention, despite the vitriolic attacks from government and media. A defining moment came when the riot police surrounded the Athens Law School, where the strikers had sought asylum after their arrival from Crete. Their arrest and removal was stopped by thousands of students and militants, who surrounded the police, thereby stopping the strikers' ejection and arrest. The protesters' determination obliged the authorities, looking for ideological gains in the xenophobic part of the population, to guarantee the peaceful exodus of the exhausted strikers and their safe passage to *Hepatia*, where they continued their struggle.

The hunger strikers wanted to make people notice their meagre, insignificant existence. They were asking for residence rights, basic labour protections and minimum living standards. More importantly, they were demanding the minimum recognition of the fellow human. Identity is built through the reciprocal recognition between self and other. The immigrants' lack of basic rights of work and life destroys all recognition, making them less than human. They were being punished not for what they had done (criminal acts) but for who they were, not for their evil nature or activity but for their abject being and innocence. They were *homines sacri*, legally non-existent and therefore non-persons who can be treated in the most cruel way by state, employer and the man on the Athens omnibus.

The Greek government claims that it fully respects human rights. According to liberal jurisprudence, human rights belong to humans precisely because they are human rather than members of narrower groups such as nation, state or class. Nation and state give political and civil rights to their citizens according to their law and constitution. Human rights on the other hand are given to people who don't have the protection of state and law. This is a comforting thought. The treatment of the *sans papiers* shows these claims to

145

be ideological half-truths. In theory, human rights are given to all humans, in practice only to citizens. This is further confirmed by the treatment of asylum seekers. In January 2011, the European Court of Human Rights held that sending refugees back to Greece amounted to torture, inhuman and degrading treatment, because of the living and detention conditions in immigration camps.[25] Greece almost never gives political asylum to refugees. Belgium was also condemned for considering Greece a humane place and sending back an Afghan refugee under the Dublin refugee treaty. Belgium and other European states, including Britain, no longer return asylum seekers to Greece. But the treatment of asylum seekers and economic migrants deteriorated further. The mainstream parties used xenophobic rhetoric in the 2012 election campaigns, legitimizing the neo-Nazi Chryssi Avgi, which followed its electoral success by setting up 'storm troops' and launching pogroms against immigrants.

The hunger strikers were humanity reduced to degree zero. They were martyrs in the double sense of the word, both witnesses and sacrificial victims. As witnesses, they gave evidence that there are truths higher than life. Life is worth living for values worth dying for. In this sense, the strikers were exercising what philosophers from Rousseau to Derrida consider the essence of freedom: acting against biological and social determinations in the name of a higher truth.[26] It is the prerogative of the sovereign, as the heir to God, to demand martyrdom from his subjects and to sacrifice his enemies. The sovereign negotiates the link between secular and holy by making sacred (*sacer facere*): war, the death penalty, rituals of sacrifice and consecration are ways through which the transcendent absolute is both acknowledged and kept at a distance. The mediation, exemplified by the King's two bodies and his power to take life and offer mercy, introduces the divine into the secular in a symbolic form and places limits on its action, both necessary for the conduct of social life. Sacrifice, making the ordinary sacred, bridges everyday life with what transcends it. The truth the hunger strikers defended at the personal level was the dignity of humanity, what makes each unique in our human similarity. At the collective level, their sacrifice brought the Greek state and people before an infinite justice and hospitality, preconditions of law and policy. The great law of hospitality, writes Derrida, is 'an unconditional Law, both singular and universal, which ordered that all borders be open to each and every one, to every other, to all who might come, without question'.[27] This unconditional law must be negotiated with the conditional rights of migrants to hospitality.[28] This is what justice demands and the hunger strikers asked.

In Greece, however, justice has miscarried in the austerity measures and the Athens ghettos, the treatment of refugees and the wall built on the Greco-Turkish border to keep the poor out and the Greeks in. Neither unconditional nor conditional, hospitality is drowning in the boats of immigrants sinking in the Aegean.

Protesting against the worst abuses, asking to be seen, heard and acknowledged in a minimum way was the great service the *sans papiers* offered to Greece. They fought to be recognized as living by going to death. They reminded the Greeks that the theologico-political order, based on the ability to take life and let live, can be disrupted by removing the power of life and death from the Sovereign. In Hegel's master and slave dialectic, the master achieves his position by going all the way in his struggle for recognition, prepared even to die; at that point the slave, fearing for his life, capitulates and accepts his servitude. The strikers reversed the dialectic. Servants and quasi-slaves legally, without any formal recognition, they faced death in order to remove from the master the power to kill. In doing so collectively, they traced the promise of a new type of power not based on imposed or voluntary sacrifice. This type of power goes to the edge of finitude and touches it but does not pierce or transcend it, as Jean-Luc Nancy puts it, because it does not need a bridge to an absolute outside or transcendent Other.[29] Their gift to the immigrants all over Europe was to tell them that they can take their lives in their hands against the iniquities and humiliations of governments, authorities and human rights fanatics. In those hard days of February and March 2011, the hunger strikers were the only truly free people of Athens. Their struggle and victory was the victory of everyone.

Syntagma

On 25 May 2011, a group of men and women of all ideologies, ages, races, occupations, calling themselves *aganaktismenoi*, a translation of the Spanish *indignados*, began occupying Syntagma – the central square in Athens opposite Parliament; the area around the White Tower in Thessaloniki; and public spaces in sixty cities. The response of the organized Left was initially confused and embarrassed. The orthodox Communist Party, one of the most doctrinaire in the world, attacked the mobilization as petty bourgeois and ineffective and escalated its attacks when the occupations became permanent encampments. For the communists, protests and insurrections are insignificant and even counter-productive if they are not led by the revolutionary vanguard. The radical Left, after the initial shock and some wavering, adopted the occupations as a new type of resistance continuing the earlier struggles of the world social forum and anti-globalization campaigns in which it had participated.

The rallies and assemblies in the squares were peaceful, with the police observing from a distance. The occupiers attacked the unjust impoverishment of working Greeks, the loss of sovereignty that had turned the country into a neo-colonial fiefdom and the decline of parliamentary democracy into corruption, cleptocracy and clientelism. Thousands of people came together daily in popular assemblies to discuss the next steps. The parallels with the classical Athenian demos, which met a few hundred metres away, are striking. Aspiring speakers were given a number and called to the platform if their number was drawn. This was a reminder that 90% of office-holders in classical Athens were selected by lots. The speakers stuck to strict three-minute slots to allow as many as possible to contribute. The assembly was efficiently run without the usual heckling of public speaking. The topics ranged from organizational matters to politics, economics and ideology, local and international solidarity, education and health. A different person was elected every evening to chair the debate. The topics were approved at the start by vote after a short presentation by the proposer. No issue was beyond proposal and disputation and no censorship or control of any kind was exercised. At the end of each assembly, resolutions with suggestions for action were put to the crowd and voted upon. Consensus was the favourite way for reaching decisions; majority vote was rarely used. Political parties and banners were discouraged. No leaders and spokespersons emerged; no manifestos were issued. Press releases to the eager media reproduced only those resolutions voted by the assembly. In well-organized weekly debates on specified topics of wide interest, invited economists, lawyers, political philosophers and activists presented alternatives for tackling the economic crisis and discussed them under strict time limits. Both panel topics and panelists were chosen through nomination and voting. On 17 June, the day after one of the riot-police assaults on the assembly, I was invited with three others to speak on the idea of direct democracy. The experience of addressing thousands who heard in church-like silence and then contributed fully to the debate was life changing. Standard political science had not and could not understand the significance of the events. Radical political philosophy had much better but insufficient insights. A couple of months later the first version of this book was written.

The mainstream media commonly blame the protests and the limited violence that follows them on the divided Left, the anarchists and the 'hoodies' of the black bloc. This tactic could not work with the *aganaktismenoi*. They came from all parties and none. The popular assembly repeatedly declared the non-violent character of the occupation and protected the square from the attacks of the riot police and occasionally from the small minority of violent youths. This repudiation of violence was in evidence during the unprecedented events of late June 2011. On 28 and 29 June, the *aganaktismenoi* attempted to encircle Parliament and put pressure on MPs enacting the second memorandum's austerity measures. Trade unions and parties had also called for a two-day general strike and a march on Parliament. When the marchers reached Syntagma, the riot police attacked the protesters indiscriminately, using tons of tear gas and other chemicals. A few youths and hoodied militants started lobbing stones, pieces of marble and the odd firebomb, affectionately known as 'Molotov cocktail'. The *aganaktismenoi* tried to stop the youths and defended the square. The police attack in and around Syntagma turned the centre of Athens into a battleground, sending sensational photos around the world. The Greek Medical Association and the Athens Bar stated that such extensive use of chemical weapons in times of war amounts to a war crime. The peaceful spirit of the square carried the day however. Despite attacks on the health and media centres and on masses of people gathered for protection in the metro station, the *aganaktismenoi* returned after the police withdrew, cleared the debris and continued the occupation.

The condemnation of violence by government and media became a major weapon for the demonization of resistance. Spectacular acts dominated news reporting and scared people by giving the impression that Greece was on the verge of civil war. It was not true. The most shocking incident happened in May 2010 early in the resistance cycle. Three bank employees died of asphyxiation when their branch in central Athens was set on fire by passing demonstrators. The crime was universally condemned and led to an intense debate about violence in the anarchist community, with many participants rejecting violence against persons. Despite the intensity of the anti-austerity protests over a two-year period, no other fatalities were reported; serious injuries were mainly the result of police action. Limited attacks on shops and banks did take place; they were exaggerated by the media and rejected by the occupations and the Left. Following the late June police attack on Syntagma, the popular assembly condemned the police and 'all extreme action, which uses the conflict with the riot police as an excuse to carry out the destruction of public or private property'.[30]

The occupations declined in July as the heat wave descended on Athens and the failure to stop the enactment of the measures deflated the enthusiasm. As the numbers shrank tensions developed between the protesters and others who were using the square opportunistically without political intent. The police removed violently the remaining occupiers and tents at 5 a.m. on 1 August. After the removal, the riot police kept Syntagma empty. The *aganaktismenoi* returned to popular assemblies in the suburbs and provincial cities with the slogan 'we are the squares, we are everywhere'. But the balance of power had already shifted and new radical subjects had emerged. The effects of the resistances became tangible in the 2012 elections. The experience and historical memory of the occupations had created a legacy which has changed the meaning of politics.

The sequence December-*Hepatia*-Syntagma

Let us compare Syntagma with the December insurrection. December was characterized by time, Syntagma by place, December by transience, Syntagma by permanence, December by (limited) violence, Syntagma by repudiation of violence, December by mobility, Syntagma by static presence. Syntagma's relationship to space and time differed from December. Public spaces, squares in particular, are given to leisure, commercial activities and mild erotic encounters. Syntagma turned the square into a public space where multiple singularities lived in common, discussed, decided and acted together. The crowd in the square was a multitude or counter-power – something that occupations of universities or other buildings could not achieve.

As far as time is concerned, December was a spontaneous, unpredictable and timely response to the killing. Its temporality was organized around institutional time, university and school terms, Christmas shopping, with the Christmas break marking its end. Syntagma too started in spontaneous fashion, the catalyst being a rally of solidarity to the Spanish *indignados*. Its organization of time followed the regularities of work. The thematic groups and popular assemblies met in the evening after work. According to opinion polls, 47% of the population went to the squares and 83% approved their actions. Syntagma time was organized in strictly equal segments and was allocated according to the axiom of equality. The random choice of speakers similarly adopted the equality of randomness. Every intervention was given equal time, discussed with equal vigour and put to the vote for adoption. Time limits were strictly kept. A new political culture emerged in the squares all over the world which cannot be repressed or forgotten. The articulate debates discredited the banal mantra that economics, public policy or political philosophy are too technical and complex and must be left to experts. The belief that the *demos* has more wisdom than any party, leader or intellectual, a constitutive belief of the classical *ecclesia*, returned to Athens.

Let us finally compare the subjects of resistance. Three types of resisting subjectivity emerged: firstly, those reacting to the status of expendable, redundant humans; secondly, the biopolitically excluded; finally, the democratically disenfranchised. The *immigrants* realized that minimum humanity is created through what they lacked, *papiers*, documents, files. In a biopolitical world, life is registered life, while undocumented life does not exist. To retrieve their life from this administrative void, they had to come to the threshold of death. The *sans papiers* became martyrs in order to enter humanity. They confirmed that human rights do not belong to humans. They construct a gradated humanity, between the fully human, the lesser human and the non-human.[31]

The December insurrection was a reaction to a society of consumption and hedonism combined with police repression and extreme control for those who do not conform. It brought together the poor, unemployed and radicalized youth with more affluent pupils and students who cannot find existential meaning or moral value in the dominant culture. The majority were people whose interests are never heard, accounted or represented. They did not demand anything specific. They simply said, 'enough is enough', 'here we stand against'. Not 'I claim this or that right', but 'I claim the right to have rights'. Those invisible, outside the established sense of what exists, speaks and is acceptable, must perform their existence, through a Bartleby-type 'I would prefer not to.' They are people who exist socially but not politically. They are 'neither absolutely outside nor really within the social system, but only in the paradoxical terms of an *internal exclusion*'.[32] The first step in the emergence of political subjectivity is the rejection of the established order. Caught between insatiable desire and brutal repression, they performed an absolute but ineffective freedom. If will and necessity cannot be dialectically united, they remain opposed in a disjunctive synthesis; the result is often violence. This was politics at degree zero, the first but insufficient step in people and movements 'becoming political'.

The mainstream media called the December protesters 'rabble'. In

Syntagma the mob became a multitude. Young people were told for twenty years that if they study and get degrees, they would get a better life than their parents. In a historical first, over 60% of European youth have post-secondary education and exactly the same skills as the elites. They are now told that they will never get a proper job. One thousand unemployed lawyers, engineers and doctors are more revolutionary than one thousand unskilled workers. When the two combine the mixture is inflammable. The physical coming together of bodies was a de-*monstration* or *manifestation* in French. If for Hegel the first step in the emergence of subjectivity is the negation of the world, the second is precisely the stepping out or alienation of self in the world, which then returns to self-consciousness enriched. A *monstration* or manifestation is precisely the public appearance of common political desire. A new type of political subjectivity started emerging in the squares. Syntagma 'sublated' or brought together and transcended the (in)human subject of *Hepatia* and the invisible person of December. The Syntagma citizen exercised the right to resistance in a form appropriate for post-industrial and post-democratic societies.

Naming resistance

Nomen est Omen. The name is destiny, a blessing or a curse that conditions a life or project. For medieval theology, a good name was half the way to paradise. There is nowhere that this applies more than in politics. Naming is the business of politics. Names are marks of identification (Marxism–Leninism), symbolic reminders (Tiananmen Square) and signs of identity (Pasok, New Labour). Nomination brings together and makes actual the virtual by constructing a political subject out of social diffusion (the working class, the capitalists etc.). Nomination is therefore an imaginative political act indicating what the group, party or organization stands for, rather than any specific policies and manifestos. Giving a name is a hegemonic practice, by choosing a signifier that will unite the greatest number of people, causes and groups. Nomination takes a determinate particularity and makes it universal. A good name constructs its own foundation myth; it acts performatively, by bringing to life what it names. The name 'National Patriotic Front', the resistance organization during the German occupation of Greece, for example, was such a hegemonic operation, bringing together nation and emancipation under the banner of a popular front. Pasok (Panhellenic Socialist Movement), by calling itself a movement instead of a party, was able to co-opt and combine the radicality of de-colonization struggles with the modernizing appeal of social movements.

The politics of resistance, like all politics, operates through the giving of names. A demonstration, rally or strike is transient and effervescent. To survive and acquire permanence, it must be nominated. According to Saul Kripke names are 'rigid designators'. They do not describe or represent referents but designate one and the same object in all possible worlds. A foundational naming or 'primal baptism' gives the name this quality. Theseus' boat, for example, is identified through its given name and remains the same, although all its parts have been changed in the voyage from Crete to Athens. The three types of resistance discussed here were named December, *Hepatia* and Syntagma. As rigid designators, they have turned transient happenings into enduring entities. December is a temporal identification, the others toponymies. December's designation is apt. Its tactics used time and movement to unsettle the propriety of official temporality. *Hepatia* and Syntagma on the other hand used the stability of place, turning it into a haven and power base.

We have named the occupations *Stasis* (Station) *Syntagma*. *Stasis* is a strange word. It means, first, the upright posture, standing tall and serene, holding your stance. This first meaning is present in the English word 'stasis', stillness or immobility. The Greek word *stasis* has a second meaning, in one of those tricks of the cunning of language: it means sedition, revolt or insurrection, the opposite of stillness. *Syntagma* is a combined word from *syn* and *tassein,* putting together. In politics and law, *syntagma* is the constitution or polity; in linguistics, a syntagmatic relationship arranges linguistic units sequentially. The *syntagma* brings together and arranges a multiplicity of people. *Syntagma* means being together and becoming political, of the polis. Syntagma Square was named after a nineteenth-century demonstration, which demanded a Constitution from the Bavarian King. This is what the *aganaktismenoi* repeated: they were standing together demanding a new political arrangement to free Greece from neo-liberal domination, political corruption and post-democratic malaise.

Stasis Syntagma (literally the bus and metro station in the square) is a symbolic nomination. The *aganaktismenoi* bring together place (the square and the public transport station), posture (standing together opposite and against Parliament) and demand (a new constitutional practice). The etymological root *sta in the word stasis or con-sti-tution has metaphysical connotations. *Sta is the root of stance,

153

sub-stance, hypor-stasis, con-sti-tution. It is the foundation on which self and collective stand together and take the stance of resistance. *Stasis Syntagma* is philosophically, politically, topographically the name of the present insurrection and of the coming democracy.

— 10 —

DEMOS IN THE SQUARE

The alter-globalization movement moved around nomadically in the early 2000s, following shadow-like the summits of world leaders. Its landmarks were places as far away as Porto Alegre, Seattle, and Genoa. Mirroring globalized and mobile capitalism, the anti-globalizers organized dissent on a planetary scale. Recent resistances from Tahrir to Syntagma and the Occupy movement are nationally based, emotionally intense and firmly located in particular places. The occupations allowed the itinerant protesters to settle down in permanent encampments and assemblies. The national base is a major difference from the previous period. It allows the utilization of social, political and historical specificities that the earlier multinational campaigns lacked. The slogans were universal in scope: *que se vayan todos, dégage*, 'we are the 99%'. But their meaning was adjusted to the circumstances of each country: Ben Ali and Mubarak represented political dictatorship and impoverishment, the IMF or the Spanish/Greek government the injustice of austerity and the destruction of democracy. Despite differences, most movements expressed an emerging anti-capitalist feeling. Ethnic and religious antagonisms were absent. Moslems and Christians stood together in Tahrir Square. Immigrants were fully integrated into the Greek and Spanish occupations and had their own stalls, debates and music.

Globalized capitalism exploits people locally. Despite the hopes of Left internationalism and liberal cosmopolitanism, effective politics still takes place at home. The resistances reminded us that radical politics, faced with a hostile international environment, can win victories only in its own *polis*.

155

Constituent demos

Let us examine the Syntagma occupation in the light of radical philosophy. For Negri and Hardt, the multitude is a social category, not a public assembly. For Rancière, on the other hand, the *demos* combined the totality of citizens with those excluded from the affairs of the polis. *Stasis Syntagma* brought the two together. The people who work, produce, and create value were there. Their views were perfunctorily discussed and summarily rejected by the government. As a result, the overwhelming majority of the population was excluded from democratic consultation and decision-making. Their demands were not sectional or regional but universal. Political exclusion, normative universality and the creativity of immaterial labour were joined in Syntagma. In this sense, the multitude became the contemporary form of the Athenian demos. Aristotle called the Athenian constitution *politeia*. 'When the multitude (*plethos*) acts politically for the common good, the common name of all citizens is *politeia*.'[1] Antonis Manitakis describes the Athenian *demos* as 'the unity of the many embodied in a representation of politics and power as common deliberation, in a common place, in the midst of a public agora'.[2] The classical *demos* was a multitude assembled in a public place, debating and deciding the common affairs. Syntagma became the contemporary *Pnyx* – the place a few hundred metres from the square where classical Athens assembled. Stasis Syntagma was the multitude in assembly, the demos in the square.

The first call to the Syntagma and Thessaloniki occupations adopted the term *aganaktismenoi,* a translation of the Spanish *indignados*. The term differentiated the occupiers from political parties and trade unions. 'We declare peacefully our outrage at the crisis, at all those who brought us to this. Spontaneously, without parties, groups and ideologies.' *Stasis Syntagma* used the rich experience of the social movements and local occupations but it was not a movement in the same way. It did not target a particular policy or set of policies but the overall austerity package and the system of power behind it. The popular assemblies discussed specific issues and grievances but did not address separate parts of the population like the identity movements. The first resolution adopted on 27 May defined the aims of the occupation in broad terms: 'For a long time decisions are taken on our behalf without us. *We* are working people, unemployed, pensioners, youth who have come to Syntagma to fight for our lives and future. *We* are here because we know that we only can find solutions to our problems ... *We* are not leaving

156

the squares before those who brought us to this state have left. Governments, troika, banks, memoranda and all those who exploit us. *We* tell them that the debt is not ours. DIRECT DEMOCRACY NOW!'[3] It was a new type of action confronting state power with a counter-power. The terms 'people', 'citizens' or 'society' had been proposed as alternative definitions of the subject of occupation; eventually the 'we' prevailed and framed the resolution. The choice was apposite. The 'we' includes non Greeks, unlike 'citizens'; it reflects the visceral character of physical presence, unlike 'people' or 'society'. It was the term that could include the largest number of people.

Most states and legal systems are founded in breach of the protocols of constitutional legality. They are the result of revolution, victory or defeat in war, liberation from colonialism or occupation. The constituent power of the people, most evident in a revolution, suspends existing constitution and law and justifies itself by claiming to found a new state, a better constitution or a just law. It appeals to the right to resistance, which accompanies like a ghostly shadow every established order. At the point of its occurrence, constituent power is condemned as illegal, criminal, evil. If it succeeds, it is retrospectively legitimized in the declarations and constitutions that inaugurate the new order. The Syntagma multitude acted in the same way. Its resolution mirrored the declarations of collective self-legislation. Its 'we' was a political baptism; it was juxtaposed to 'they', the Parliament and politicians opposite, bankers and the troika. The resolution both stated the existence of the multitude and performatively instituted it in juxtaposition to a 'constitutive outside'. 'There is no hegemonic articulation without the determination of a frontier, the definition of a "them"', writes Chantal Mouffe.[4] Syntagma's 'they' was the power system *tout court*. The multitude's constituent power did not lead to Mouffe's 'agonistic politics', however. It was constructed in a deep antagonism towards the power elites that cannot be negotiated through the institutions of 'democratic pluralism'. As Jodi Dean put it, in relation to Occupy Wall Street, the occupation

> asserts a gap by forcing a presence. This forcing is more than simply of people into places where they do not belong ... It's a forcing of collectivity over individualism, the combined power of a group that disrupts a space readily accommodating of individuals. Such a forcing puts in stark relief the conceit of a political arrangement that claims to represent a people who cannot be present, a divided people who, when present, instil such fear and insecurity that they have to be met by armed police and miles of barricades.[5]

Before the resolution's 'we', the square was another protest rally. After its public pronunciation, the multitude became a constituent counter-power. As constituent, it created what it announced: 'we', the new collectivity. As counter-power it emerged in opposition and conflict with 'them', the political and economic elites. Creating its own constitution, it set out a minimal set of principles and rules about its operation, aims and action. This imbrication of constituent and constituted turns Syntagma into an instance of the 'paradox of constituent power': it founds a polity or collective by acting as constituted or legislative power.[6] The act retrospectively creates its own ground and splits the social space.

Constituent power is self-legitimating, groundless. It succeeds if those the 'we' evokes accept the act as their own. Let me explore further this act of self-creation of a political subject that lifts itself from its own bootstraps. According to a crucial semiotic distinction, the subject of enunciation and the subject of statement are two separate speaking positions. In literature, for example, the subject of enunciation is the author of a novel; the novel's fictional narrator, on the other hand, is the subject of the statement, (s)he who tells the story. Something similar happens in inaugural acts of constituent power, typically in constitution making. The legislator enacts the constitution but its text is attributed to a different author, God, humanity, nowadays the people. Similarly, the 'we' of the squares rolled the particular and the universal into one. The 'we' referred first to the three thousand people present debating and adopting the resolution. But once this new collectivity had demarcated its place and time, its intension and extension, the 'we' became the whole suffering population. The subject of enunciation, the Syntagma assembly, and the subject of statement, the Greek people, were merged. Once constituted, Syntagma spoke for every suffering person in the country. The multitude in assembly and the whole of Greece joined in this 'we'. As Judith Butler put it, 'we are coming together as bodies in alliance, in the street and in the square. We're standing here together making democracy, enacting the phrase "We the people"'.[7]

Stasis Syntagma was the 'demos in the square'. Unlike its classical predecessor, its decisions did not bind the state; but it was the only popular body that debated the commons and prefigured a different, 'bottom up' type of democracy. The metaphysics of constituent power was confirmed by the social composition of the multitude. Every part of the population was present. The young and the old; Greeks and foreigners; high school pupils and university students; the unemployed, unemployable and low paid; civil servants, private sector employees and the self-employed; the Left, the Right and the apolitical; army officers and conscripts, priests and policemen. Women – a majority in *Stasis Syntagma* although the 'expert' panels did not always have a female presence, reminding us that patriarchy dies hard – alongside children, immigrants and pensioners gave the occupation its rainbow character. The presence of whole families and many children was particularly striking. The occupation 'attracted young people, and especially young single mothers, who realize that this crisis is going to hit them very hard; also elderly people whose pensions are shrinking. I don't say they're apolitical though. They are all well aware that only their presence in this symbolic place can change things.'[8] Syntagma was the Greek people. But unlike the 'people' in the constitutional text, the occupiers did not merge in a single 'body politic' claiming an imaginary sovereignty. They remained unique in their common desire. 'Party member, we want you here, but not your party', said a prominent banner. The occupation was a coming together of the multiple, plural and singular.

The constitutional lawyer Hans Lindahl has coined the term 'alegality' to describe acts of constituent power. Alegal acts are neither legal nor illegal. They 'contest the distinction between legality and illegality as drawn by a legal order, intimating another way of distinguishing between these terms . . .' Importantly the 'a' of alegality does not mean the other of legality, for this is illegality. Alegal acts set legal boundaries and inaugurate the new collectivity by creating an inside ("we") and an outside ("they"). They intimate the possible legality of what counts as illegal and the possible illegality of what counts as legal'.[9] I have argued elsewhere that the theological form of sovereignty is partly due to the organization of *juris-diction*, law's speech. A unitary entity with the power to speak must be seen to announce the law.[10] The demarcation between 'we' and 'they' unravels this unitary principle and starts a process of 'deactivation of the legal theology of sovereignty'.[11] Similarly, 'the 'can't pay won't pay' movement, the acts of solidarity with the unemployed and the immigrants, the electricians' reconnection of power supply are cases of alegal legality. Successful challenges to the power of the sovereign in the name of universal principles undermine its *raison d'être* and prefigure a different legality.

The 'we' of the occupations constructs a constituent counter-power; alegal acts create a fold within state legality. In this sense, Syntagma developed a new theory and practice of constituent power. Only a democratic counter-power can initiate radical change in conditions of late capitalism and parliamentary democracy. We can call the constituent power of the squares, the sovereignty of being together, a non-sovereign anomic or bare sovereignty. 'Bare sovereignty is the name of community opening to itself, in its self-institution or constitution.'[12] The sovereignty of the demos is not singular but multiple; it speaks in tongues, one could say. It is not the awe-inspiring source of the state of exception but a multitude of dignity, care and solidarity. The 'demos in the square' is the auto-immune syndrome of theological sovereignty. It prefigures the democracy to come.

Standing indignation

The *aganaktismenoi* adopted initially the name of an emotion instead of a class position, ideology (many expressed opposition to all ideology) or belief system. From Baruch Spinoza to Stéphane Hessel, outrage has been interpreted as an ethical response to injustice and evil. For Spinoza, indignation is 'hatred towards someone who has injured someone else'.[13] This concern for others makes indignation an ethical and active emotion. In the phenomenology of indignation, tolerance of unjust, immoral or evil action has a limit. When it is reached, tolerance turns into emotional turmoil. If unjust and evil acts escalate, an 'indignation capital' is created, the first step towards anger. 'Anger is the emotion that produces motion, the mood that moves the subject.'[14] This capital can be quietly consumed in the moralism of the 'beautiful soul' or can be invested in specific actions. When our existence rebels in indignation, we discover the power to act. Outrage is an emotional-ethical response, anger ethico-political. Indignation is the necessary propaideutic for resistance, 'the ground zero, the basic material from which movements of revolt and rebellion develop'.[15]

When indignation becomes moralistic or personalized, it leads to linguistic insults, swearing and heckling, 'pieing' or the Greek equivalent of 'yoghurting' (the throwing of pies or yogurt at enemies). The conspiracy theories widely circulating during the crisis are part of this moralistic and impotent outrage. It does not turn to action because the great and many powers allied against the people are invincible. But, as Carl Schmitt insisted in his definition of politics as a friend/enemy relationship, political enmity is not personal hatred or desire for revenge but an attack on an enemy who rejects and tries to destroy our way of life. Only when outrage becomes anger addressed at systemic faults rather than individuals can emotion turn into political action. Collective anger leads to resistance. Indignation and anger are politically active emotions, perhaps the most political of emotions.

Alain Badiou disagrees. 'Being indignant has never sufficed. A negative emotion cannot replace the affirmative idea and its organization, any more than a nihilistic riot can claim to be a politics.'[16] This is a case of philosophical monolingualism – the desire to apply the same theoretical tools to all situations. Indignation led to Tahrir Square, the overthrow of the *ancien régime* and the beginning of a new era. Indignation motivated Syntagma Square, leading to the unseating of government and the best electoral result of a radical Left party in Europe. Badiou's commitment to the 'subtraction from the state' (but how can the people resist a dictatorial government except through a revolt that overthrows it?) and the 'subtraction from economics' (but how can people stop the economic austerity that destroys a nation except by voting its promoters out of power?) makes him miss the pedagogic contribution of indignation.

Crowd sociology and psychology have different reservations. The crowd is emotional, feminine, angry, a congregation of bodies, touching, pushing against each other, kneading and knotting, losing autonomy and privacy. Indignation falls perfectly within the litany of the crowd's sins. And yet, the occupations undermined these views. Against Le Bon's or McDougal's worries, the Syntagma multitude remained multiple and tactile, the opposite of a mute beast or a led mass. Elias Canetti has captured the positive aspect of the crowd's life. The crowd and the mass express the enduring desire to fuse with others in common action and strong identification against the capitalist tendency towards individualization and privacy. These are not 'archaic' remnants but a constant human trait. Passion, affect and the visceral aspects of embodied living determine political commitment and action as much as interests and reason. As Freud put it, 'it is always possible to bind together a considerable amount of people in love, so long as there are other people left over to receive the manifestation of their aggressiveness'.[17] There was *cupiditas*, libidinal investment, in the squares but not on a leader or a common ideology. The political desire was manifest in practices of direct democracy, in the determination to stop the social catastrophe, in the imagination of new ways for organizing the social bond. The multitude was thinking and deliberating, speaking and self-governing. *Cupiditas quae ex ratione oritur, excessum habere nequit* – a desire that emerges out of reason cannot be excessive – wrote Spinoza.[18] The combination of radical desire and reason characterized all aspects of the occupations. Liberal autonomy was replaced by unmediated decision-making and collective self-determination. Ideas and emotions circulated through bodily proximity and led to new types of collective self-awareness.

161

Participants reported a heightened sense of perception, feelings of familiarity and solidarity towards strangers and a hitherto undiscovered ability to speak in public. In London, Athens and New York, a sense of joy and exhileration was evident. People smiled and laughed, kissed and hugged strangers, told personal stories and shared food, water and cigarettes. The collaboration, co-ordination and good humour led Paul Mason to call Syntagma 'Glastonbury without Bono'.[19] The 'affect deficit' of democratic politics, so lamented by political science, was replaced by a surfeit of reason-driven emotion and commitment.

Syntagma moved outrage and anger to a higher plane. The *aganaktismenoi* is a novel entity. It does not exist in normal politics and cannot be counted in opinion polls. Indeed the gap between the common presence of the multitude and the methodology of opinion polls is unbridgeable. The measurement of 'public' opinion is based on a sample of people representing the different components of the population such as gender, income, profession, residence etc. Such a sample must not include people who know each other, meet and discuss common affairs. The 'public' of opinion polls is an aggregation of the views of private persons; it excludes physical co-presence, the core meaning of publicity. Syntagma on the other hand was the public – the people – assembled, discussing and acting in public. Eventually the name *aganaktismenoi* was sidelined by the more positive *apofasismenoi* – determined. The Syntagma occupier was both citizen and excluded from politics, formally citizen but substantively *apolis* (without city); the *apofasismenoi* were the excluded whole of the population. Tahrir and Syntagma turned from geographical centres of Cairo and Athens into the heart of Egypt and Greece, for a short while perhaps of the whole world.[20] The assemblies, debates and resolutions were contemporary versions of Jean-Jacques Rousseau's *volonté générale*.[21] The people in Syntagma were closer to the *ecclesia* than the Parliament opposite. It was the House of Commons by and for the commons, located below Parliament's Upper House. Decisions about the commons, the multitude declared, cannot be taken without the active participation of those who are asked to carry their burden.

Syntagma as toponymy, concept or action stood for radical change. The whole of Egypt and Greece became for a few weeks a square. In this sense, the multitude was assembled in Syntagma but it became visible everywhere. 'Wherever you go, you will be the polis' was the saying that accompanied ancient Greeks in their travels. It was unknowingly repeated by the succinct slogan 'we are the squares and we are everywhere'. The Syntagma demos was the Greek people.

The aesthetics of multitude

Squares and greens are places for strolling, leisure activities and mild erotic experiences. Crowds assemble for festivals, carnivals and the election campaign rallies still taking place in Southern Europe. In Greece, the big rally of the ruling parties is held in Syntagma Square just before the elections and marks the end of the campaign. These rallies juxtapose the leader's speech with the crowd's speechlessness. The leader 'gags' the crowd, whose muteness is exaggerated by the demand that they applaud, chant and celebrate at regular intervals, while jeering political opponents. A rally is successful if TV news presents a crowd massive in size and enthusiasm. The mute crowd symbolizes the role of the people in contemporary democracies: they are passive recipients of rhetoric, instructions and occasional rewards.

In the occupations, the crowd became a speaking multitude. The idea of the 'public sphere', developed by Jürgen Habermas, returned to the original meaning of publicity as the material co-presence of people in an open space. The 'dialogical will formation' escaped the wiles of metaphor and ideological exaggeration and became physical. The rejection of representation for presence and presentation as well as the respect for speakers and audience characterized *Stasis Syntagma*. People spoke but also listened. Interruptions and heckling were rare. The success of the leader's address in election rallies is counted by the minutes of interruption by the enthused crowd – something like the standing ovation of leaders at British party conferences. In Syntagma, approval and disapproval were expressed through a rhythmic wave of arms and hands. These practices marked an unprecedented public commitment to thinking, debate and common action. In the *Human Condition,* Hannah Arendt distinguished work into *poiesis* and *praxis*. Poiesis produces something, a table, chair or book. Praxis, on the other hand, finds its telos internally, in its own becoming and self-referentiality which, according to Arendt, is the essence of politics. The success of poiesis depends on the excellence of the outcome, cooking a tasty meal or writing a good book. Praxis succeeds in the perfection of its own execution. Poiesis is teleological and spatial; it has a telos, a produce and endpoint. Praxis is a becoming, a temporal unravelling in the world. Such is the dancer's performance of a choreography or the actor's interpretation of a play. The dancer and the dance, the play and the acting cannot be prised apart. The success of the dance perfects the dancer and the virtuosity of the dancer presents the score in its ideal form. For Arendt, politics is closer to a self-perfecting public performance. 'The political realm rises directly out of acting together, the "sharing of words and deeds" ... The polis is not the city state in its physical location; it is the organization of the people as it arises out of acting and speaking together, and its true space lies between people living together for this purpose.'[22] This is not the definition of politics in Whitehall and Westminster. For Arendt, 'politics is a *techne*, belongs among the arts, and can be likened to such activities as healing or navigation, where, as in the performance of the dancer and play-actor, the "product" is identical with the performing act itself'.[23]

Syntagma returned to this forgotten sense of the public, the political and the aesthetic. Speaking and performing were the central activities of the occupations. They posed a double challenge. First, to the usual silence ordinary people are condemned and, secondly, to the politicians, experts and 'celebrities' who monopolize public speaking. Maurice Blanchot, commenting on the May 1968 events, wrote that they 'gave back to all the right to equality in fraternity through a freedom of speech that elated everyone.'[24] It was the same in the occupations. The saying was more important than the said. People spoke in public to strangers; speaking created the common space of being together. It was a new aesthetic of public performance. The speeches were both praxis and poiesis, autarchic communication and purposive activity. The poems recited, the personal stories and histories narrated transformed public speaking from instrumental and demagogic into artistic and political. The 'politicized' members thought that the artistic interventions were 'irrelevant', 'a waste of time' or just 'silly'. But it was this novel approach to debating and acting that transformed it from instrumental to practical in the original meaning of the term. 'Following the assemblies of direct democracy with people squatting in a circle, devoted to the monologues of the speakers, I found elements of a living theatre in which the public participates' writes a member of the artists' group.[25] The theatricality of speech and performance carried the hallmarks of an aesthetics which 'requires spectators who play the role of active interpreters, who develop their own translation in order to appropriate the "story" and make it their own story. An emancipated community is a community of narrators and translators.'[26]

Jean-Jacques Rousseau suggested that civil festivals are theatres of popular sovereignty. People become 'actors and enactors of their own sovereignty' in public spectacles and festivals.[27] The theatre more than any other art has been linked, since German Romanticism, with a living community and an active politics. Theatre is the aesthetic constitution of community, 'a way of occupying a place and a time, as the body in action as opposed to a mere apparatus of laws; a set of perceptions, gestures and attitudes that precede and preform laws and political institutions.'[28] Syntagma enacted popular sovereignty in the form of public theatre. It reminded Friedrich Schiller's call for an aesthetic revolution to accompany the political insurrection.

Artistic activities marked every aspect of life and complemented the political performance. Art materials were freely available and people were encouraged to use them and show the results. Paintings, graffiti, reading and posting of poems and novellas, music and dance, murals on walls made with laser beams and human installations on the street created the sense of an immense arts festival. Unknown and famous artists gave music concerts regularly but did not use a stage. 'The philosophy was to abolish the stage so that there is no separation between artist and public, both artist and audience/actors on the same level.'[29] This is Antonin Artaud and Berthold Brecht's idea of the theatre: spectators abandon their passivity and are drawn into an action that restores their collective energy. As Jacques Rancière puts it, emancipation means 'the blurring of the boundary between those who act and those who look; between individuals and members of the collective body.'[30] *Stasis Syntagma* was an 'event' of political aesthetics which changed the meaning of both politics and public art.

The place and time of demos

The 'public sphere' as a physical space linked work, aesthetics and politics. A new configuration of political time and space emerged which removed the monopoly of professional politicians. Popular assemblies started after the end of the working day and attracted large numbers at the weekends, with the first three Sundays bringing out close to a quarter of a million people. The free time normally used for leisure, rest and training became a time of collective creation and action. The networking and horizontal connectivity of post-Fordist capitalism exited the logic of profit and exploitation and became political collaboration, virtuoso performance and productive action. According to Negri and Virno, the socialized language, knowledge and communication of immaterial labour have turned the general intellect into a force of production. But the atomization of working people and the strict disciplining of economic activity prevent political co-operation. It is a strange paradox, exploited by capitalism, that networking at work leads to political isolation and solitude at home. The occupations reversed the order.

Stasis Syntagma mobilized the skills and knowledge demanded by late capitalism against its principles of representation and hierarchy. The decay of representation was exposed by the proximity and juxta-position of Parliament and Syntagma. Parliaments everywhere form the central political place, expressing the autonomy and superiority of politics *vis-à-vis* the rest of society. They are frequented by pro-fessionals, who follow strict institutional and party discipline. But Parliament also stands for the principle of representation, the vertical relationship between the elected members and the people outside. Power is topographically arranged on the floor of the House, Right-Centre-Left, acting as a social map with classes and interests allocated to strictly designated places. When MPs, under instruction by the troika and their leaders, voted into law measures in total disregard of popular feelings, they could not step into the street without being verbally and occasionally physically attacked. More significantly, the idea of representation fell into disrepute. The political system could no longer claim to 'represent' popular interest. It turned into a mechanism for the legitimation and communication of decisions made elsewhere. The decay of parliamentary democracy, a permanent topic of conversation in political science circles, became evident to the people themselves.

The space of the occupation was arranged in a different manner. The gathering of people in the same place and the resulting bodily proximity and emotional intensity strengthened political identity and commitment. Topographically, the square was ringed by the tables of thematic groups and political campaigns, artistic displays, a lending library and various food-selling stalls. The tents were placed on the green surrounding the square, like sleepy suburbs around a busy city. There was no central point and people tended to move around. There was motion and fluidity, people moved in and out, groups were formed and dissolved, impromptu debates and unplanned actions started and continued into the night. At 1 or 2 a.m., after the last group stopped its planning and the last dance was danced people retired to their tents. Spending the night there, ensuring that the occupations con-tinued despite hardship and police attacks became the physical and symbolic manifestation of resistance. 'Square, sweet square' was the motto of the occupants, who defended place and tent like home. After the army or the riot police had withdrawn from Tahrir or Syntagma following one of their usual attacks, the occupants returned, cleared the debris and resumed normal life. The square was not an incidental place but a central element in the creation of identity.

Unlike the dedicated 'political place' opposite, the square replaced the verticality of representation with the horizontality of presence. Politics became a social activity, relations were politicized. Against decaying representation, the squares operated direct non-hierarchical collaboration. The horizontal association of working practices was put into political service. Networking and computing skills were used to create superb websites, radio stations and information networks. The social media and live streaming disseminated debates and announcements and called for support when the riot police attacked. In this sense, the occupations both demanded and performed direct democracy. The multitude was not an abstract social category, as in Hardt and Negri, but a material gathering, a crowd with a common political desire. But unlike the crowd of Le Bon and the sociologists, this was not a silent but a speaking crowd, it was not dictated and manipulated but debating, deciding and acting. It did not have representatives and leaders but its own direct action.

Stasis Syntagma mirrored and reversed the organization of the state. Fourteen thematic and service groups supported the occupation and covered every major need. The 'cleaning' group was created first. It ensured that every night and soon after police attacks the square returned to its tidy state. On 16 June, after the riot police withdrew, people formed a human chain passing bottles of water to those cleaning the square; famous artists and singers joined in a practical display of equality. Thematic groups were formed as the need arose. When an old lady was told that the occupation did not accept financial donations, she offered to cook and started the 'food' group, which kept the permanent campers in superior cuisine throughout the occupation. This was another innovation. Capitalist time is linear and controlled; the price of labour is calculated according to the exchange value of the commodity. The time of the occupations on the other hand was open-ended. Work was organized according to needs and skills; it produced use value. Volunteers provided all necessary services. Medical staff created a well-supplied centre and offered twenty-four-hour support, the main reason why relatively few people were seriously injured despite the massive teargas and chemical attacks by the police. The 'serene' or 'cool' group in charge of security was an oasis of friendly calmness and sound advice and ensured that no drink or drugs fuelled conflict developed. The media group consisted of twenty people, half of them with PhDs in various fields, who had set ten laptops on a couple of trestle tables and worked furiously away. They had not met in advance but they worked in a highly integrated way, discouraging people from approaching, chatting and disturbing their work. If this highly skilled group of unemployed young people were transferred

167

to the Ministry of Economics, tax evasion would be seriously reduced.

Throughout history rulers have justified their rule by claiming superior knowledge. For the first time, the ruled have the some knowledge and skills as their rulers. Highly qualified engineers, lawyers and doctors used to be the backbone of the power system. As they join the other side, a revolution of the professions becomes a real possibility. This politicization of knowledge led to the emergence of a new political epistemology. Dominant methodologies and knowledge hierarchies were undermined. The thematic assembly speakers were invited because of their expertise. But even in those debates, the multitude did not act as an ignorant mass awaiting illumination. Technical aspects were discussed but did not dominate. It was made clear that the economists disagree as to the right solutions because they start from radically different premises and follow antagonistic schools, left or right-wing, Keynesian or Marxist. The solution will not be given by the most knowledgeable economist but by the collectivity which, listening to the conflicting schools and views, will judge technical positions with political and moral criteria. Admittedly, the radical experts could not always set aside their institutional positions, didactic roles and occasional displays of arrogance, usually a symptom of insecurity and vulnerability rather than of achievement and confidence. But the assemblies and thematic debates proved that the wisdom of the multitude is often much greater than that of political or intellectual leaders.

In Syntagma the multitude recovered a sense of debate, and politics exited its normal 'post-democratic' condition. Speakers and audience were transformed, new subjectivities were born, the biopolitical project stalled. A new type of political appreciation of knowledge is emerging after the occupations. It has to confront the claims of epistemic and disciplinary authority which, even when expressed by radicals, wish to retain the privileges of power. As this book has argued throughout, biopower constructs obedient subjectivities and normalizes knowledge. Resistance keeps deconstructing them, a difficult task when pitted against the threats or rewards of power. Syntagma was a novel and unexpected experience, after which politics could not return to its previous practices.

'Upper' or 'lower' square?

Public assemblies give the multitude the emotional tension and bodily closeness discussed by Freud and Canetti. But against the fears of Le

Bon, bodily proximity and fleshy contact does not lead necessarily to the abandonment of reason or blind submission to leaders. Bodies and emotions are not an enemy of argument and deliberation. They form their material ground and support as feminism and post-colonial theory have compellingly argued. Different bodies, classes, ideologies, sexualities, ages and ethnicities converged in Syntagma. This plurality of singularities helps understand a divide that developed in the squares between the radicals and the rest. This juxtaposition was reflected in the 'upper' and 'lower' parts of Syntagma Square. The 'upper square' occupants were presented as right-wing nationalists, religious and apolitical. They were criticized for one or more of the following: swearing and gesticulating at the Parliament opposite and calling it a 'brothel'; attacking politicians and journalists; being aesthetically and historically challenged with their badly drawn banners and clichéd references to past glories. The argument went further. The 'upper square' did not participate in popular assemblies and degraded the occupation with its antics. The upper square was a mob or mass, the lower, where the daily popular assembly and the thematic debates took place, a multitude.

The arguments were drawn from the rich arsenal of fear and hatred of the crowd or mob. Abandoned terms such as *lumpen* and sub-proletariat or the more recent 'chavs' were recovered from the ample depository of crowd abuse. These attacks 'proved' the aesthetic sensibility and political propriety of commentators continuing the age-old contempt of intellectuals towards the *hoi polloi*.[31] Yet, the neo-fascist Chryssi Avgi was not allowed to enter Syntagma; immigrants were welcome and participated fully. Despite the lack of elaborate economic analyses and debates, the 'upper' square consistently attacked the parasitic and corrupt nature of the political elite, emphasized the importance of national independence and criticized the moral collapse of the power system, including the mainstream media. Its contribution to the hegemonic intervention of Syntagma was central in areas the Left had abandoned or trodden with great care. If the multitude as a social category is the multi-coloured whole of the people, it cannot but include right-wing and religious people, patriots and the apolitical. If, at the same time, the multitude is the excluded from politics, the unemployed, the 'plebs', the uneducated and the immigrants will be there. Without these 'others', the multitude would have ended a rather oversized rally reproducing the protest strategies tested and failed over forty years. Only someone 'recognized as part of the establishment was not welcome'.[32] The 'indignation capital' the occupants of the upper square built, preserved and invested (rather badly for some) became a common resource for both sides. *Stasis Syntagma* was the multitude and crowd become demos.[33] Not in the sense that some were part of a 'lower' crowd while others of a 'sophisticated' multitude. Every participant was a member of crowd, multitude and demos. A disciplined and led crowd is homogeneous and agrees on most things. Democracy on the other hand introduces active and effective disagreement; the tensions in Syntagma were expected and welcome. This was the main difference of Syntagma from a rally or demonstration of trade unionists and Leftists.

Syntagma brought together people radically divided in the past and drew a line of antagonism with the elites. Its plurality and appeal across traditional divides was an important achievement. Conflicts and tension are unavoidable. Antagonisms and disagreement nourish the popular pole. Consensus was sought throughout the occupations but minorities did not block decision-making. Disagreement was either synthesized or temporarily suspended. The determination to decide and act while accepting disagreement separated the occupation of Athens from London. Occupy London prioritized horizontal and decentralized procedures and avoided making demands that could polarize the people. In Athens, direct democracy was the central organizational principle and prefigured future institutional arrangements. It was both a process and a demand addressed to the state. Syntagma started a debate about the meaning of democracy and made it an object of hegemonic contestation. But democracy was one in a series of demands and did not stand in the way of decisions and action. Constituent power emerges only when demands are agreed, often impossible demands, and the multitude undertakes the necessary action. The occupations in Egypt and Greece accepted the integrity and authenticity of disagreement and attempted to synthesize it without abandoning action. This is the model of constituent power in late capitalism.

The axiom of equality

The axiom of equality formed the theoretical and practical foundation of the occupations. The people occupied because they assumed that, despite huge social differences, they are politically equal with politicians and elites. The occupations were actions of political equalization; equality permeated every aspect of their life. Topics were chosen and thematic speakers selected by the multitude democratically, speakers adhered strictly to equal time limits, the time given to invited speakers was not disproportionately greater than that of assembly members. It was the contemporary manifestation of the classical principles of *isonomy* and *isopolity*. Isonomy is not the same as our weak 'equality before the law'. It means that the law must create equality. Modern democracy enforces substantive equality (each counts as one and none more than one) only in elections. The universal franchise radically individualizes the population and then reassembles it into the 'people' through a simple aggregation of votes. This double trans-substantiation of socially embedded people into isolated monads and their subsequent gathering into a 'sovereign' people is the great achievement of representative democracy. As I used to tell my students of Constitutional Law on election Thursday, 'we, the people' are sovereign in the few seconds we spend in the polling booth placing the cross against the candidate's name. But the miraculous transformations elections carry out do not extend to political life before and after the elections. Party organization, manifesto planning, and post-election delivery are largely immune from popular intervention.

Stasis Syntagma radicalized the principle of electoral equality and introduced it to every part of its activities. The axiom of equality applied to the occupations is this: whoever is in the square, everyone and anyone, is entitled to an equal share of time to put her views across, have them debated and acted upon if accepted. The views of the unemployed and the university professor are given equal time, discussed with equal vigour and put to the vote for adoption. This is precisely the action of direct democracy: it declassifies pre-existing 'natural' inequalities and hierarchies and subjects the 'objective' knowledge of 'experts' to the equality of intelligence and the challenge of disagreement. Representation and substitution were replaced by presence and presentation. The multitude could debate and decide every question and argument.

Starting from direct democracy, equality is transferred to social and economic rights creating a duty to set aside inegalitarian structures. One may object that this axiom or presupposition sounds false or 'utopian'. It is the only principle, however, that takes account of the simple fact that man is a speaking animal. Thought and language create humans and unite humanity; subjectivity is inter-subjective and is mediated by the object.[34] In a famous joke, there is a knock on the door of a particularly stupid person (it has a different nationality depending on the country it is told). 'Who is there?' 'I' comes the response. 'I?', repeats the bemused idiot. Self-consciousness, every 'I', presupposes implicitly and addresses explicitly a 'You'; in turn, every 'You' gives rise to an 'I'. Basic linguistic and grammatical practice incorporates human equality. We *are* all equal; consciousness starts in recognition and response to this basic fact. What needs explanation is not axiomatic equality but the history of its distortion and decline. The theoretical attempts to legitimize this anomaly form perhaps the greatest perversion of human thought.

What did the squares achieve?

Civil servants and their unions, the first victims of austerity, led the early protests. By the summer of 2011, wage and pension cuts had been imposed in the private sector. Large indirect and property tax hikes, increases in transport fares, road tolls and fuel price had affected every part of the population. The many grievances and demands converged in Syntagma and the other occupations. The popular assemblies and debates developed over a short period of time a series of ideological themes that made people feel that, despite differences, they were part of a common struggle. Three lines of antagonism were put forward: rejection of austerity, defence of national independence and direct democracy. The catastrophic economic measures were the first and obvious line of attack. Economic demands cannot lead to broad alliances on their own, however. Conflicting interests of groups and professions create tensions. Civil servants (accused of corruption and inefficiency) and private sector employees and professionals (accused of tax evasion and uncompetitive protections) or the working population and the unemployed appear to have diverging interests. A hegemonic intervention must marginalize sectional differences and local rivalries. A central antagonism that traverses society diagonally must be turned into the central line of confrontation uniting classes, groups and people. The attack on austerity was therefore broadened. It did not target exclusively the debt or the economic crisis but the desire of debt and its exploitation by the rulers to rearrange the social bond against the interests of ordinary people. The size of debt and deficit combined with official silence about its provenance made people suspicious. The occupations demanded a formal debt audit commission which would examine the legality of the loans and the way the money was spent. When it was denied, the antagonism expanded from opposition to austerity to an attack on the corrupt political elites and eventually to predatory capitalism itself.

This widening of the target was helped by the second line of confrontation, the defence of popular sovereignty and national independence. Greece had not experienced colonialism but now found itself in a neo- or postcolonial condition. The troika and the assorted task force 'experts' act like colonial administrators dictating high and low policy. Historical experience tells us that self-determination is a contested concept. It can be interpreted in a radical way, as in the decolonization struggles, but it can also lead to xenophobia and racism. In times of crisis, the familiarity of national identity and nationalism, with its potential racism, becomes an attractive haven for people. This was prevented in part by the occupations which stepped in ideological areas the Left tends to avoid. The distinction between patriotism and nationalism remains vulnerable and the two sides can easily collapse into each other. Only if national independence becomes linked with popular sovereignty and democracy can its conquest and use by the extreme right-wing be prevented. The third line of attack therefore placed the defence of democracy at the centre. Globalized capitalism has persistently undermined parliamentary democracy. The replacement of democratically accountable governments by technocratic governance has turned citizens away from the machinations of elites and parties and has eviscerated politics.[35] Only a different conception of democracy could gather popular resistance for its defence. This is precisely what happened. Democracy as a form of life permeated all aspects of the occupations. It was performed in the squares and also announced as a future model of constitutional organization. Institutional innovation was one of the greatest achievements of the squares.

The connection of economic with wider political demands was encapsulated in the slogan 'we don't owe, we don't sell, we don't pay', a masterful combination of the particular and the universal. Specific claims about the debt ('we don't owe') and economic deprivation ('we can't pay') became linked with public property and the common good ('we don't sell'). The slogan was a response to the European request to sell off most publicly held assets. Other slogans and chants expressed generic opposition to the decay of democracy and representation. The former was expressed by the upper square's 'let this brothel of a Parliament burn', a slogan disowned by the Left. Representative government had failed the people it claimed to represent. The anti-government anger was pithily expressed: 'take your memorandum and go'. 'Your' memorandum combined the foreign and domestic elites into a common enemy against which those assembled became 'We, the people'. For Ernesto Laclau, the popular pole does not pre-exist the hegemonic intervention and must be created in confrontation with the power system. The two camps, the people and the elite, are created on the sides of the line of antagonism. The Syntagma strategy was a textbook case of hegemonic intervention. The rejection of 'their' power and right to control and destroy 'our'

173

lives split the social field. A hegemonic struggle succeeds, if claims, grievances and protests come together and become a central anti-systemic demand elevated into the 'universal equivalent' of all others. This function was performed by the 'memorandum': both as a slightly sinister signifier and as the series of measures it became the symbol of the evil that befell Greece. The political space was split between the old pro-memorandum and the new anti-memorandum forces. It was the most successful hegemonic intervention in recent history.

The resistances corrected the theory of hegemony. The popular bloc had been preconstituted as a social category by the violent impoverishment of the population before the hegemonic intervention. Laclau is right to insist that a social class or category becomes politically effective when it acquires identity. But this identity existed *in nuce* before the occupations. The degradation of many groups had already mobilized people and had been expressed in union strikes and political rallies. The political subject that emerged in the squares was possible because class consciousness had already created a receptive ground. They were the social whole and the political nothing, those whose speech has no meaning or historical significance. In Syntagma, they became agents of history. If communism is the reappropriation and socialization of the (privatized) commons, *Stasis Syntagma* amounted to a proto-communist event.[36]

Postscript. In late 2012, the Greek government and mainstream media started blaming the occupations for the rise of the neo-nazi Chryssi Avgi. It was a desperate and transparent attempt to delegitimize popular resistance by attacking the high point of the anti-austerity opposition. Following the historically ignorant iden-tification of Right and Left 'extremes', it tried to equate the radical Left which participated in the occupations with the fascists, who were chased away every time they appeared openly. The powerful often try to defame and delete from historical memory major acts of popular resistance considered as threats to their rule. In Greece, attacks on Syntagma have joined diatribes against the protesters of the 1973 Athens Polytechnic uprising for allegedly leading to the post-dicta-torship cronyism and corruption. Parts of the Left too continue to treat the Syntagma legacy with hostility because the occupations did not follow the rhetorical and ideological tropes of Marxist dogma or the organizational disciplines of old style communism. Like all spon-taneous acts of popular protest and counter-power, *Stasis Syntagma* started hesitantly, had no model, pre-existing plan or leadership. The occupiers were taken aback by their success, were unprepared for the numbers they attracted and had often to develop their strategy on the hoof. But it was precisely this lack of previous examples, of worked out plan or common ideology that turned Syntagma into such an unprecedented triumph of popular initiative, imagination and organization. The risible attacks are evidence of the power of its legacy and its continuing effects.

—11—

LESSONS OF POLITICAL STRATEGY

Radical philosophy reads the uprisings

After the end of the 'postmodern' period with its emphasis on the local, the relative and the modest, radical philosophy returned to the tradition of grand theory. Badiou, Hardt and Negri, Žižek, Rancière and Laclau have all attempted global reconstructions of political philosophy. Their work offers important insights used extensively in this book. Nevertheless, they did not anticipate the recent events. The Left has often dismissed the crowd, the plebs or the *lumpen* proletariat. This *hauteur* has affected its contemporary heirs. Negri and Hardt's *Empire* and *Multitude* were indifferent to the crowd and the 'mass'. Alain Badiou dismissed the Paris, Athens and London insurrections. Slavoj Žižek was quite critical of the various occupations he visited. In December 2010, Žižek warned the resisting Greeks at a large meeting in Athens that after they have had their 'fun' in the streets they would go back home and in twenty years time, middle aged and affluent, they would reminisce nostalgically about their adventures, hypocritically mourning their youthful enthusiasms. Žižek's message to the Occupy Wall Street movement in New York was similar.[1] The resistances were a superficial response to the crisis, Žižek feared, closer to a 'hippy' or 'anarchist' happening than to a properly organized, realistic and efficient opposition claiming power. Recalling past defeats of insurrections and revolts, Žižek insists that the radical act must break away from 'the vicious cycle of revolt and its reinscription . . . an eventual explosion followed by a return to normality.'[2]

The failure to anticipate the resistances was redressed by a series of books published after their eruption. Michael Hardt and Toni Negri's

Declaration,[3] Alain Badiou's *Rebirth of History*[4] and Slavoj Žižek's *The Year of Dreaming Dangerously*[5] are an implicit apology for the absence of the 'street' from the earlier work. The responses to the uprisings offer a clear view of respective strengths and weaknesses. Let me start with Antonio Negri and Michael Hardt, the theorists of constituent power and the multitude. They released their *Declaration*, a statement about the achievement and prospects of the uprisings, in the summer of 2012. It is not a manifesto, they claim. Manifestos 'provide a glimpse of a world to come and also call into being a subject . . . [they] work like the ancient prophets, who by the power of their vision create their own people'. This order has been reversed; the multitude has created its own visions and has declared a 'new set of principles and truths.'[6] Hardt and Negri want to systematize these principles and turn them into foundations of a constituent process that will organize new and lasting social relations. Negri's historical trajectory, prolific writings and charismatic public performances bring him closest to a contemporary prophet. Despite protestations, the *Declaration* is his modern-day manifesto, influenced by the American prototype and its founding fathers. The fascination with everything American is a permanent aspect of Hardt and Negri's *oeuvre*. The *Declaration* aims to discover the common elements of the worldwide uprisings but concentrates on American themes (its politics, media, debt, prisons, judicial system etc.), and keeps returning for inspiration to Occupy Wall Street. The Egyptian, Spanish, Greek and Latin American movements are given walk-on roles.

The second characteristic of the *Declaration* is the relentless attack on the Left. American radicalism is equated with the Occupy movement. The European Left, on the other hand, is counterfactually identified with the mainstream socialist parties. Gerhard Schroeder and Tony Blair undermined the values and principles of the Left in collaboration with the emerging neo-conservatives. Papandreou and Zapatero were the socialist Prime Ministers who introduced the most aggressive neo-liberal policies into the European South. Based on this false identification, the authors proceed to accuse the Left of a 'combination of nostalgia and old-fashioned Left moralism' and of corruption on the 'almost unavoidable path to election'. Left leaders and organizers were 'displeased or at least wary' of the 2011 events, the authors claim. 'Until there is a party and an ideology to direct the street conflicts . . . there will be no revolution' such leaders apparently reasoned. The repeated failures have turned the Left into parties of lament: 'Eventually they also lament the corruption of their own representatives and their own lack of representative legitimacy.'[7] Negri and Hardt conclude that 'we need to empty the churches of the Left even more, and bar their doors, and burn them down!'[8]

It is true that melancholy descended on the Left after 1989. The bricks and mortar of the Berlin wall fell hardest on the heads of the Leftists who criticized the Soviet empire. But the attack on the Left is only partly justified. Radical parties were the main opposition to the socialist governments in Spain, Portugal and Greece. This opposition was widened in the squares. People without previous political involvement, Rightists, Leftists, extra-parliamentary groups and anarchists found themselves together in the occupations and a creative osmosis developed. The Left was in the squares, learned from the multitude and helped with its long experience in organization and struggle. Negri and Hardt rightly diagnose the Left's 'lament', but their exaggerated attacks are symptoms of an equally problematic syndrome, the 'narcissism of small differences'. The theorists whose ideas are closest to the movement of the squares chose to abandon successes to which the Left contributed in favour of theoretical purity. The unsupported ferocity of the attack is perhaps the result of personal histories and traumas. But their diagnosis is wrong. Some *indignados* in Spain did not vote in the 2011 elections. Hardt and Negri celebrate their political maturity, since the non-voters 'have larger battles to fight; in particular one aimed at the structures of representation and the constitutional order itself . . . a kind of exodus from the existing political structures'.[9] The idea that the people whose lives are destroyed by neo-liberal policies would contemplate voting for socialist parties who authored the policies is counter-intuitive, as is the inclusion of these parties in a fantasy 'Left'. The absence of a credible Left party led to the Spanish abstention. In Greece, the *aganaktismenoi* massively abandoned the socialist party, which was reduced from 42% in 2009 to 12% in 2012, and 'adopted' the radical Left Syriza party. The participation of Syriza in the occupations had prepared the ground for its great results in the elections.

The positive programme of the *Declaration* proposes a constituent process, which will institutionalize the principles of the occupations. Struggles are constituent if they take place on the 'terrain of the common' and chart the path to a 'new constitutional process', in which the commons become the 'central concept of the organization of society and the constitution'.[10] It is true, that the occupations discussed the idea of the 'commons'. Negri and Hardt's theories were present and inspired the multitude, whether people had read *Empire* or not. But as the authors rightly claim, the resistance movements did not have leaders or common ideology, including that of the 'commons'. The main concern of the occupations was to defend public services, the social state, and to reject wholesale privatizations of state assets. Despite Negri and Badiou's advice, nobody suggested seriously in Syntagma that people should 'subtract' from the state or abstain from elections. The squares used an eclectic and highly effective combination of ideas and tactics, some libertarian and anarchist others from the Left, still others from the patriotic tradition. On the radical side, groups and ideologies that had not conversed in the past learned to co-habit and act together. The mix of libertarian methods and Left commitment, of horizontal and vertical organization is the greatest legacy of occupations.

Is the constituent process, proposed in the *Declaration*, the condensed wisdom of the squares? Toni Negri's *Insurrections* is perhaps the most brilliant exposition of the idea. For Negri, the American and French revolutions, the radical events of modern history, were victories of popular power. In the great revolutions, constituent power reached an intensity that only a 'little Dutch Jew', as he calls Spinoza, could have imagined. It was 'a freedom born from appropriation, a freedom that spread throughout the multitude, that potentially spread into equality'.[11] But when popular power becomes institutionalized, the constitution turns into a machine that 'each time chooses the cult of the state, imperialism, social division, or exploitation as alternatives of reproduction, all equally fierce and interchangeable'.[12] The American principle of 'checks and balances' is another attempt to tame constituent power. 'The division and the reciprocal control of the organs of the state, the generalization and formalization of the administrative processes consolidate and establish this system of the neutralization of constituent power.'[13] All three constituted powers contribute to the reassertion of traditional sovereignty which 'bring[s] the constitutive process to an end'.[14] The executive ends the insurgency, re-incorporates the principle of sovereignty and replaces the King. The legislature has little power compared with the executive, while the judiciary is constituent power's 'death knell'.[15] The American constitution tried to pacify political conflicts by assigning them to a 'juridical machine so sophisticated that it is manipulable and soon distorted'.[16]

The *Declaration*'s proposals follow the criticized separation of powers into executive, legislative and judicial parts. Federalism, direct democracy and workers councils should be introduced in the legislature; the executive should enact planning and development processes democratically conducted and focusing on the commons. Finally, the judiciary (presented as elected, despite the fact that only the United States among the major powers have an elected judiciary) should continue to provide 'checks and balances' on the government and interpret the constitution. Appropriate education should be given 'to enable the entire multitude to participate in such interpretation and decision-making'.[17] These are admirable ideas and could perhaps work in the future. They diverge somewhat from the wild energy of *Insurrections*. Constituent power is rooted in the right to resistance and revolution; its shape is 'irresistibility, the impossibility to restrain it'.[18] It is a collective subjectivity with a passion for renewal, a 'democratic living God' who escapes the rigidities of institutions, becoming a permanent thorn in their flesh.[19] The creative strength of the multitude (*potenza*) cannot be constrained in constitutions, nor can it assume the stifling power (*potere*) of institutional sovereignty. Its strength is that of '"much" but also the strength of "many", that is, the strength of singularities and differences'.[20]

Compared with this lyrical promotion of people power, the constitutional proposals of the *Declaration* are somewhat modest. Negri's early work insisted that constituent power decays once it is captured by constituted power. The recent proposals may be inspired from the principles of constituent power, but they have a touch of constitutionalism about them. This is both a problem and an advantage. They express the imagination and force of constituent power but their relatively prudent nature makes their institutionalization possible. The Syntagma debates and reform proposals moved in similar directions even though they did not become so detailed. The occupiers used their own evolving practices to imagine what constitutional reforms direct democracy requires. The assemblies recognized, however, that progress in this direction necessitates participation in the political process. Radical new structures can be introduced only if the Left has scaled the heights of state power and the balance has shifted in favour of the people. Hardt and Negri are right to emphasize that the experience of resistance fertilized radical thinking. The end of the occupations did not stop this mutual enrichment. The debates in the squares have continued formally in Syriza and informally among activists, workers and intellectuals. This major debate about democratic socialism will influence the European Left and the future of Europe by developing new strategies and ideas to replace the failed neoliberal model.

There is a slight naiveté in Hardt and Negri's belief that the reform of legal procedures and institutions can take place without a radical government or that it can change the world on its own. It is closer to American constitutionalism than European radicalism.

The constitution expresses and sanctifies principles and procedures that protect, promote and reproduce the dominant social order. In *Commonwealth*, Negri and Hardt argue rightly, for example, that the right to property has become the transcendental precondition of the entire legal and constitutional system because it protects the dominant socio-economic order.[21] No legal reform can erode this principle before the political balance of power has radically changed. The *Declaration* adopts John Rawls' 'difference principle' as a guide for economic distribution.[22] According to Rawls, income and asset inequalities should be permitted if they benefit the least advantaged. But Rawls' difference principle comes after his first principle, which prioritizes individual freedom. Safeguards of the right to property – and the structural inequalities of capitalism – take precedence over redistribution. No resistance movement or radical party can guarantee property relations unqualifiedly in order to start using taxation and other redistributive policies. The radical changes Negri and Hardt support can be realized only when the diverse and horizontal resistance movements are supported by 'vertical' organizations which place the question of state and political power on the agenda. A constituent process starts and can be completed only when the movement in the streets and representatives in Parliament act in parallel and co-ordinated ways.

The concluding part of the *Declaration* returns to the 'despair' the authors had originally attributed to the Left. Entitled the 'event of the commoner', it argues that miracles and unforeseeable events happen in history and radically change the world. 'We must prepare for the event', they advise, 'even though its date of arrival remains unknown.'[23] They are right. Preparing for the event, however, means participating in resistance, articulating the principles and processes emerging and injecting these values in individuals and parties. Very little can happen unless the new Left is prepared to challenge and form a government, leaving behind its melancholy and 'lament'. Without the 'vertical' involvement of parties, unions and movements with electoral politics and governmental institutions the constituent process of the *Declaration* cannot take roots in the lives of ordinary people. Negri and Hardt have made key contributions to our understanding of immaterial labour and the multitude. In conditions of serious economic crisis, however, the multitude cannot abandon the state politics that condemn people's lives to dramatic deterioration. Austerity can be reversed only through the capture of the state. The counter-power of the squares can institutionalize its principles by means of governmental action. The multitude's wisdom turns it into a people, supporting and voting the parties of the Left. The multitude and the party are not enemies; they should combine and learn from each other.

Let us move to Alain Badiou. Despite great differences and his criticisms of Negri, Badiou's position on the occupations is almost the mirror image of the *Declaration*. In a 2002 interview, Badiou explained that the 'resistance' (in ironic quotation marks) of the anti-globalization movement was creation and part of power. The movement is 'a wild operator' of globalization and 'seeks to sketch out, for the imminent future, the forms of comfort to be enjoyed by our planet's idle petite bourgeoisie.'[24] Warming to the theme, Badiou proceeded to attack Negri ('a backward romantic') who is fascinated by capital's 'flexibility and violence'. The multitude is a 'dreamy hallucination', which claims the right for our 'planets idle . . . to enjoy without doing anything, while taking special care to avoid any form of discipline, whereas we know that discipline, in all fields, is the key to truths'. Finally, Badiou dismisses the category of the 'movement' because it is 'coupled to the logic of the state'; politics must construct 'new forms of discipline to replace the discipline of political parties'.[25] Badiou's rejection of identity politics and the anti-globalization movement was total in 2002. A few years later, the *Rebirth of History* welcomes the recent uprisings which are partly inspired by the earlier campaigns. We are at the end of an interval between revolutionary periods, Badiou argues. After the last revolutionary age of the 1960s and 1970s, reactionary capitalism triumphed under the guise of liberal democracy. The possibility of a world popular insurrection against neo-liberal and imperial capitalism has risen again. The uprisings guard the history of emancipation during these intervals. History has placed radical change on the agenda; its realization needs a strong 'idea' and an organization that will sustain it politically.[26]

Badiou classifies the recent riots and uprisings, which reopened history, into immediate, latent and historical. The 'immediate' riots, such as Paris 2005, Athens 2008 and London 2011 are assemblies of angry youth reacting to an event, usually a police killing. They erupt in the poor suburbs where rioters live and do not move to the centre of the city. Immediate riots are negative, nihilistic, and destructive; they cannot give rise to a concrete insurrectionary subject. The subject of riots is not political, it is 'composed solely of rebellion, and dominated by negation and destruction, it does not make it possible clearly to distinguish between what pertains to a partially universalizable intention and what remains confined to a rage with no purpose'.[27] At best, the immediate riot prepares the way to a historical revolt. 'Latent' uprisings started with the militant activism of autonomous workers.

The best examples are French factory strikes and occupations carried out by their workers and others not working in that particular factory. They bring together 'students, youth, working people, unionists and non unionists, pensioners, intellectuals' in a specific place, creating a new type of popular unity. Finally, the 'historical' uprising of the Arab spring is characterized by duration, persistence, coherence and independence from parties. It occupies a place in the centre of the city and moves from the cacophony of immediate riot to a central slogan such as 'Mubarak go' which brings together almost all popular forces. The occupiers created a self-affirming and self-legitimizing 'popular dictatorship'. This localized, united and intense minority expressed the general will. The militants in Tahrir Square had the authority of truth on their side, imposed their decisions on everyone and justifiably treated dissidents as traitors.

Badiou's analysis is full of insights. The prognosis is not optimistic however. To avoid the defeats and co-optation of the past, the revolts must be inspired by an affirmative idea. Without the idea, they remain negative and become counterproductive riots. Only the 'idea of communism' can confront capitalist democracy today. Its absence, aggravated by the lack of political organization, means that insurrections cannot mature into emancipatory politics. The political organization Badiou fantasizes is highly disciplined and, although not attached to a class, acts towards the people in a directive and authoritarian manner. This is the type of organization that recent resistances categorically rejected.

Badiou's formalization and periodization of resistances makes him underestimate their successes. His approach underplays both socio-economic similarities and historical and political differences. Badiou's dislike of state politics leads him to dismiss left-wing parties, many of which are actively involved in the uprisings; his lack of interest in the economy makes him neglect the contribution of the financial and economic crisis to the world-wide explosion. Differences and nuances are forgotten in the search for a common diagnosis. Badiou's classifications suffer from what we could call 'positive orientalism'. The last revolutionary age finished with the end of the Chinese cultural revolution and the Iranian revolution. The historical uprising has arrived (and can only arrive) in Egypt. Europe is still (and perhaps for ever) in the age of riots. Greece and Spain, however, find themselves in a historical conjuncture not dissimilar to that of Egypt. Badiou hopes that a political organization embodying the communist idea will rise to meet the historical challenge. His call for an institutional structure to move the uprisings forward is right. But the distaste of existing

Left parties and organizations leads to a rather unrealistic eschatology. Badiou joins the long list of Leftist prophets and groupuscules promising the refoundation of the correct communist organization. The age of uprising has firmly placed radical change on the historical agenda; desperately seeking the (impossible) party is an admission of failure and defeat.

Badiou as well as Hardt and Negri consider the production of militant subjectivity central to the radical project. But only the small number of militants who accept his idea of communism can change the route of history. The question of subjectivity, however, is not about the militant subjects of a particular version of political truth. The production of radical subjects starts with the disarticulation of people from the economy of pleasure and consumption and their gradual introduction into an ethics of disobedience and a politics of resistance. This happens in Occupy London and New York as well as in Cairo and Athens. The question of motivation is central. For Badiou, radical subjectivities are created when an individual determines the place of truth in relation to her own vital existence and the world. How does that happen? Why, how and when do people who live in an economy of consumption and a moral economy of personal gratification abandon it? These are the questions Badiou neglects and the resisting multitude addresses as chapter 6 explained. The squares confirmed Badiou's claim that politics is a type of thought that creates its own truth; they rejected his version of truth created in some considerable distance from the politics of resistance.

Finally, Žižek. Unlike Badiou, Žižek does not advise withdrawal from state politics. His theory of the 'radical act' targets state power in order to change it radically and introduce a 'new order' that challenges capitalist 'worldlessness'.[28] This can only happen after the victory of the Left. Žižek's main worry is that the Left is either incapable of winning power, or has no idea what to do with it. With an eye to the world Occupy movement, Žižek wrote that 'the success of a revolution should not be measured by the sublime awe of its ecstatic moments, but by the changes the big Event leaves at the level of the everyday, the day after the insurrection'.[29] But the difference between Cairo and Athens on the one hand and New York or London on the other was great. Throughout 2011 and 2012, Žižek and I argued publicly over the future of the resistance with special emphasis on Greece.[30] I explained that behind the *aganaktismenoi* stands a powerful political and popular movement, which can help translate indignation into action and protest into politics. Žižek doubted the ability of the Left to take central stage and kept asking about the 'day after'. Žižek fears the well-known paradox of constituent power: as soon as it becomes constituted, it loses its dynamism and becomes the target for repression. Žižek generalizes the critique. Capitalism keeps changing and revolutionizing the world. Its late globalized and 'worldless' phase can attach itself to dissent and resistance and make them masquerade as 'subversive'. Communitarian localism and cosmopolitan liberalism, for example, despite their apparent opposition, are fully integrated into the capitalist vortex and offer no ground for resistance. With its constant reversals, crises, and reinventions, capitalism 'carnivalizes' normal life. What we need is a critique of capitalism 'from a stable "ethical" position'.[31] Only the imposition of a new order against capitalist disorder can guarantee the change. But this cannot happen at a distance from the state. In a clear criticism of his friend Badiou and of Negri, Žižek argues that the attempt to abandon the state and replace it with 'direct' non-representative forms such as councils was a main cause of past failures. 'If you have no clear idea of what you want to replace the state with, you have no right to subtract/withdraw from the state.'[32]

The reactions of Negri, Žižek and Badiou to the uprisings offer a clear view of their theoretical differences. Three lines of disagreement emerge. First, the composition of the political subject and the revolutionary potential of the multitude. Secondly, the relationship between the multitude's horizontal organization and the vertical structures of party and state. Finally, the potential of recent resistances to bring about radical change. Negri and Hardt celebrate the uprisings, discovering in their operation the principles of constituent power. Žižek has the greatest reservations about spontaneous, leaderless movements, the 'subversive' abilities of which match the chameleon like self-revolutionizing nature of late capitalism. For Žižek, social movements may become part of a capitalist reorganization, which turns difference, identity and locality into profitable use for capital. Finally, Badiou adopts the most pessimistic reading of Foucault's theory of resistance, claiming that its recent forms are generated and used by power. Badiou dismissed identity politics, anti-globalization campaigns and found major problems in the recent insurrections. Even the 'historical' uprising of Egypt will end up in the 'phenomenon of Western inclusion [which] cannot be regarded as genuine change.' What would be a genuine change would be an *exit from the West*, a de-Westernization, and it would take the form of an *exclusion*'.[33] 'History's rebirth', Badiou's title, sounds like a stillbirth.

Negri and Hardt believe that the occupations have opened the way for the transformation of the multitude into a radical political subject.

No possible compromise can be found between Badiou's claim that anti-capitalist movements are creations of power and Negri's celebration of the multitude as the only subject that can bring about the demise of capitalism. Yet below the surface the differences are not so pronounced. Badiou and Negri find themselves on the same side in their attitudes to democracy and the state. Badiou dismisses the Spanish *indignados*' call for 'real democracy' because it remains too close to parliamentary democracy and unlike the 'authority of the True, or an unconditional Idea of justice', does not create an 'enduring dynamic'.[34] He celebrates, like Hardt and Negri, the proclamation by some *indignados* of the *'utter vacuity of the electoral phenomenon, and hence of representation'*. A historical movement does not care about the state. It 'wants to celebrate its own dictatorial authority – dictatorial because democratic ad infinitum . . . It subordinates the results of action to the value of intellectual activity of action itself, not to the electoral categories of a programme and results.'[35] Negri and Hardt share Badiou's dislike of representation and the detestation of the state. They too celebrate the raw energy of the occupations, emphasize their direct democracy – not different from Badiou's 'democracy ad infinitum' – and praise the *indignados* for not participating in parliamentary elections. They both dismiss representative democracy and share the analysis of the relationship between movement/multitude and state or party politics. Badiou calls the militants to 'subtract' from state politics; Negri and Hard reject the 'notion of taking power in the sense of laying hold on the existing, ready-made state machinery'.[36] The multitude has no interest in capturing the state, not even to direct it to other ends; it just wants to dismantle the state apparatus. Finally, they both call for a political organization to lead after the uprising (Badiou) or an institutional process to protect the victories (Hardt and Negri). 'Just as insurrection has to become institutional, so too must revolution, in this way, become constitutional . . .'[37] But their rejection of the party form and the Left makes their call unconvincing. Badiou's philosophical idealism and Negri's romanticism have made important contributions to radical thinking. The resistance, however, has brought to the surface their strange dogmatism that dismisses politics if it does not conform with the theory.

Žižek's reservations are almost the opposite of the other two. Leaderless movements without clear aims and identifiable results exercising direct democracy and scorning participation in elections (the main advantage of recent resistances for Badiou, Hardt and Negri) are powerless, if they have not been already co-opted into the capitalist machine. The party form is necessary because state power is central to the radical project. The dilemma for or against state power is therefore false. It assumes that the state form will stay the same forever. On the contrary, the task of the Left is to 'transform [state power], radically changing its functioning, its relationship to its base'.[38] Žižek supported and visited resistance movements and despite his criticisms used their experience to finesse his theory. He proved closest to the concerns and achievements of protesters and insurgent. Political experience has made Žižek amend and adjust earlier views in order to respond to the contingencies of the situation. In this sense, he is both more political and a better philosopher.

A good example of Žižek's ability to revise earlier positions when the facts do not support them was his change of heart over the Greek resistance and the role of the Left. His earlier reservations were removed on 6 May 2012, when the Coalition of the Radical Left (Syriza) increased its share of the vote from 4.5% to 17%, making the prospect of a first ever radical Left government in Europe realistic. Žižek admired the statement of the party, a small protest movement before 2010, that it was willing and prepared to take power. After the minor political earthquake of the May elections, Žižek, in an act of implicit self-criticism, came to Athens. On 3 June, a fortnight before the second elections, Žižek gave full support to Syriza at a rally with its leader, contributing to the party's success. The Greek resistance, unlike the Occupy movements, posited clear and achievable political ends, developed a hegemonic strategy and, adopting Syriza as its institutional expression, achieved a major victory. Žižek's change of mind was an admission that his earlier theoretical reservations towards the ability of the multitude to act politically were perhaps mistaken. Žižek has been accused for repeating himself and for lack of consistency. Bruno Bosteels, for example, has recently tried to reconstruct Žižek's 'four' versions of the 'radical act' in order to show that, despite apparent contradictions, they can be synthesized into a coherent narrative which acknowledges their differences.[39] The attempt to iron out differences and apparent contradictions in a prolific *oeuvre* that spans many disciplines and themes is perhaps impossible, as Derrida has intimated.[40] It reveals the impasses of the reader more often than those of the text. If the Left is thinking in action, Žižek proved the only philosopher prepared to accept that political events can correct theoretical constructions.

Let me conclude. The most important reason why radical theory was unable to comprehend fully recent resistances is perhaps the 'anxiety of the grand narrative'. A previous generation of radical intellectuals such as Jean-Paul Sartre, Bertrand Russell, Edward

Thompson and Louis Althusser had close links with the movements of their time. Contemporary radical philosophers are found more often in lecture rooms than street corners. The wider 'academization' of radical theory and its close proximity with 'interdisciplinary' research and cultural studies departments has changed its character. These fields have been developed as a result of university academic and funding priorities. Media studies or cultural studies are disciplines in search of their object. They happily welcome the appeal of radical philosophers contributing to their celebrity value. But this weakening of the link between practice and theory has an adverse effect on theory construction. The desire for a 'radical theory of everything' caused by the 'anxiety of influence', the previous generation of philosophical greats generates, does not help overcome the limitations of disembodied abstraction.

The recent offerings of Badiou, Hardt, Negri and Žižek offer great insights into the age of resistance. Their attempt, however, to use resistances as examples of their theories proves problematic. Cases that cannot be seamlessly inserted into the theoretical edifice are neglected or rejected. They join a well-known tradition of the academic Left which corrects the movement, leaving the theory intact. Instead of the theory fitting in and helping to change the world, the world is made to fit the theory. To paraphrase Brecht, if the movement does not act according to the theory, we should elect a new movement. Alain Badiou has insisted that politics is a type of thinking; its truth emerges in political action. Philosophy takes this 'truth' and universalizes it. Žižek is the best example of this attitude. Radical philosophy concentrates on building grand theory while Leftist organizations exhaust themselves in often thoughtless activism. The insights offered by recent resistances could help improve both radical philosophy and radical strategy.

Lessons of political strategy

Political ontologies are neither abstract foundations of Being, nor historicist instantiations of political desire or relativist anthropology. Left ontology involves an active political and normative intervention. It starts from particular contingencies and conjunctures and proceeds to elevate the ethos of community and the morality of solidarity to the level of the universal – not as *a priori* logical proposition or normative maxim but as the claim to universality of a situated ethico-political demand. A Leftist ontology 'expresses a coherent system of beliefs about the world and calls for a particular course of action commensurate with those beliefs'.[41] Political struggles construct their ground or subject not in some abstract or metaphysical fashion but from within the context and conditions they find themselves in. 'A Leftist ontology therefore recognizes that everyday political practice – and not just the "political" – is defined by this daily struggle about the very nature of our world and its lines of communication, about who possesses the right and the power to delineate its borders and enforce its rules.'[42]

Let us examine briefly the ontologies we discussed above from the perspective of political struggle. Virno and Negri's multitude helps us to understand the social composition of late capitalism. However, the revolutionary hope placed on constituent power without political organization failed. Each instance of uprising started with the crowd assembling in a public place and rejecting the established socio-political order and its injustice. Victories were achieved when the revolting crowd moved from negation to affirmation, becoming a political subject. To do so, it adopted a party or parties and entered the central political stage, against the advice of Negri and Badiou. Change came in Tunis, Cairo, partly in Athens; not in New York and London. The physical presence of people was a determining characteristic of recent uprisings, bringing them closer perhaps to sociological and psychological theory than to the sophisticated post-Marxist analysis. The occupations confirmed that emotional intensity nourishes crowds. But the crowd was not irrational, fearful, easily led. It was a multiplicity of bodies debating, deciding and acting. Passionate reason and rational desire helped revitalize the autonomy promised and betrayed by liberal individualism and representative democracy. The multitude acted in common and defined what is common, the common good. The direct democracy of the occupations was pivotal in constructing the opposition and the eventual overthrow of governments. A type of political practice modernity had exorcised has now returned.

The theory of the social multitude gives useful analytical tools. But only the multitude in assembly, the people as demos, can initiate radical change. The multitude is the social foundation; the *demos* the political subject. Rancière's emphasis on exclusion, disagreement and conflict corrects Hardt and Negri's obsession with the multitude's capitalist immanence. His categories of political and cultural exclusion must be complemented, however, with class exclusion and hegemonic politics. Physical co-existence created the public space of dialogue, collective decision-making and action. The multitude developed a hegemonic policy without hegemons and parties. In this sense, an original political strategy gradually emerged. Greek resistance drew eclectically from radical philosophy, displaying the wisdom of the multitude who had not read Badiou or Negri. It confirmed certain aspects but also amended and moved the theory forward. It accepted political ontology without returning to the outdated analyses about the working class and its party leadership. It recognized the deep structural antagonism between the rulers, the ruled and the excluded, which splits the social space and could become the front line in a politics of confrontation. At the same time, Syntagma called the whole population to the anti-memorandum pole – or created the people through the antagonism with the elite, according to Laclau – as the subject of a proto-constituent power. Conflict was not abandoned. The political subject came together in opposition to political and economic elites; the exclusion of large parts of the population was confronted and contested in a strategy of radical but not violent confrontation. Excluded and marginalized groups became representatives of the wider social catastrophe. Two strategies emerged and coalesced therefore in those amazing days: a narrower of conflict and a wider of hegemonic intervention. Radical identities, prepared in the various resistances, converged in the squares and became constituent power. Hegemonic intervention was crucial for the construction of the popular pole. Without class analysis, however, the theory of hegemony risks losing its radical potential, becoming descriptive and axiologically neutral. Hegemony needs a normative supplement. It needs the equality maxim and an analysis of exclusion in order to distinguish radical from reactionary populism.

The successful uprisings in Tunisia, Egypt and Greece moved from massive occupations to parliamentary elections. The Occupy movements in New York or London on the other hand did not make that transition and have not achieved major victories yet. In Greece, hegemonic nominalism and the strategy of confrontation cracked the glass ceiling that had contained the Left after the end of the civil war in the 1940s. To use an expression that will put a smile on many a cynical lip, the end of the power system and the rise of the radical Left is a matter of historical necessity. Throughout history, revolutions succeed when a power system has run its course and has become obsolete and harmful. At the time of happening, uprisings and insurrections are condemned as violent, criminal, illegal. If they succeed, they become sanctified and celebrated. Historical necessity is recognized retrospectively, after its consummation. Necessity provides the context but is not enough. The *ancien régime* may survive for a while and even frustrate the 'spirit' of history through rearguard action. To succeed, radical change requires three elements. First, a strong popular will for change. Secondly, a political agent who is prepared to take power; this political subject often appears by happenstance. Finally, a catalyst which combines the other elements into a combustible whole and gives the final push to the moribund system of power. All three elements converged in Tunisia and Egypt.

In Greece, the horizontal organization of the occupations prepared radical change but could not succeed on its own. *Stasis Syntagma* indicated the need for complementary strategies and overlapping tactics of resistance, some coming from the multitude, others from organized collectivities. Was there a link between the resistance and the election results? After all, the 2012 elections returned a coalition of the old parties to power. Without the resistance and the rise of the radical Left, however, the power system would have survived intact. It now lives on half dead. Let me explain. The resistance brought to an end the post-civil-war divides between a victorious Right and a defeated Left, which sustained the balance of power for seventy years. People with opposed and antagonistic ideologies found themselves in the same place for the first time. They realized that an unemployed Leftist and an unemployed Rightist suffer the same; patriotic and internationalist pensioners are equally hurt by pension cuts; a Greek and an immigrant are similarly offended by attacks on their dignity. People concluded that their common interests were greater than ancient enmities and recent rivalries. The post-civil war divide between victors and defeated dissolved in mass assemblies and clouds of teargas. After that, the power system had reached its end. Only the final push was required. On 6 May and 17 June, the multitude became again a people and voted massively for the Left. Direct democracy acquired its parliamentary companion.

We can now identify the 'work' of history in Greece. The desire for a radical overhaul of the political system and a new beginning was expressed in the 2011 occupations that led the Papandreou government to resign twice and again in the 2012 elections. The multitude in the occupations started the constituent process and adopted Syriza as the political subject in the elections. The catalyst was provided by the escalating austerity measures that have brought the constituted system to the edge of abyss. It was a rendezvous with history; it had to confront a major campaign of blackmail and fear aiming to frustrate the consummation. *The Financial Times*, *Deutschland* and *Bild* published articles in Greek on their front page asking people to reject the Left. Merkel, Baroso, even George Osborne, ordered the

Greeks to vote the 'right way'. This direct intervention followed a plethora of threats and rumours, secrets and lies, telling the Greeks that if they voted for the Left, the country would be ejected from the euro, savings would be seized, milk and bread would disappear from supermarket selves. The campaign prevented the election of a Syriza government. Still the result was a major surprise. Syriza fought hard in the past to gain the 3% threshold necessary to enter Parliament. The party did not change radically between 2009 and 2012 to justify a seven-fold jump in its vote. It was adopted by those determined to give the final push to the power system. Why Syriza and not some other anti-austerity party?

Two reasons come to mind. Party members joined the resistance movement from the start. Syriza used to be a small party concentrating on protest activities. Participation in the anti-globalization movement and the world social forum had prepared it for multiform and dynamic action. Syriza joined the resistance without hegemonic ambitions. It did not try to lead or use the squares to recruit members. Secondly, Syriza had adopted internally the ideology of pluralism and direct democracy well before the crisis. The party is a coalition of twelve parties and groups. The largest (Synaspismos) hails from the Eurocommunist tradition; others have ecological, Marxist, Trotskyist, radical democratic and post-anarchist roots. Tendencies and factions are allowed; each constituent group has one vote in the party committees, creating an atmosphere of dialogue, negotiation and compromise. It is a 'new type' of party that has jettisoned the characteristics of the original Leninist model and comes closest to the ethos of the multitude and the organization of the occupations. When elections were called, the people of the squares adopted Syriza as their obvious choice. The Presidents of Brazil, Venezuela and Bolivia were elected with the help of independent social movements. Something similar happened in Greece without a formal agreement between the resisters and the Left. This way a dual track strategy developed: social mobilization and parliamentary presence, direct and representative democracy, in and against the state. The meeting between the occupations and the radical Left was serendipitous; it was prepared by the 'cunning of history'.

The attack on the Greek life and ethos continued after the 2012 elections under the new coalition government. The withdrawal of a further €14 billion from the public sector in the autumn of 2012 turns the humanitarian catastrophe into an unprecedented civic collapse. The major social services (health, education, social security) can no longer provide a minimal safety net. Families and individuals are thrown back to a search for the basics in a brutal literalization of the survival of the fittest. The last remnants of the ethos of friendship and community are shredded; the atomization of affluence and consumption is turning into a defensive individualism of bare life. This is a capitalist final solution, the implementation of the nominalist dream: there will be no collectivities, only individuals and the sovereign. Fascism and racism flourish on this ground, with the Chryssi Avgi gang masquerading as a political party that combines the politics' blood and soil with anti-systemic rhetoric. Violent daily attacks on immigrants, gays and Roma, often tolerated by the authorities, proliferate and create a sense of lawlessness. The ruling elites, sensing their pending end, have started equating the fascists with the Left, perceived as a greater threat. It is a textbook case of the moral, political and intellectual collapse of a power system that Samson-like tries to take the whole country down with it.

Žižek has consistently warned that the Left will fail unless it has a clear plan for the day after victory. 'Today's global capitalism, precisely insofar as it is "world-less", involving constant disruption of all fixed orders, opens up the space for a revolution which will . . . break the vicious cycle of an evental explosion followed by a return to normality, but will instead assume the task of *a new "ordering" against the global capitalist disorder.*'[43] He is right and wrong. The Left in Southern Europe must develop and publicize immediate plans for confronting the crisis, reversing the humanitarian catastrophe and putting people back to work. But in this bleak situation, a potential Left government cannot rely on a gradual return to normality. Workers, private sector employees and the lowly paid want to see the state functioning properly. They pay their taxes and have no rewards to hand out corruptly; they have been the electoral fodder of the mainstream parties in return for paltry bribes. The rationalization of the state, an end to corruption and patronage, the collection of taxes and the punishment of tax evasion should be main planks of Leftist policy. They will align the social movement with popular feelings and inject the necessary pragmatism. Left strategy must mitigate the catastrophic effects of austerity while starting at the same time to heal the torn social fabric. A Left government will face a hostile European Union; political time will be compressed and the 'window of opportunity' limited. Palliatives and limited reversals of the most offensive austerity measures will not be enough. The Left will be obliged to move towards a democratic socialist order, something that has not been achieved before and for which no blueprint or experience exists. The dual democratic strategy of social mobilization and representative politics means that the day after will be the continuation of the day before. The difficult task is to get to that day by building party and movement on the principles of direct democracy and equality. Žižek's insistent questioning contributes to the debate on democratic socialism. He keeps reminding us that economic crisis and austerity, the undermining of democracy and police repression, the 'revolutionizing' of social life and the destruction of communities are not side-effects but central products of late capitalism. The debt crisis may be resolved, austerity mitigated but the catastrophic effects will continue until democratic socialism has radically changed economic activity and rebalanced social life. In this difficult environment, the energy of the resistances and the constituent power of the occupations are the best hopes for success.

What are the lessons of the squares? First, the rediscovered principles of publicity and equality. The multitude as social category became a force of radical change when it met in public. Public assemblies, direct democracy and collective action have revived the power of the people. Can this energy be maintained and institutionalized? Place, time and intensity were central in the construction of the multitude. Protests, demostrations and rallies are 'natural' activities of social movements. The defence of the poor, solidarity networks helping the vulnerable and the immigrants, union strikes and occupations remain staple Leftist tactics. They are no longer enough. The age of leaders, of centralized parties and unions, of solid and conscious political subjects awaiting representation has passed for good. The global anti-political and anti-party popular feelings, fuelled in Greece by endemic cronyism and corruption, combined with the domination of financial priorities over politics have led the principle of representation to further decay. The squares changed the dynamic of earlier resistances and should remain a focal point, their spirit spread everywhere. Co-operation and solidarity, sharing of knowledge and skills, discussing in public and deciding in common are the guiding principles. If encampments have been abandoned, they should be replaced by virtual camps and local gatherings. Regular assemblies in neighborhoods, suburbs and towns, solidarity networks and cultural events could turn transient occupations into a permanent feature of politics. The skills and knowledge of the multitude finds continually new ways of collaboration, networking, new ideas for life. The social ethos of horizontal work should be institutionalized and disseminated, keeping the citizenship of the squares active.

From space to time. The second legacy of the occupations is the aesthetics of praxis. Praxis is the temporal dimension of constituent power. The linear time of work was replaced by the teleological temporality of creation. Praxis produces new subjects, collective praxis changes the world. But how can constituent power survive the emptying of the squares? The resistance disarticulated subjectivities from capitalist biopolitics. The production of subjectivity must now move from the squares to communities. Our discussion of social ethos and the morality of resistance could be of help. The modernizing elites offer a choice between East and West, communitarianism and individualism. In this Manichaean division, people are either fully attached to thick identities and inescapable communities, or they are free-floating individuals creating their identities at will following rational calculations. These are wrong alternatives. The juxtaposition between reason and passion or between individual and community was deconstructed a long time ago and no longer convinces. The individualism of universal principles forgets that every person is a world who comes into existence in common with others; we are all in community. Being in common is an integral part of being self: self is exposed to the other, it is posed in exteriority, the other is part of the intimacy of self. My face is always turned towards another, faced by her, never facing myself. Being in community with others is the opposite of common being or of belonging to an essential community. Most communitarians, on the other hand, define community through the commonality of tradition, history and culture, past crystalizations whose inescapable weight determines present possibilities. The essence of the communitarian community is often to compel or 'allow' people to find their 'essence', defined as the spirit of the nation, the people or the leader. We have to follow traditional values and exclude the stranger and the alien. This type of community as communion helps submerge the *I* into the *We*, destroying its singularity.

From our perspective, identities start with the homely, protective and socializing ethos of early life. Family, friends and community are inescapable components of identity. The mature self develops in a dialectical confrontation of our early socialization with cognitive horizons and normative principles which subject our commitments to the test of the universal. We are both attached and detached, both Greek or English and European, if we were to consider for a moment rather rashly Europe as the representative of the universal. Every *I* is a cosmos, the unique combination of past events, current projects and future aspirations, of intimate and stranger encounters, of roads traversed and paths missed, of emotions and reasons, ethics and passions. The uniqueness of self is the result of all those others who have touched, spoken and acted with me. I am because I have been in common with others. As Gilles Deleuze put it, individuality is not a 'point' but a 'minimum of incompressible social relations', a capacity to act and to be acted upon, to affect others and be affected by them.[44]

This analysis helps develop a progressive strategy for revitalizing communities. Biopolitical capitalism undermines the social ethos in order to construct disciplined bodies and controlled populations. For the individual of late capitalism, the other is a tool to be used or a hindrance to be defended agaist. The de- and reconstruction of subjectivity remains a principal field of intervention. Despite attacks, ethos and ethics remain a major source for social renewal. Its betrayal and corruption by modernization and austerity can be reversed and combined with a new sense of social morality. *Filia, filotimia* and *filoxenia* (friendship, love of honour and hospitality), the surviving components of social ethos, can help reverse the ideology of possessive individualism and capitalist conformism. Friendship helps reactivate communities, dignity combats the corruption of elite cynicism and anomie. Finally, hospitality promotes social solidarity and the spirit of care and empathy. But the social ethos needs repair and revitalization. Both its communitarian perversion and its individualist distortion must be confronted. Nationalism and nepotism are the other side of individualism and greed; both sides corrupt the singularity of selfhood, our uniqueness created in continual conversation and being with the other. The ethos, the common, togetherness lie at the foundation of self and community. Žižek's 'new order' must be ontological before it becomes political and economic. It will be built on the remains of social ethos turned into foundations of a new culture. There is no Left identity without indignation and anger at the injustices of the world. But there is no Left commitment, if it is does not submit feelings and emotions to the strict test of universal equality. The 'idea of communism' must recreate and strengthen community and social ethos not as dead tradition but as the coming together of unique selves. Socialism will be ethical and democratic or it will not be.

The combination of *filia* or friendship in its widest meaning with the skills and networking abilities of working people should be a priority. The organizational principles of the squares should be extended to all areas of economic, social and cultural life. Initiatives from below, direct democracy, physical and virtual collaboration, bringing people and skills together would revive the faltering sense of community. Economically profitable and socially useful enterprises would be based on these principles. Workers in failing industries, for example, could take over their place of business and run it as a co-operative. A special bank, funded by a solidarity levy, would finance projects that promote collaboration and networking. 'Universities of the squares' would meet regularly in suburbs and towns, continuing the dissemination of alternative views about epistemology and methodology and the dissemination of knowledge that started in the occupations. Open and public meetings would act as a kind of second chamber scrutinizing policy proposals discussed in Parliament. Direct democratic methods could be introduced in local and eventually central government. Public debate and voting of council budgets and all important local issues could be a start. Public art, film shows, music performances, literary readings and debates in squares would introduce an alternative political culture. These proposals aim at repoliticizing politics and introducing the ethos of the collective into all aspects of public life. After the catastrophes of austerity, Greece needs a cultural and moral renaissance. Deepening democracy and making it the form of every type of activity and life is the main lesson of the squares.

The Greek resistance offers a corrective to radical philosophy and indicates a future direction for the Left. Necessary pragmatism must be accompanied with an unwavering commitment to principle. The Greek Left has a major moral advantage compared with other political forces. It is based partly on its clean past but, more importantly, on its commitment to equality and justice. Every policy proposal must be assessed therefore against universal principles. Democratic debate, political activism and popular mobilization will help combine principle and pragmatism, both necessary for radical reform. Only such a combination of politics with radical intent and social mobilization can succeed. It means representative politics, electoral campaigning combined with solidarity campaigns, social movements, activism and trade union pressure. Democratic creativity and instrumental rationality must come together. The task of the Greek Left is to develop the 'idea of communism' for an age of capitalist crisis and violent social rearragement. It is a tall order for a small country and organization. It can succeed only if the European movements learn from the Greek experience and follow similar strategies. In such case, the Greece of resistance will become the future of Europe.

EPILOGUE:
THE EUROPE TO COME

How different Europe looks today from some ten years ago. In 2000, influential commentators hailed the dawn of the 'new European century' to replace the 'American' twentieth century. Europe was on the way to becoming the model polity of the new world order. The reunification of Germany, the successful introduction of the euro and the expansion eastwards were ushering in a new age of prosperity and freedom. Jurgen Habermas and Ulrich Beck enthused about the European model and prophesied its exportation to the world. Many were the successes of the Union, they claimed.[1] Old nationalism and xenophobia had been left behind, former enemies collaborated in peaceful competition, creating the most successful economic region in the world. The European Union's principles of democracy, human rights and multiculturalism were a beacon of hope. Europe was the model for the future of humanity. The reality is so different today. The European Union is no longer a model but a dysfunctional organization that has betrayed its founding principles of economic stability and prosperity based on social solidarity and respect for human rights and justice. Recent attacks by economic and political elites and the European administrators on the Mediterranean people dismissively called PIIGS (Portugal, Italy, Ireland, Greece and Spain) show that the foundations of Europe are shaking.

Europe is at a crossroads, Europe is in crisis. But the idea of Europe at a crossroads or in crisis is not new. Europe is a crossroads. The name and idea of Europe were inventions of people in the eastern Mediterranean around the Aegean Sea. The etymological root of the word Europe is *ereb*, the darkness after the sun has gone down. The Greek Ionians, who lived in what we now call Asia Minor, were the first to call Europe the lands on the western shores of the

Aegean – Greece and further west – where the sun sets. If we turn to mythology, Europa, the beautiful daughter of a Phoenician king, was born in the city of Tyre, now in the Lebanon. She was abducted and ravished by Zeus, the king of gods, metamorphosed into a bull, who took her to Crete. The origin of Europe's name is non-European. Not just the name. Europe was united politically for the first time in the Roman Empire and culturally through its Chistianization into a holy Roman Empire. The founder of Rome was Aeneas, a wandering exile from Troy. Jesus was a Jewish prophet. Europe is the creation of non-European travellers, wanderers and mystics. They came from the Mediterranean, the *Mesogeios* in Greek, literally the centre of the earth, the world's navel.

The Mediterranean lands, a hospitable haven for nomads and immigrants, was also a place of departures. The European boats of discovery, conquest and colonization departed from Mediterranean ports, on the Greco-Latino-Iberian shores. As Paul Valéry put it, the same ships carried merchandise and goods, ideas and methods. The Mediterranean has been a machine for making and spreading commerce and civilization. On the shores of the Mediterranean, spirit, culture and trade came together.[2] In 1830, the philosopher Hegel called the Mediterranean the centre of world history.[3] In 1960, the historian Fernand Braudel called it the 'radiant centre' of the entire globe 'whose light grows less as one moves away from it, without one's being able to define the exact boundary between light and shade'.[4] If the Mediterranean is the *medius terra*, she is also the heart and begetter of Europe.

And yet, the European nations are sick; Europe itself in a critical condition. This is how the German philosopher Edmund Husserl opened his famous Vienna lecture entitled 'Philosophy and the Crisis of European Man' in 1935.[5] Husserl, a German Jew, had already been expelled from Freiburg University. His death in 1939 spared him the experience of war and the Holocaust. In his 1935 lecture, he diagnoses the present sickness as a temporary deviation from the idea of Europe. For Husserl, Europe's idea represents truth and the universal, what transcends local and parochial attachments and commitments. The purpose of European history is to seek truth behind passing appearances and partial opinions. Its spiritual birthplace was Greece. Greek philosophy and science created a disinterested view of the world and explored the universal unity of all beings. A special type of humanity spread out from Greece, which, while living in a particular place, was oriented towards the infinity of the future in a constant spiritual renewal. Truth is the gift of Greeks to Europe and of Europeans to humanity. Europe is the *telos* of humanity, it helps humanity become itself.

The European idea leads to the abandonment of local, ethnic or religious differences and the construction of a genuinely universal humanity. Philosophy emerged in Greece against *doxa* and orthodoxy as the call to explore and live according to universal ideas. When truth becomes a practical task, it leads to democracy and the demand to give reasons (*logon didonai*) for beliefs and actions, to be responsible to others and publicly accountable. The spiritual task of European 'man' is to create freely himself and his history under the guidance of reason. Europe means the infinite task of self-creation and the continual improvement of nations and individuals. Europe is therefore not just the name of a landmass but a 'spiritual geography'. Humanity will be reached when the idea of Europe becomes global; we, Europeans, the functionaries of the human spirit. What is the role of non-Europeans, outsiders and aliens in Europe's task of infinite self-creativity? The universal vocation of truth, philosophy and science does not belong to a particular nation. They are open to all. And yet, the Greek birth and European heritage are quite unique in their universality. No similar idea or vocation worthy of the name philosophy has emerged in India or China, Husserl claims. 'Therein lies something unique, which all other human groups, too, feel with regard to us, something that apart from all considerations of expediency, becomes a motivation for them – despite their determination to retain their spiritual autonomy – constantly to Europeanize themselves, whereas we, if we understand ourselves properly, will never, for example, Indianize ourselves.' If Europe designates the unity of spiritual life and creative activity, the Eskimos or Indians of the country fairs or the constantly wandering gypsies do not belong to it.[6]

Let us now move from 1935 to 2010. On 13 September, a European commissioner called the French deportation of one thousand Roma a disgrace and likened it to Vichy France's treatment of Jews. Pierre Lellouche, a French minister, responded in kind. France is 'the mother of human rights . . . not the naughty pupil of the class whom the teacher tells off and we are not the criminal before the prosecutor'.[7] If France is the mother of human rights, if human rights are the noblest normative universal, if the universal is the future task of humanity, France is nascent humanity. France has claimed this position at least since Napoleon, who claimed that what is good for France is good for the whole of humanity. Hegel agreed. Hearing the sound and fury of the Jena battle, he wrote that Napoleon was spirit on horseback, freedom and modernity spreading through the barrel

of a gun. Spanish prisoners of war met Napoleon's inspecting officers with banners declaring 'Down with Freedom'. Our contemporary
humanitarian emissaries, soldiers and NGO operatives are similarly
met in parts of the world with the cry 'Down with your human rights'.

The French deportations of the Roma are exemplifications of
Europe's and humanity's history. Racism, xenophobia and deportation are as part of Europe as are humanity and human rights. Husserl
and Mr Lelouche point to a secret at the heart of Europe and perhaps
of humanity. Fear and hatred of the foreigner is both an integral part
and the greatest enemy of universal Europe. Greece and Europe came
from elsewhere themselves, from Asia and the East. We are heirs of
this history, children of Europa, our primordial mother. Her journey
from Tyre to Crete introduced her to other people, civilizations and
cultures. So did the voyages of Mediterranean seafarers. Greece, the
Mediterranean, Europe represent separation and movement, being
cut off from and leaving your proper and property behind. Departure
from hearth, home and the homely can be voluntary or violent, emi-
gration or deportation. De-*portation*, departing or expelled from the
port (Pireas, Porto, Paris or Paros) is the fate of the Mediterranean
and by extension the European. Sophocles described Greek man as
pantoporos aporos, sailing everywhere but nowhere at home.[8] The
voyage can be cyclical Ulysses-like or nomadic Abraham-like. But
in both cases, uprootedness, the Mediterranean fate, makes the exile
or migrant always glance into the distance, into the darkness of the
West, the gaze always ahead of itself, in touch with the other at or
beyond the horizon. Original uprootedness, separation from the
homely, passage to what is not and is always to come captures the
idea of Mediterranean and Europe. And yet today our sea has become
a wall, a controlled and policed borderline, where migrants, following the winds that transported Europa, Aeneas and the numberless
generations of Mediterranean sailors, are left by patrol boats and
border guards to drown.

It was exposure to different laws, customs and gods that triggered
the Greek vocation to transcend the local and parochial towards what
is universal and common to all. It taught the voyagers that there are
different vocations and truths, different ways to the universal. From
the very beginning the Greeks questioned their identity, disrupted by
the Egyptian other and the wholly other. Greek philosophy intro-,
duced otherness into the reason of logos. Sailing into foreign lands
leads to self-estrangement; philosophy is the way of the sea. European
identity is always established in relation to its other, the non-European. Europe means exposure to the other, the foreigner and stranger

and to what is other within self. We are responsible for our identity, for the universal and infinite task of imagining humanity. We are also responsible for our repeated atrocities, in the New World, in the Asian and African colonies, in our genocides and holocausts, in our expulsion of the Roma. Kidnapped Europa's journey from the Phoenicians to the Greeks symbolizes Europe's mobility. But perhaps it also signifies something darker. We have been in mourning for the abduction and rape of Europa, our primordial mother. We have interiorized this original crime, like Freud's parricidal band of brothers. They killed the father and created law, we purify and avenge the mother by visiting her atrocious fate upon others.

This is how the inner paradox in Husserl's celebration of universality and truth, which is however exclusively credited to the Greeks and Europeans, can be explained. If the Europeans are the functionaries of humanity, if their rationality gives them superior power, they have the obligation to raise to humanity those lesser souls who have not developed ways of thinking the universal. Europe represents the infinite task of leading humanity home, of humanizing humanity. Historically however humanity has been used consistently as a strategy of ontological separation and ordering into a full, a lesser humanity and the inhuman. The infinite task of humanity to reshape itself, what used to be called 'the civilizing mission', has always been accompanied by a history of conquest, domination, extermination and colonialism.

Let us return to Husserl's diagnosis of the European crisis in 1935 and link it to our present woes. For Husserl, the crisis, with its countless symptoms of corruption, was not an inescapable fate. It resulted from a mistaken turn in Enlightenment rationalism. The scientific and technological triumphs, the perfection of mathematics and geometry, have made Europeans approach nature and spirit, object and subject, as if they were identical. We use the same type of instrumental rationality and method to examine both the natural and the human worlds. The sciences have been formalized and mathematized but they lost their relationship to universal truth and are unable to understand humanity. The crisis lies therefore not in the collapse of reason but in the imperialism of one type of reason for which man is a natural object. The essence of the human is spiritual not material. Man has intentions and creates meaning, he is not the result of physical causes or chemical reactions. Universal truth exists because there is one cosmos, a common horizon encompassing local and partial human worlds. It is built out of the incessant critique of everything particular, continual departing and sailing away, deported from natural belonging and becoming strangers to ourselves. The infinite process of self-creation passes through self-alienation. Psychologists and other policemen of the soul, on the other hand, have naturalized the human spirit and examine it as if it were an inert material entity. The Greek idea of universality must be rediscovered and revived. Husserl believed that only his transcendental phenomenology can understand a rationality specific to human consciousness. One may disagree with the prescription. Husserl's idiosyncratic approach however reopens the question of the universal idea freed from the arrogant Eurocentric version.

We find clear parallels in the contemporary crisis. The idea of Europe, the universal vocation of spirit, is being undermined, 'corrupted' to use Husserl's term, by the orthodoxies of the European Union. The underlying cause is the same, the instrumentalization of reason, in this case of practical reason. Let us go back again to Greece, Husserl's birthplace of Europe and truth, to examine its other great invention, politics and democracy. If the invention of philosophy introduced truth and the universal into the heart of Europe what did the invention of democracy achieve? As chapter 7 discussed, democracy means, the *kratos* power of the *demos*, the power of those who have no qualification, no knowledge, skill or wealth to exercise power. The *demos* is a group without a fixed place in the social edifice. They became a group when they demanded to be included, to be heard on an equal footing with the rulers and be recognized as partners in decision-making.[9] Democracy destabilizes the 'natural' order which routinely follows the hierarchies of wealth, knowledge and power. It takes place when a group of excluded (the demos, women, workers, immigrants, the Roma, the unemployed youth) puts itself forward as stand-in for the universal. This is universality in politics.

The Athenian *demos* excluded slaves, women and *metics*. The axiom of equality of everyone and anyone was strictly limited. It was Christianity, this other stranger to Europe, which universalized equality and introduced it to the idea of Europe. St Paul's statement, that there is no Greek or Jew, man or woman, free man or slave (Epistle to the Galatians 3: 28) removed restrictions and introduced universalism and equality into Western civilization. This was of course a spiritual equality, accompanied by strict socio-political hierarchy. All people are equally part of humanity; they can be saved in God's plan of salvation. But only if they accept the faith, since non-Christians have no place in the providential plan. This radical divide and exclusion founded the ecumenical mission of Church and Empire. Christ's law of love turned into a battle cry: let us bring the pagans to the grace of God, let us impose the message of truth and love upon the whole world. The road from spiritual to political equality was also the way of imperialism colonialism and genocide; the normative universal always accompanied by the brutally parochial.

If universal truth is the task of humanity, it can be guaranteed only by a politics of incessant disagreement and conflict. Here we reach the contemporary crisis of Europe. In late capitalism, politics has been trumped by the supposed objective knowledge of economists, managers and accountants, disagreement by fake consensus, argument by the diktat of experts. Politics is made to resemble the market-place: the propertied and those in employment accept the overall socio-economic balance, despite its huge inequalities, and pursue marginal improvements to their income and status. Governance has become the administration of economics according to neo-liberal recipes. Here we find Husserl's contemporary relevance. Neo-liberal mathematized financial models, based on rational expectations and objective calculations, are presented by national and European elites as an exact science. They can predict and control human behaviour, leading with mathematical precision to growth and prosperity, despite the huge inequalities they create. The economy has been naturalized, the rationality of physics and mathematics applies to social relations and human behaviour. Managed consensus replaces conflict, the formulas of economists the disagreements of democracy, obscene inequalities the egalitarian idea. Politics should not interfere with 'objective' truths, it should act as the simple administration of economic prescriptions, a kind of extensive public relations enterprise.

All great ideas in modernity, from human rights to popular sovereignty to the nation and socialism were advanced originally by intellectual and political elites but were able to inspire people and turn them to action. This has palpably failed in Europe. Elites have become European but the people have not followed. The loss of nerve of intellectuals in this context is quite striking. Social justice, the single issue that most consistently defined the public intellectual and brought together Sartre and Russell, Camus and Derrida, has been forgotten in the quest for the latest EU research grant. No wonder nationalism is on the rise.

One response to the structural problems of the monetary union is to propose greater economic integration, which necessarily leads to closer political union. But a closer European polity would have to address the famous 'democratic deficit' of the Union. This is a euphemism however. The EU suffers an absence of democracy. Every single principle of a democratic constitution from the separation of powers to democratic accountability and executive transparency is breached. The government-appointed commission exercises the exclusive power of legislative initiative, Parliament-like, but also enforces the law, executive-like. Government representatives and council of Ministers emissaries legislate in collaboration with government appointed commissioners. The Parliament is still a talking shop with minimal powers despite a recent increase in its competencies. Throughout the recent crisis, Parliament has been absent from summits and negotiations, its views on the greatest challenge to the Union's survival non-existent or unknown. The combination of unaccountable Eurocrats and national bureaucrats has led to a mountain of legislation amounting to more than 100,000 pages. They are imposed on states without even a minimum discussion by national Parliaments and amount to 70% of legislative production in Britain. European citizens realizing the impotence of Parliament have turned their back on European elections.

The European lack of democratic accountability has been welcomed by national governments, which can agree unpopular measures in Brussels without having to get MPs to vote in Athens or London. Citizens' participation in European affairs is limited to lawsuits and lobbying. This is a sad remnant of the original vision of democratic European integration. On the few occasions the public was asked to vote on the European construction, it decidedly rejected the proposals. The referenda over the European 'constitution' in France, Holland and Ireland confirmed extensive popular distaste and the one in Britain had to be cancelled as a result. The typical and angry response of the frustrated elites was to repackage the 'constitution', offer bribes to the Irish and the Poles, and impose a President and Foreign Secretary, whose only quality was that they were universally unknown. This European attitude to democracy shows postmodern cynicism at its worst. It combines Brecht's dictum that if the people do not vote for the government, the government should dissolve the people and elect a new one with the principle of 'as if': the more you have your proposals rejected the more you should act as if they have been unanimously approved. Based on these reversals, academic propagandists for the Union argue that popular participation is undesirable because it is 'ignorant, irrelevant and ideological'. Andrew Moravcsik argues that 'social Europe is a chimera' and democratic participation should be discouraged because it 'runs counter to our consensual social scientific understanding of how advanced democracies work'.[10] Economic and scientific expertise is not open to debate and voting. Indeed, all democratic participation and mobilization is expensive, counter-productive and gives the impression that there may be more than one solutions to problems that have objectively right answers. The great advantage of the Union is that it is so 'boring' that people do not care about it.

No prospect of a European democracy exists because no European demos has been created. The failure has emboldened neo-liberal apologists to propose a new type of integration. Jan Zielonka announced in 2006 that Europe is becoming a benign Empire.[11] Its complex governance, neo-medieval maze of jurisdictions and committees of experts, which find their equilibrium through spontaneous market adjustments, is closer to the Holy Roman Empire than a modern democracy. Policy networks and lobbying are more effective for decision-making than popular sovereignty and elections. As Perry Anderson sarcastically comments, this is a 'return to medieval petitions submitted to the prince'.[12] This complacency has been undermined by the austerity measures. Europe can no longer be seen as a remote bunch of bureaucrats dealing in esoteric rules of trade, competition and product regulation. Its diktat now reaches the basics of popular well-being. To smooth its passage, Eurocrats and national governments followed identical tactics. The politics of fear (bankruptcy, exit from the euro, non-payment of salaries) mimicked the war on terror. The monotonously repeated claims about the 'objective character' and unavoidability of austerity exploits the trust scientists generate. Why ask for social justice, if you can get a good ombudsman?

In 2009, Jean-Claude Trichet, the president of the European Central Bank, gave a lecture on European culture.[13] The lecture consisted of a long series of clichéd and unrelated quotes about the greatness and diversity of Europe. They ranged from Aquinas, to Valéry, Husserl and Derrida. Their incoherent arrangement indicates that they were perhaps unearthed and compiled by unfortunate assistants. The concluding part is entitled 'the aspiration of European culture to universality'. Trichet quotes Renan's well-known essay on a nation's identity: 'in the past [the nation] was a heritage of glory and regrets to share together; but in the future it will be the same programme (*un meme programme*) to be realized'.[14] For the banker, Europe can now be compared to, if it has not replaced, the nation, and its future lies in its 'same programme'. But what is the European 'same programme'? Despite references to Husserl and Derrida, it is 'the single currency . . . the essential part of this programme to be realized'. We shall continue to offer the euro, he concludes, as a 'unique and irreplaceable anchor'. Monetary union is the new European universal, exchange value has replaced the idea of Europe. This is what remains from Europe's aspiration to universality. Historically all cosmopolitanisms ended up in empire. Stoic philosophy ended up in Rome, Christian spiritual universalism became conquest, genocide and conversion, modern reason and progress degenerated into colonialism and the 'civilizing mission'. Similarly today Western cosmopolitanism ends up in the imperialism of the market, the strong-arm tactics of the IMF and the Iraq war.

Husserl argued in 1935 that the inappropriate naturalization of spirit infected universalism and brought Europe to its near destruction. Today the naturalization of economics is the end of politics and of the idea of Europe. Universality presupposes a common world of meaning and value, a common horizon that encompasses our different worlds. The answer to the European crisis lies in the transcendental community, the subjectivity of a universal *we* for which Europe is the name and mission. Jacques Derrida, on the other hand, the Jewish Algerian French philosopher, introduces a different axiom: what is proper to a culture is not to be identical with itself. Europe is double.[15] I cannot say I or we, without at the same time identifying with the other. We must learn again what it means to be at home with the other. The Europe of the French deportations and capitalist fanaticism, much worse than any religious fundamentalism, represents the lack of common world, the imperialism and empiricism of a culture that claims the mantle of the universal for the most particular interests. We must remain vigilant against the Stoic, Roman and Eurocentric filiations with their patriarchal and colonial legacies. But we should not give up the universalizing impetus of the imaginary, the *cosmos* that uproots every polis, disturbs every filiation, contests all sovereignty and hegemony. We must invent or discover in the European genealogy of universalism whatever goes beyond and against itself, the principle of its excess. This means going back to the beginning, the Mediterranean and its ports of departure. It is the return of the ontology of singular equality and the culture of hospitality and openness. The Mediterranean, the navel of the earth, can become again a physical or symbolic bridge for bringing people and cultures together, instead of a floating cemetery for the wretched of the earth.

Dissatisfaction with state and European institutions comes from a bond between singularities that cannot be turned either into community, state or union and cannot be contained in traditional concepts of community or cosmos or of polis or state. The Europe to come is a bond between singularities, the world of each unique one, of whoever and anyone, those infinite encounters of singular worlds creating a cosmos.[16] But each world is penetrated by the world of the other, the other in me, myself in the other. What binds me to a Roma, a Palestinian, a *sans papiers* migrant or a Greek or Spanish unemployed youth is not membership of state, Europe or humanity but a protest against a meaningless European citizenship, resistance against fake economic orthodoxy, against a false ethnic mono-culturalism. It was resistance to orthodoxy and the diktats of priests and ancestors that allowed the Greeks to imagine a universal truth beyond custom and law. This vocation of truth and equality calls us to resistance today against the oppression of contemporary common sense and the commands of power. The Europe to come is not some future utopia; it is happening here and now in cities and villages, in Greece, Spain and Italy, where we, tired old Europeans, link back again to our beginning and birthplace, to a universalism that was never one and can never become a tool for the powerful. This is our responsibility today, as European, to the name and idea of Europe; Europe as a universal created always in a self-relation with the other, the other in self and the self in other. Resistance and/for equality are its two foundational maxims.

NOTES

PROLOGUE: THE AGE OF RESISTANCE

1 Costas Douzinas, 'Greeks must fight the neoliberal EU', *Guardian*, 4 February 2010, http://www.guardian.co.uk/commentisfree/2010/feb/04/greece-eu-fiscal-policy-protest?INTCMP=SRCH; For an early overview see a transcription of a debate at the Birkbeck Institute for the Humanities in May 2012 with interventions by Etienne Balibar, Stathis Kouvelakis, Costas Lapavitsas, Akis Bratsis, Kevin Featherstone and Costas Douzinas in 'The Greek Crisis', *Journal of Modern Greek Studies*, Vol. 28, No. 2, 2010, 285–310.
2 Costas Douzinas, *The End of Human Rights* (Oxford, Hart, 2000), chs. 8 and 9.
3 Costas Douzinas, 'Greece can fight back against neoliberals', *Guardian*, 27 April 2010, http://www.guardian.co.uk/commentisfree/2010/apr/27/greece-imf-eu-welfare-state.
4 Costas Douzinas, *Resistance and Philosophy in the Crisis: Politics, Ethics and Stasis Syntagma* (Athens, Alexandria Press, December 2011), back cover.
5 Jean-Luc Nancy, *Being Singular Plural* (Stanford University Press, 2000) has been an inspiration in writing this book.
6 Paul Mason, *Why it's Kicking off Everywhere: The New Global Revolutions* (London, Verso, 2011), 26.
7 Michael Hardt and Toni Negri, *Declaration* (e-book, 2012).
8 Alain Badiou, *The Rebirth of History: Times of Riots and Uprisings* (London, Verso, 2012).

1 THE QUEEN'S QUESTION

1 E. M. Forster, *Two Cheers for Democracy* (Harmondsworth, Penguin [1951] 1972), 237.
2 Giorgio Agamben, 'In this Exile (Italian Diary, 1992–4)' in *Means without Ends* (University of Minnesota Press, 2000), 142.
3 Yannis Varoufakis, *The Global Minotaur* (London, Zed Books, 2011); Costas

Lapavitsas et al., *Crisis in the Eurozone* (London, Verso, 2012); Euclid Tsakalotos and Christos Laskos, *Beyond Neo-Liberalism: Greece, the EU and the World Economy* (London, Pluto Press, 2013); Nuriel Roubini, *Crisis Economics* (Harmondsworth, Penguin, 2011); Micahel Lewis, *Boomerang* (London, Allen Lane, 2011).

4 Heather Stewart, 'This is how we let the credit crunch happen, Ma'am ...', *Observer*, Sunday 26 July 2009 at http://www.guardian.co.uk/uk/2009/jul/26/monarchy-credit-crunch

5 Michael Grynbaum, 'Greenspan Concedes Error on Regulation', *New York Times*, 23 October 2008, http://www.nytimes.com/2008/10/24/business/economy/24panel.html

6 Dean Baker, 'For Greece there is an alternative to austerity – as Argentina proved', *Guardian*, 30 July 2012, http://www.guardian.co.uk/commentisfree/2012/jul/30/greece-alternative-austerity-argentina-imf-germany?INTCMP=SRCH

7 Dimitris Yannopoulos, 'Debt Chief blames ex-PM for 2009 deficit', *Kathimerini*, 16 March 2012 (in Greek), http://www.athensnews.gr/issue/13487/54161

8 'Former IMF Representative Testifies', *Athens News*, 22 August 2012, http://www.athensnews.gr/portal/11/57774

9 Christian Marazzi, *Capital and Language*, Gregory Conti, trans. (Los Angeles, Semiotext(e), 2008).

10 Quoted in Andy Bennett, 'Britannia unchained: The rise of the new Tory Right', *Guardian*, 22 August 2012 at http://www.guardian.co.uk/politics/2012/aug/22/britannia-unchained-rise-of-new-tory-right?INTCMP=SRCH

11 Athena Athanassiou, *The Crisis as a 'State of Exception'* (Athens, Savvalas, 2012), 11–27 and at 16 (in Greek).

12 Wendy Brown, *Walled States, Waning Sovereignty* (Cambridge, Mass., MIT Press, 2010).

13 Alenka Zupančič, *Ethics of the Real* (London, Verso, 2000), 234–6.

14 Mark Fisher, *Capitalist Reality* (London, Zero Books, 2009), 16–20.

2 THE BIOPOLITICS OF PLEASURE AND SALVATION

1 Michel Foucault, *The History of Sexuality* (Harmondsworth, Penguin, 1981), 96.

2 Preface to *The Uses of Pleasure: The History of Sexuality*, Vol. 2 (Harmondsworth, Penguin, 1989), 203.

3 Michael Hardt and Antonio Negri, *Empire* (Cambridge, Mass., Harvard University Press, 2000), 1.2.

4 Giorgio Agamben, *Homo Sacer: Sovereign Power and Bare Life*, D. Heller-Raozen, trans. (Stanford University Press, 1998); Roberto Esposito, *Bios: Biopolitics and Philosophy*, Timothy Campbell, trans. (Minneapolis, University of Minnesota Press, 2008).

5 Hardt and Negri, op. cit.; Paolo Virno, *A Grammar of Multitude*, Isabella Bertoletti, James Cascaito and Andrea Casson, trans. (Los Angeles, Semiotext(e), 2004).

6 Costas Douzinas, *The End of Human Rights* (Oxford, Hart, 2000), ch. 8.

7 Christian Marazzi, *The Violence of Financial Capitalism* (Los Angeles, Semiotext(e), 2007), 40.

8 Ibid., 44.
9 Stavors Lygeros, *From Cleptocracy to Bankruptcy* (Athens, Patakis, 2012), 51 (in Greek).
10 Angelique Chrysafis, 'Greeks fall back on family ties amid debt crisis', *The Guardian*, 2 August 2011, http://www.guardian.co.uk/world/2011/aug/02/greece-family-ties-debt-crisis?INTCMP=SRCH
11 Richard Sennet, *The Corrosion of Character. The Personal Consequences of Work in the New Capitalism* (New York, W. W. Norton & Co., 1999).
12 Efi Avdela, 'Gender in the crisis; or what happens to "women" during hard times', *Journal of Modern Greek Studies* (forthcoming) in file with author; Athena Athanassiou, 'Becoming precarious through regimes of gender, capital and nation' in *Beyond the Greek Crisis*, Cultural Anthropology, Hot Spots Forum, 2011, http://www.culanth.org/?=node/445
13 Aditya Chakrabortty, 'Athens protests: Syntagma Square on frontline of European austerity protests', *Guardian*, 19 June 2011 http://www.guardian.co.uk/world/2011/jun/19/athens-protests-syntagma-austerity-protests?INTCMP=SRCH
14 Michel Foucault, *Society Must be Defended*, David Macey, trans. (London, Penguin, 2003), 65–86.
15 Athanassiou, op. cit., ch. 6.
16 Quoted in Joanna Bourke, *What it Means to Be Human: Reflections from 1791 to the Present* (London, Virago, 2011), 99.
17 Ibid., 98.
18 Minister of Education Diamantopoulou, quoted in Athanassiou, op. cit., 48.
19 Athanassiou, op. cit., 40–50.
20. This part draws on Costas Douzinas and Adam Gearey, *Critical Jurisprudence* (Cambridge, Hart, 2005) and Costas Douzinas, *Human Rights and Empire* (Abingdon, Routledge, 2007).
21 Jürgen Habermas, *The Inclusion of the Other* (Cambridge, Polity, 1998), 125 (first italicization in original, the second mine).
22 The World Bank, *Governance and Development* (1992).
23 Jean-Marie Guehenno, *The End of the Nation-State*, Victoria Elliott, trans. (Minneapolis, University of Minnesota Press, 1995), 99.
24 Michel Foucault quoted in Colin Gordon, 'Afterword' in *Power/Knowledge* (Brighton, Harvester, 1980), 257.
25 Costas Douzinas, 'The poverty of (rights) jurisprudence' in Conor Gearty and Costas Douzinas, eds, *The Cambridge Companion to Human Rights Law* (Cambridge University Press, 2013), 56–78.
26 Agamben, *Means*, op. cit., 133.
27 George Katrougalos, 'The "para-constitution" and the other way', *Constitutionalism*, 22 March 2011 (in Greek) http://constitutionalism.gr/html/ent/967/ent.1967.asp
28 Constitutional Law professor George Kasimatis offers an exhaustive list of the constitutional defects of the agreement and implementing laws, George Kasimatis, *The Loan Agreements between Greece the EU and the IMF* (Athens, The Athens Law Society, 2010) (in Greek).
29 Kerin Hope, 'Greek privatization chief predicts bonanza', *Financial Times*, 17 September 2012, http://www.ft.com/intl/cms/s/0/b4f6b8e2-fa62-11e1-b775-00144feabdc0.html#axzz27NGuKLDY

30 The Eurogroup 'welcomes the intention of the Greek authorities to introduce over the next two months in the Greek legal framework a provision ensuring that priority is granted to debt servicing payments. This provision will be introduced in the Greek Constitution as soon as possible.' Eurogroup statement, 21 February 2012.

3 ANOMIE I: SOCIAL ETHOS AND POLITICAL CYNICISM

1 'Minister attacks anomie', *Kathimerini*, 6 February 2011 (in Greek).
2 Emile Durkheim, *The Division of Labour*, George Simpson, trans. (New York, Free Press, 1933); *Suicide*, John Spaulding and George Simpson, trans. (New York, Free Press, 1951). Stephen Marks, 'Durkheim's Theory of Anomie', 80/2 *American Journal of Sociology*, 329 offers an excellent review of the topic and has informed the following discussion.
3 Emile Durkheim, *Professional Ethics and Civic Morals*, Cornelia Brookfield, trans. (New York, Free Press, 1958), 13.
4 Hans-Georg Gadamer, *Truth and Method*. J. Weinsheimer and D. G. Marshall, tans. (New York, Crossroads, 1990).
5 Carl Schmitt, *Political Theology: Four Chapters on the Concept of Sovereignty*, (Cambridge Mass., MIT Press, 1985), 13.
6 Paolo Virno, *Multitude. Between Innovation and Negation,* I. Bertoletti, J. Cascaito and A. Casson, trans. (Los Angeles, Semiotext(e), 2008), 119.
7 Julian Pitt-Rivers, 'The Law of Hospitality', HU: Journal of Ethnographic Theory 2(10, 501–517 (2012).
8 Jacques Derrida, *Politics of Friendship* (London, Verso, 1997), 1.
9 *Suicide*, 369.
10 Virno, *Grammar*, 42–3.
11 Katerina Rozakou, 'The Biopolitics of Hospitality in Greece: Humanitarianism and the Management of Refugees', 39/3 *American Ethnologist*, 562–577.
12 Gadamer, *Truth and Method*, 354.
13 Ibid., 343.
14 Peter Sloterdijk, *Critique of Cynical Reason*, M. Eldred, trans. (London: Verso, 1988), 5.
15 Michael Herzfeld, *The Poetics of Manhood; Contest and Identity in a Cretan Mountain Village* (Princeton University Press, 1988); Efthymios Papataxiarchis, 'The World of the Coffee Shop: Identity and Exchange in Male Conviviality' in Papataxiarchis and Paradellis (eds), *Identities and Gender in Contemporary Greece* (Athens, Kastaniotis Press, 1992, 209–50 (in Greek).
16 Greece was 25th in the OECD league table when the crisis started. By now of course austerity and recession have downgraded it.
17 Christian Marazzi, *Capital and Language: From the New Economy to the War Economy,* Gregory Conti, trans. (Los Angeles, Semiotext(e), 2008), 23.
18 George Soros, *The Crisis of Global Capitalism* (London, Little Brown, 1998), 48
19 Costas Douzinas, *Human Rights and Empire* (London, Routledge, 2007),

ch. 7; Gilbert Leung, 'Towards a Radical Cosmopolitanism' in Matthew Stone, Illan Wall and Costas Douzinas, eds, *New Critical Legal Studies* (London, Birkbeck Law Press, 2011), 229–40.
20 Sloterdijk, op. cit., 218.

4 THE CRISIS AS SPECTACLE

1 Naomi Klein, *The Shock Doctrine: The Rise of Disaster Capitalism* (London, Penguin, 2007).
2 Zizek, *First as Tragedy*, 18–19.
3 Costas Douzinas, 'Identity, recognition, rights: what can Hegel teach us about human rights', *Journal of Law and Society*, 29 (2002), 479–505.
4 John Gray, *Straw Dogs* (London, Granta, 2003), 110.

5 *ADIKIA*: THE ETERNAL RETURN OF RESISTANCE

1 Quoted in Paul Mason, *Why It's Kicking off Everywhere: The New Global Revolutions* (London, Verso, 2012), 65.
2 Ibid.
3 Alain Badiou, *The Rebirth of History: Times of Riots and Uprisings* (London, Verso, 2012), 38.
4 This translation combines elements from a number of translations emphasizing both the ontological and normative character of the fragment with its abundance of terms such as *dike, adikia* and *tisis* (reparation). Martin Heidegger, 'The Anaximander fragment' in *Early Greek Thinking*, D. F. Crell and F. Capuzzi, trans. (New York, Harper and Row, 1975) examines the various (mis)translations of the fragment.
5 Ibid., 41.
6 Jacques Derrida, *Spectres for Marx: The State of Debt, the Work of Mourning and the New International* (New York, Routledge, 1994), 23–9.
7 Jean-Francois Lyotard in *Heidegger and the 'Jews'*, A. Michel and A. Roberts, trans. (Minneapolis, University of Minnesota Press, 1990); S. Ross, *Injustice and Restitution: The Ordinance of Time* (New York: State University of New York Press, 1993), 4. See also a superb exegesis of Heidegger's text in Jacques de Ville, 'Rethinking of the notion of a "higher law": Heidegger and Derrida on the Anaximander fragment', 20, *Law and Critique*, (2009), 59–78.
8 Heidegger discusses the *Ode on Man* in *Introduction to Metaphysics*, R. Mannheim, trans. (New York, Doubleday Anchor, 1961), 155 ff.
9 Ibid., 163.
10 Ross, op. cit., 10.
11 Costas Douzinas, 'Antigone's death and law's birth', *Cardozo Law Review*, 16 (1995), 1325.
12 'That is what is unjust. Not the opposite of the just, but that which prohibits that the question of the just and the unjust be, and remain, raised', Jean-Francois Lyotard, *Just Gaming*, W. Godzich, trans. (Manchester, Manchester University Press, 1985), 66–7. Derrida's 'indeconstuctibility', 'incalculability' and unconditionality of justice lead to the same conclusion. Justice

is always to come, but we do not know its nature and cannot theorize it besides proclaiming its radical otherness. See Douzinas and Gearcy, *Critical Jurisprudence*, op.cit., ch. 4.

13 J.-F. Lyotard, 'A l'Insy (Unbeknownst)' in Miami Theory Collective, eds, *Community at Loose Ends*, (Minnesota University Press 1991), 42–8, 46.

14 Ibid., 44, 43.

15 Slavoj Žižek, *For They Know Not What They Do* (London, Verso, 2008), 101.

16 Michel Villey, *Le droit et les droits de l'homme* (Paris, PUF, 1983), 118–25.

17 Douzinas, *End*, chs. 2 and 3.

18 Hanna Arendt, *On Revolution* (London, Penguin, 2006), 30.

19 Norberto Bobbio, *The Age of Rights* (Cambridge, Polity, 1996), 88 quoting Mirabeau.

20 Immanuel Kant, *The Metaphysics of Morals* (Cambridge University Press; 2nd edn, 1996), 162. See Illan Wall, *Human Rights and Constituent Power* (Abingdon, Routledge, 2012), ch. 4; Stathis Kouvelakis, *Philosophy and Revolution* (London, Verso, 2008), passim.

21 Wall, op. cit. discovers traces of constituent power in the practice of human rights.

22 Samuel Moyn's *The Last Utopia* (Harvard University Press, 2011) charts in detail the way in which human rights and radical change have developed in opposed ways.

23 Costas Douzinas, 'The poverty of (rights) jurisprudence' op. cit.

24 Eric Santner, *The Royal Remains: The People's Two Bodies and the Endgames of Sovereignty* (Chicago University Press, 2011), xxi, fn 15.

25 Richard Tuck, *Natural Right Theories* (Cambridge University Press, 1979).

26 'Declaration of the right to insubordination in the Algerian war (Manifesto of the 121) in Maurice Blancot, *Political Writings*, Zakir Paul, trans. (New York, Fordham University Press, 2010), 15–17.

27 Ibid., 33–4.

28 Costas Douzinas and Slavoj Žižek, *The Idea of Communism* (London, Verso, 2011).

29 Rancière, *Hatred*, 57.

30 Alain Badiou, *Metapolitics* (London, Verso, 2005), chs 6, 7 and 8.

31 Quoted in Jason Barker, 'Translator's introduction' in Alain Badiou, *Metapolitics*, xv.

32 Art. 19 of ECHR bans foreigners from exercising political rights.

33 Badiou, 'Truths and Justice' in *Metapolitics*, 96–106.

34 Douzinas, *End*, chs. 8 and 9.

35 Peter Halward in Douzinas and Žižek, eds. *The Idea of Communism*, 117.

36 Walter Benjamin, 'Critique of Violence' in *Reflections*, Edmund Jephcott, trans. (New York, Schocken Books, Benjamin 1978), 277–300.

37 Badiou, *Metapolitics*, 24.

6 ANOMIE II: DISOBEDIENCE, RESISTANCE, SOVEREIGNTY

1 Hannah Arendt, 'Civil disobedience' in *Crises of the Republic* (Harmondsworth, Penguin, 1972), 61.

2 Ibid., 54.

3 H. A. Bedeau, *Civil Disobedience* (New York, Pegasus, 1969); Peter Singer, *Democracy and Disobedience* (Oxford, Clarendon, 1973).
4 Arendt, 'Civil disobedience', op. cit.
5 John Rawls, *A Theory of Justice*, 363–5; Rawls, 'The justification of civil disobedience' in *Revolution and the Rule of Law*, E. Kent, ed. (Princeton Hall, Spectrum, 1971), 29–45.
6 Ronald Dworkin, *A Matter of Principle* (Cambridge, Mass., Harvard University Press, 1985), 105.
7 Richard Nixon, 'If mob rule takes over in the U.S.', quoted in Kevin Yuill, *Richard Nixon and the Rise of Affirmative Action* (Oxford, Rowman and Littlefield, 2006), 222.
8 Domenico Losurdo, *Liberalism: A Counter-History*, Gregory Elliott, trans. (London, Verso, 2011), 431.
9 Dworkin, ibid.
10 Rawls, op. cit., 372; disobedience confronts 'especially the infringement of the fundamental equal liberties', 366.
11 Ibid., 360 ff.
12 Ronald Dworkin, *Taking Rights Seriously* (London, Duckworth, 1977), 186 ff; *A Matter of Principle*, 104 ff.
13 Op. cit., 112.
14 Jean-Jacques Rousseau, *On the Social Contract*, (St Martin's Press, 1978), 53.
15 Giovanna Borradori, *Philosophy in a Time of Terror: Dialogues with Jürgen Habermas and Jacques Derrida* (Chicago University Press, 2003), 41.
16 Colin Crouch, *Post-Democracy* (Cambridge, Polity, 2004).
17 Etienne Balibar *Masses, Classes, Ideas*, James Swenson, trans. (London, Routledge, 1994), xiii.
18 Balibar, op. cit., 347.
19 Aristotle, *The Constitution of Athens*, H. Rackha, trans. (Cambridge, Mass., Harvard University Press, 1996), viii, 5, 30–1.
20 Daniel Markovits, 'Democratic disobedience', *Yale Law Journal*, 114 (2005), 1897 at 1941.
21 Ibid., 1950.
22 Todd May, *The Political Thought of Jacques Rancière* (Edinburgh University Press, 2008), 52.
23 Mario Tronti, 'Towards a critique of political democracy' in Alberto Toscano and Lorenzo Chiesa, eds, *The Italian Difference* (Melbourne, repress, 2009), 104.
24 Badiou, *Rebirth*, 41.
25 Douzinas, *End of Human Rights*, ch. 13.
26 Hannah Arendt, *Eichmann in Jerusalem: A Report on the Banality of Evil* (Harmondsworth, Penguin, 1994), 136.
27 Balibar, op. cit., 354.
28 Simon Critchley, *Infinitely Demanding: Ethics of Commitments Politics of Resistance* (London, Verso, 2007), 42.
29 Rancière, *Disagreement*, 39.
30 Ernesto Laclau, 'An ethics of militant engagement' in Peter Halward ed., *Think Again: Alain Badiou and the Future of Philosophy* (London, Continuum, 2004), 134, 135.
31 Simon Critchley, *The Faith of the Faithless* (London, Verso, 2012), 244.
32 Brown, *Walled States*, op. cit.

33 Carl Schmitt, *Political Theology*, op. cit.
34 Giorgio Agamben, *State of Exception*, Kevin Attell, trans. (Chicago, University of Chicago Press, 2005).
35 John Williamson, 'What Washington means by policy reform' in Williamson, ed., *Latin American Readjustment: How Much has Happened* (Washington, Institute for International Economics, 1989).
36 Dani Rodrick, 'Goodbye Washington consensus, hello Washington confusion' (2006), *Journal of Economic Literature*, 974.
37 David Harvey, *The New Imperialism* (Oxford, Oxford University Press, 2003), 137–82.
38 Jacques Derrida, *Rogues* (Stanford University Press, 2005), 168.
39 Arendt, op.cit, 56.
40 Wall, op. cit., 20

7 POLITICAL ONTOLOGIES

1 Wendy Brown, 'Resisting left melancholy', *Boundary 2*, 26.3 (1999), 26.
2 Douzinas, *Human Rights and Empire*, op. cit., chs. 7 and 8.
3 John Holloway, *Crack Capitalism* (London, Pluto, 2010).
4 Alain Badiou, *The Communist Hypothesis* (London, Verso, 2012); *Metapolitics*, Jason Barker, trans. (London, Verso, 2005).
5 Carsten Strathousen, ed., *A Leftist Ontology: Beyond Relativism and Identity Politics* (Minneapolis: University of Minnesota Press, 2009).
6 Rancière, *Disagreement*, 65.
7 Badiou, *Metapolitics*, xxxix.
8 Bruno Bosteels, *The Actuality of Communism* (London, Verso, 2011), 92.
9 Philippe Lacoue-Labarthe and Jean-Luc Nancy, *Retreating the Political*, Simon Sparks, ed. (London, Routledge, 1997).
10 Oliver Marchart, *Post-Foundational Political Thought: Political Difference in Nancy, Lefort, Badiou and Laclau* (Edinburgh University Press, 2007), 5.
11 Chantal Mouffe, *On the Political* (London, Routledge, 2005), 8–9.
12 William Rasch, *Sovereignty and its Discontents* (London, Birkbeck Law Press), 6.
13 Alain Badiou, *Ethics*, Peter Halward, trans. (London, Verso, 2001); *Being and Event*, Oliver Feltham, trans. (New York, Continuum, 2005).
14 Badiou, *Saint Paul. The Foundation of Universalism*, Ray Brassier, trans. (Stanford, Stanford University Press, 2003).
15 Badiou, *Being and Event*, 193.
16 Douzinas, *Human Right and Empire*, ch. 11.
17 Jacques Rancière, *Disagreement*, Julie Rose, trans. (Minneapolis, University of Minnesota Press, 1998); *On the Shores of Politics*, Liz Heron, trans. (London, Verso, 1995); 'Who is the subject of the rights of man?' in Ian Balfour and Eduardo Cadava, 'And Justice for All?', 103, 2/3 *South Atlantic Quarterly*, (2004), 297.
18 Slavoj Žižek, *Tarrying with the Negative: Kant, Hegel and the Critique of Ideology* (Durham, Duke University Press, 1993), 209–10.
19 Jacques Rancière, *Disagreement* (Minnesota University Press, 1999), ix.
20 Rancière, 'Subject', op. cit., 304.

21 Rancière, *Disagreement* op. cit., 1–42.
22 Rancière, 'Subject', op. cit., 305.
23 Bourke op. cit., 137 (italics in original).
24 Ibid.
25 Alain Badiou, 'Homage to Jacques Derrida' in Costas Douzinas, ed., *Adieu Derrida* (London, Palgrave Macmillan, 2007).
26 Rancière, *Disagreement*, 90.
27 Ibid., 16, 27.
28 Ernesto Laclau and Chantal Mouffe, *Hegemony and Socialist Strategy* (London, Verso, 1985); Ernesto Laclau, *Emancipation(s)* (London, Verso, 1996); Ernesto Laclau, *On Populist Reason* (London, Verso, 2005). For a friendly introduction and critique see Oliver Marchart, op. cit.
29 Ernesto Laclau, *New Reflections on the Revolution of our Time* (London, Verso, 1990), 160.
30 Laclau, *Emancipation(s)*, 90.
31 Ernesto Laclau, 'Why constructing a people is the main task of radical politics', 32/4 *Critical Inquiry* (2006), 646.
32 *On Populist Reason*; in the Greek context, 'populism' has become a passpartout negative term. The early Pasok government of Andreas Papandreou was 'populist' because it supported the 'non-privileged' petty bourgeois and farmers. In the 2012 elections, the radical Left Syriza party was accused of populism because it promoted the people's interests against the machinations of the elites and the IMF. Everything that refers to the 'people' is labelled 'populist' and is dismissed as part of the 'oriental' backwardness of the Greeks. Populism is an empty signifier in Laclau's terms, hegemonized by the modernizers and liberals. After Laclau's critical intervention, a battle for reconquering the term has been joined. See Etienne Balibar, 'Europe is a dead political project', *Guardian,* 25 May 2010, http://www.guardian.co.uk/commentisfree/2010/may/25/eu-crisis-catastrophic-consequences
33 Laclau, *Populism*, xi.
34 Mouffe, *The Political*, 18.
35 Žižek, 'Against the populist temptation', 32/3 *Critical Inquiry*, (2006), 551.

8 PEOPLE, MULTITUDE, CROWD

1 Key references in the theory of multitude include Antonio Negri, *The Savage Anomaly*, Michael Hardt, trans. (Minneapolis, University of Minnesota Press, 1991); *Insurrections: Constituent Power and the Modern State*, M. Boscagli, trans. (Minneapolis, University of Minnesota Press, 1999); Michael Hardt and Antonio Negri, *Multitude* (London, Hamish Hamilton, 2004); Michael Hardt and Antonio Negri, *Commonwealth* (Cambridge, Mass., Harvard University Press, 2009); Paolo Virno, *A Grammar of the Multitude* (Los Angeles, Semiotext(e), 2004); Paolo Virno, *Multitude: Between Innovation and Negation* (Los Angeles, Semiotext(e), 2009).
2 Thomas Hobbes, *De Cive* in *Man and Citizen*, Bernard Gert, ed. (Indianapolis, Hackett, 1991), ch. XII, section VIII, 250.
3 Jacques Rancière, *Disagreement:* op. cit.
4 Hobbes, *De Cive,* ch. 14, s. 21, 286.
5 Ibid., 287.

6 Ibid., ch. 14, s.5, 275; ch. 14., s. 22, 287.
7 Ch. 14, s. 11, 279.
8 Virno, *Grammar*, 23.
9 Hobbes, op. cit., ch. 12, s. 8, 250–1.
10 Antonis Manitakis, 'The meaning of multitude and the utopian perspective of global democracy (in the context of the "democracy of the multitude" in the work of Hardt and Negri)' at www.constitutionalism.gr/html/ent/910/ent.1919.asp (in Greek).
11 Antonio Negri, *Insurrections,* op. cit.
12 Ibid., 304.
13 Negri, *Savage Anomaly* (Minneapolis, University of Minnesota Press, 1999), 222, 226.
14 Niccolo Machiavelli, *Discourse on Livy* (London, Penguin, 2007), 99.
15 Baruch Spinoza, *A Theologico-Political Treatise* (Cambridge University Press, 2007), 216.
16 Jacques Rancière, *The Philosopher and his Poor*, Andrew Parker, ed., John Dury, Corinne Oster and Andrew Parker, trans. (Durham, Duke University Press, 2003), 9–10.
17 Virno, op. cit., 21 (italics in the original).
18 Ibid., 43.
19 *Multitude*, 348–58 and 353.
20 Slavoj Žižek, 'How to begin from the beginning' in Costas Douzinas and Slavoj Žižek, eds, *The Idea of Communism* (London, Verso, 2010), 221.
21 Virno, *Grammar*, 87.
22 Carlo Vercellone quoted in Žižek, op. cit., 224.
23 Antonio Negri, 'Communism. Some Thoughts on the Theory and Practice', in *Idea of Communism*, op. cit., 163.
24 Esposito, *Bios*, op. cit.
25 See generally Paolo Virno and Michael Hardt, eds, *Radical Thought in Italy: A Potential Politics* (Minneapolis, University of Minnesota Press, 1996); Lorenzo Chiesa and Alberto Toscano, eds, *The Italian Difference: Between Nihilism and Biopolitics* (Melbourne repress, 2009).
26 Alberto Toscano, 'Chronicles of insurrection: Tronti, Negri and the subject of antagonism' in Toscano and Chiesa eds, op. cit. 120.
27 Antonio Negri, *Goodbye Mr Socialism*, Peter Thomas, trans. (London, Serpent's Tail, 2009), 221.
28 *Multitude*, 192.
29 Hardt and Negri, *Commonwealth*, 380.
30 Ernesto Laclau, *On Populist Reason* (London, Verso, 2005), chs. 2 and 3. Laclau criticizes the dismissal of the 'people' and of the crowds who, according to mainstream theory, cannot rise to the autonomy of individuals, 29.
31 H. A. Taine quoted in Laclau, *On Populism*, 31–2.
32 Gustave le Bon, *The Crowd: A Study of the Popular Mind* (London, Dover, 2002), 22.
33 Elias Canetti, *Crowds and Power* (New York, Farrar, Straus and Giroux, 1984), 15ff.
34 Sigmund Freud, *Group Psychology and the Analysis of the Ego* (New York, W. W. Norton & Co., 1975), 70.
35 William McDougal, *The Group Mind* (Cambridge University Press, 1973).
36 *Insurrections*, 324.

37 Ibid., 100.
38 Ibid., xiv.
39 William Mazzarella, 'The myth of the multitude, or, who's afraid of the crowd?', 36, *Critical Inquiry*, 697 (Summer 2010) at 713. Mazzarella offers an interesting tour of crowd theory.
40 Hardt and Negri, *Commonwealth*, 237.
41 Ibid., 243–4.
42 Mazzarella, op. cit., 707.

9 *STASIS SYNTAGMA*: THE SUBJECTS AND TYPES OF RESISTANCE

1 Paul Mason, *Why it's Kicking off Everywhere* (London, Verso, 2012), 14.
2 Quoted in Yannis Kallianos, 'December as an event in Greek radical politics' in Antonis Vradis and Dimitris Dalakoglou, *Revolt and Crisis in Greece: Between a Present Yet to Pass and a Future Still to Come* (Edinburgh, AK Press, 2011), 155.
3 Ceamor, 'From innocence to awareness' in Christos Giovanopoulos and Dimitirs Mitropoulos, eds, *Democracy under Construction: From the Streets to the Squares* (Athens, A/Synecheia, 2011), 29 (in Greek).
4 David Graeber, 'The new anarchist' in T. Mertes, ed., *A Movement of Movements: Is Another World Really Possible?* (London, Verso, 2004), 214.
5 Slavoj Žižek, *Tarrying with the Negative: Kant, Hegel and the Critique of Ideology* (Durham, Duke University Press, 1993), 234.
6 Vradis and Dalakoglou op. cit; A. G. Schwarz, Tasos Sagris and Void Network, *We are an Image from the Future: The Greek Revolt of December 2008* (Edinburgh, AK Press, 2010); Andreas Kalyvas, 'An anomaly: reflections on the Greek December 2008', 17/2, *Constellations*, 2010, 351–65; Costas Douzinas, 'What we can learn from the Greek riots', *The Guardian*, Friday 9 January 2009, http://www.guardian.co.uk/commentisfree/2009/jan/09/greece-riots.
7 Hara Kouki, 'Short Voyage to the Land of Ourselves' in Vradis and Dalakoglou, 169.
8 Etienne Balibar, 'Uprisings in the *banlieues*' in *La Proposition de l' Egaliberté* (Paris, PUF, 2010), 290.
9 Kouki, ibid.
10 Michel de Certeau, *The Practice of Everyday Life* (Berkeley, University of California Press, 1988), 91–131.
11 Alain Badiou, *The Rebirth of History*, op. cit., 16–26.
12 Ibid., 21.
13 Ibid., 25.
14 Ibid., 17, 26.
15 Ed Vulliamy and Helena Smith, 'Children of the revolution', *Observer*, 22 February 2009, http://www.guardian.co.uk/world/2009/feb/22/civil-unrest-athens
16 Alain Badiou, *Homage to Jacques Derrida* in Costas Douzinas, ed., *Adieu Derrida* (London, Macmillan, 2007).
17 Balibar, op. cit., 291–315.
18 Badiou, *Rebirth*,110.
19 Ibid., 311–12.

20 LSE and *Guardian*, 'Reading the riots: investigating England's summer of disorder', http://www.guardian.co.uk/uk/series/reading-the-riots
21 Alain Badiou, *Being and Event*, Oliver Feltham, trans. (New York, Continuum, 2005), Part VIII.
22 Kaplanis, op. cit., 164.
23 Kouki, op. cit., 179.
24 Ibid., 175.
25 M.S.S. v. Belgium and Greece (ECHR, application no. 30696/09).
26 Costas Douzinas, *Human Rights and Empire* (London, Routledge, 2007), ch. 5.
27 Jacques Derrida, *On Cosmopolitanism and Forgiveness*, Mark Dooley and Michael Hughes, trans. (London, Routledge, 2001), 18.
28 Ibid., 22–3.
29 Jean-Luc Nancy, 'Church, state, resistance' in Hent de Vries and Lawrence Sullivan, eds, *Political Theologies* (New York, Fordham University Press, 2006), 102–12.
30 Resolution of popular assembly, 3 July 2011 at http://amesi-dimokratia.org/el/psifismata/item/264-ψηφίσματα-λαϊκής-συνέλευσης-3/7
31 Douzinas, *The End of Human Rights*, chs. 8 and 9.
32 Balibar, op. cit., 288.

10 DEMOS IN THE SQUARE

1 Aristotle, *Politics*, 1279a, 40–3.
2 Manitakis, 'The meaning of multitude', op. cit.
3 Giovanopoulos and Mitropoulos, op. cit., 277, 279 (italics mine).
4 Chantal Mouffe, 'Carl Schmitt and the Paradox of Liberal Democracy' in Mouffe, ed., *The Challenge of Carl Schmitt* (London, Verso, 1999), 51.
5 Jodi Dean, 'Claiming Division, Naming a Wrong' in Astra Taylor et al., eds, *Occupy: Scenes from Occupied America* (London, Verso, 2011), 91–2.
6 Martin Loughlin and Neil Walker, eds, *The paradox of constitutionalism: Constituent Power and Constitutional Form* (Oxford University Press, 2008).
7 Judith Butler, 'Bodies in public' in Taylor, *Occupy*, 193.
8 Rena Dourou quoted in Mason, op. cit., 89. Dourou was elected a Syriza MP in the 2012 elections.
9 Hans Lindahl, 'The opening: alegality and political action' in Andrew Schaap, ed., *Law and Political Agonism* (Aldershot, Ashgate, 2009), 90.
10 Douzinas, *Human Rights and Empire*, ch. 12.
11 Illan Wall, 'Tunisia and the critical legal theory of dissensus', 23/3 *Law and Critique* (2012), 232.
12 Douzinas, *Human Rights and Empire*, 279.
13 Spinoza, *Ethics*. Complete Works, Samuel Shirley, trans. (Indianapolis, Hackett, 2002), 314.
14 Simon Critchley, *Infinitely Demanding; Ethics of Commitment, Politics of Resistance* (London, Verso, 2007), 130.
15 Hardt and Negri, *Commonwealth*, 235.
16 Badiou, *Rebirth*, 97.
17 Sigmund Freud, *Civilisation and its Discontents*, Vol. XXI, standard edn (London, Vintage, 2001), 114.
18 Spinoza, *Ethics*, Part IV, Proposition LXI (NY, Dover, 1959), 229.

19 Mason, op. cit., 89.
20 Badiou, *Rebirth*, 55–61.
21 Hardt and Negri argue that the occupations express the 'will of all', which preceded the social contract and the creation of the state. After the agreement, it degenerated into the 'general will'. The main point however is the same.
22 Hannah Arendt, *The Human Condition* (Chicago University Press, 1998, 2nd edn), 198.
23 Ibid., 207.
24 Maurice Blanchot: *The Unavowable Community*, Pierre Jorris trans. (Barrytown, State Hille Press, 1988), 30.
25 Yannis Stefanakis, 'The square, an immense artistic and activist happening' in Giovanopoulos and Mitropoulos, eds, op. cit., 86.
26 Jacques Rancière, *The Emancipated Spectator*, Gregory Elliott, trans. (London, Verso, 2011), 22. I would like to thank the anonymous Polity reader of the manuscript who brought to my attention the link with Rancière's analysis of theatre and spectatorship.
27 Critchley, *Faith*, op. cit., 52.
28 Rancière, op. cit., 6.
29 Stefanakis, op. cit, 89.
30 Rancière, op. cit., 19.
31 Rancière, *The Philosopher and his Poor*, op. cit.
32 Achileas Stavrou, 'The "upper square"' in CGiovanopoulos and Mitropoulos, op. cit., 36.
33 Chapter 11.
34 Jeanne Schoeder, *The Vesta and the Fasces: Hegel, Lacan, Property and the Feminine* (University of California Press, 1998), chs. 1–3.
35 Crouch, *Post-Democracy*, op. cit.; Mouffe, *Political*, op. cit.
36 Douzinas and Žižek, *The Idea of Communism*, op. cit.

11 LESSONS OF POLITICAL STRATEGY

1 Slavoj Žižek, 'Don't fall in love with yourselves' in Astra Taylor, *Occupy*, 67–9.
2 Slavoj Žižek, *First as Tragedy, then as Farce*, (London, Verso, 2009), 130.
3 Michael Hardt and Antonio Negri, *Declaration* (e-book, 2012).
4 Alain Badiou, *The Rebirth of History: Times of Riots and Uprisings* (London, Verso, 2012).
5 Žižek's book had not been published at the time of writing. His many essays and speeches give a good idea of his position.
6 *Declaration*, 2.
7 Ibid., 15, 65, 66.
8 Ibid., 78.
9 Ibid., 36.
10 Ibid., 9, 53.
11 Antonio Negri, *Insurrections: Constituent Power and the Modern State*, Maurizio Boscagli, trans., (Minneapolis, University of Minnesota Press, 1999), 188.
12 Ibid.
13 Ibid., 312.

14 Ibid., 311.
15 Ibid., 184–6.
16 Ibid., 302–3.
17 *Declaration*, 75.
18 *Insurrections.*, 186.
19 Ibid., 304.
20 Ibid., 307.
21 Hardt and Negri, *Commonwealth*, 3–22.
22 Hardt and Negri, *Declaration*, 60.
23 Ibid., 77.
24 Alain Badiou, 'Beyond formalisation', an interview conducted by Peter Hallward and Bruno Bosteels (Paris, 2 July 2002) in Bruno Bosteels, *Badiou and Politics* (Durham, Duke University Press, 2011), 318–50.
25 Ibid., 336, 337.
26 Badiou, *Rebirth of History*, 41–3.
27 Ibid., 25.
28 Žižek, *First as Tragedy,* op. cit., 125–31.
29 Ibid., 154.
30 Gilbert Leung, 'Rights, politics and paradise', *Critical Legal Thinking*, 14 March 2012, http://criticallegalthinking.com/2012/03/14/rights-politics-and-paradise-notes-on-zizek/
31 Žižek, *First as Tragedy*, 128.
32 Ibid., 130
33 Badiou, *Rebirth of History,* 52.
34 Ibid., 97
35 Ibid., 98, 99 (italics in original).
36 Hardt and Negri, *Commonwealth*, 371, 354.
37 Ibid., 374–5.
38 Žižek, *First as Tragedy*, 131
39 Bruno Bosteels, *The Actuality of Communism* (London, Verso, 2011), ch. 4.
40 Jacques Derrida, *Spurs: Nietzsche's Styles* (University of Chicago Press, 1981).
41 Strathausen, 'Introduction' in *Leftist Ontology*, op. cit., xxv.
42 Ibid., xxvi.
43 Žižek, *First as Tragedy,* op. cit., 130.
44 Quoted in Etienne Balibar 'Résistance, Insurrection, Insoumission' in *La Proposition de l' Egaliberte* (Paris, PUF, 2010), 355.

EPILOGUE: THE EUROPE TO COME

1 Jürgen Habermas, *The Divided West* (Cambridge, Polity, 2006), 43; Ulrich Beck, *Cosmopolitan Vision* (Cambridge: Polity, 2006).
2 Paul Valéry, 'Notes on the greatness and decline of Europe' in *History and Politics* (NY: Bollinger, 1962), 196.
3 Georg Hegel, *The Philosophy of History* (London, Dover Publications, 2004), 86.
4 Fernand Braudel, *The Mediterranean,* quoted in Anthony Pagden, 'Europe: conceptualizing a continent' in Pagden, ed., *The Idea of Europe* (Cambridge, 2002), 37.

5 Edmund Husserl, 'Philosophy and the Crisis of European Man'. At http://www.users.cloud9.net/~bradmcc/husserl_philcris.html
6 Ibid., 15.
7 Lizzy Davies, 'France defends Roma expulsion policy', *Guardian*, 15 September 2010. At: http://www.guardian.co.uk/world/2010/sep/15/france-defends-roma-crackdown
8 Sophocles, *Antigone*, lines 360–1.
9 Rancière, *Disagreement* op. cit., 1–42.
10 Andrew Moravcsik, 'In defense of the "democratic deficit"', 40/4 *Journal of Common Market Studies,* (2002), 618.
11 Jan Zielonka, *Europe as Empire* (Oxford University Press, 2006), 54.
12 Perry Anderson, *The New Old World* (London, Verso, 2009), 117.
13 Jean-Claude Trichet, 'Europe – cultural identity – cultural diversity', Presidential Lecture, Center for Financial Studies, Frankfurt am Main, 16 March 2009 at http://www.bis.org/review/r090317a.pdf
14 Ibid., 9.
15 Jacques Derrida, *The Other Heading* (Indiana University Press, 1992), 9–16.
16 Douzinas, *Human Rights and Empire*, op. cit., ch. 12.

INDEX